COMPUTER
FOR LAW STUDENTS

Dr. P.K. Jain

Ph.D., (Mineral Legislation), Master of Computer Applications (M.C.A.),
LL.M. (Comercial Law), M.B.A. (HRD), M.Tech (Applied Geology),
P.G. Diploma in Yogic Science, Certificate in Environmental Study,
Central India College of Law, Nagpur (Mah.)

SCIENTIFIC
PUBLISHERS (INDIA)
www.scientificpub.com

Published by:
Scientific Publishers (India)
5-A, New Pali Road, P.O. Box 91
JODHPUR - 342 001
E-mail: info@scientificpub.com
www.scientificpub.com

ISBN: 978-81-7233-685-1 (PB)
978-81-7233-687-5 (HB)

Lasertype set: Rajesh Ojha
Printed in India

Dr. S.M. RAJAN
M.Com., MIRPM, LL.B., DBM., C.LDT.,
LL.M. (Constitutional & Administrative Law)
Ph.D. in Law, LL.D. (Registered)
Director
Nagpur Central India College of Law

CENTRAL INDIA COLLEGE OF LAW
GODHANI, NAGPUR

FOREWORD

It gives me an pleasure to write a forward for the book entitled, "Computer for Law Students" authored by one of our erudite faculties, Dr. P.K. Jain who has been teaching the subject of computer for many years at Central India College of Law, Nagpur. This book meets the great and long awaited demand of a standard book on computer which would enable the students especially, the law students to acquaint themselves with the basic concepts of computer and to understand its niceties and intricacies. The merit of this book is in its clarity, precession, certainty and conciseness. The language of the book is very simple and incisive. The author has taken so much of pain for writing such a useful book on computer for law students. It is good that curriculum and examination pattern of our universities and Bar Council of India is kept in mind while writing this book.

I firmly hope and believe that the present book authored by Dr. P.K. Jain will stand as a milestone and would certainly serve the needs of our law students and teachers.

I wish the author Dr. P.K. Jain as well as Publisher of the Book, viz. Scientific Publishers (India), Jodhpur (Rajasthan) all success.

Nagpur
5th September, 2010

Dr. S.M. RAJAN
Director
Central India College of Law

PREFACE

We are in an era of computer and internet where majority of work is being done online to save time and money. Now to bring transparency in system and for speedy disposal of writs, Supreme Court of India has advised advocates to learn application of internet. If advocate and Registrar of Courts will start use of e- mail, the pending cases since long can be disposed off as early as possible.

Bench of Chief Justice of India S.H. Kapadia, Justice K.S. Radhakrishnan and Justice Swatanter Kumar stated that fifty percent cases are pending in court because delay in services. Bench further stated that while filing writ, affidavit or other documents, advocate can give soft copy in pen drive or CD to Registrar office. This can be started immediately for commercial matter. It will be additional medium to submit documents in court.

Government of Finland has included Broadband (service provider for internet data transmission) as Fundamental Right of their citizen in addition to food, cloth and shelter. In this background, step taken by Bar Council of India and RTM Nagpur University to include a new subject i.e. *Computer*- both theory and practical in curriculum of Law students is noteworthy. It is a forward action to groom budding lawyers not only in various aspects of Law but also to make them well acquainted with computer and its application. Because every invention by man has brought advantages and perils also. The understanding of the modern age tool i.e. *Computer*, not only law students can use it in their academic and personal life but also in their career for solving cyber crimes

I intended to write this book for benefit of graduate and post-graduate students of Law, keeping in mind that though there are many books available on computer technology in market, I have not come across one single book covering all the aspects as per syllabus of Law Universities. Moreover simple language with illustrations may make technical subject interesting and easy to understand by Law students.

For the LL.B. course there are four units in Computer theory paper i.e. Computer and its basic, Window Operation System, Networking and Internet and E-Commerce. The organisation of chapters in this book has been done accordingly and I have tried to cover all the portion of syllabus so that students need not search for other books. Response and feedback from the readers, particularly students, on this book shall inspire me to write next book for students.

I take this opportunity to offer my sincere thanks to Dr. S.M Rajan, Director, Central India College of Law, Nagpur for entrusting upon me the responsibility to teach computer, both theory and practical since inception of Computer paper for LL.B. examination. My special thanks are due to Shri A.G. Patukale for critically going through the manuscript and his valuable suggestion.

I look forward to your valuable feedback to enhance the quality of this book and make it more meaningful.

Nagpur

Dr. P.K. Jain
E-mail: pkjain3661@gmail.com

CONTENTS

Foreword *iii*

Preface *v*

CHAPTER I. COMPUTER AND ITS BASIC **1-59**

Characteristics of Computers 1

Block Diagram of Computer 2

Functions of Computer 4

Generations of Computer 5

Classifications of Computer 9

Characteristics, Advantages and Limitations of Computer 14

Central Processing Unit (CPU) 17

Computer Memory 20

Type of Memory 21

Types of Data Storage Devices 23

Input Devices 28

Output Devices 34

Hardware and Software 44

Type of Languages 48

Complier and Interpreter 52

CHAPTER II. WINDOWS OPERATION SYSTEM **60-120**

Introduction 60

Benefits of Windows Operation System 68

Applications of Windows Operation System 70

Graphical User Interface (GUI) 72

Starting Applications 72

Control Panel 84

Accessories 100

Recycle Bin 109

My Documents 111

My Computer 113

Windows Explorer 115

System Tools 116

CHAPTER III. NETWORKING AND INTERNET 121-189

Computer Network and its need 121
Type of Networks 122
Concept of Network Topology 131
Classification of Network Topologies 133
Internet 144
History of Internet 150
World Wide Web (WWW) 167
Web Browsers 167
Internet Servers 176
Server Types 177
Uniform Resource Locator (URL) 178
Internet Architecture 180
Cyber Space 181
TCP/IP Internet Service Provider 182
Domain Name 184
Electronic Mail (E-mail) 186
Communication using E-mail 187

CHAPTER IV. E-COMMERCE 190-

Introduction 190
History 191
Scope 193
Definition 194
Traditional vs E-Commerce 195
Advantages and Disadvantages of E-Commerce. 195
E-Commerce and Trade Cycle 197
Functions of E-Commerce 198
Types of E-Commerce 199
E-Commerce Applications 201
Internet Payment Systems 202
Consumer Oriented E-commerce 207
Business Oriented E-commerce 207
E-Services 208
Facilitators of E-commerce in India 230
Potential of E-commerce in India 231

Syllabus for Computer 235
Question Papers 237

CHAPTER - 1

COMPUTER AND ITS BASICS

The word "computer" comes from the word "compute" which means to calculate. Computer is defined in the Oxford dictionary as "An automatic electronic apparatus for making calculation or controlling operations that are expressible in numerical or logical terms". So a computer is an electronic device that can perform arithmetic and logical operations at enormous speed and accuracy. A computer can store, process and retrieve data as and when desired.

CHARACTERISTICS OF COMPUTERS

The following are few important characteristics of computer:

1. Speed: A computer is a very fast device. While taking about the speed of a computer, do not talk in term of seconds or even milliseconds (10^{-3}). The unit of speed for computer is the microseconds (10^{-6}), the nanoseconds (10^{-9}), and even the picoseconds (10^{-12}). A computer is capable of performing about 3 to 4 million simple operations per second.

2. Accuracy: The accuracy of a computer is consistently high and degree of accuracy of a computer depends upon its design. For a particular computer, each and every calculation is performed with same accuracy. A computer performs the millions of instruction with exactly same accuracy and speed as the first one.

3. Diligence: Unlike human beings, a computer is free from monotony, tiredness, lack of concentration, etc and hence can work for hours together without creating any error and without grumbling.

4. Versatility: Multitasking and multiprocessing are most wonderful thing about computer. Computer can perform more than one instruction simultaneously.

5. Memory: A computer can store and retrieve any amount of data from its secondary storage device. Even random access memory (RAM) also helps to perform cut-copy –paste function without storing the data in secondary memory.

6. No I.Q.: Like human brain computer does not possess intelligence of its own. Its follows instruction in sequence. A computer cannot take own decision.

7. No feelings: Computer is devoid of emotions. It is machine hence no feeling and no instincts. A computer is only as good as man makes and uses it.

BLOCK DIAGRAM OF COMPUTER

The Central Processing Unit (CPU) as a part of compute contains Arithmetic Logical Unit (ALU) and Control Unit (CU). Apart of it there is Input Unit, Output Unit and Storage Device or Memory Unit.

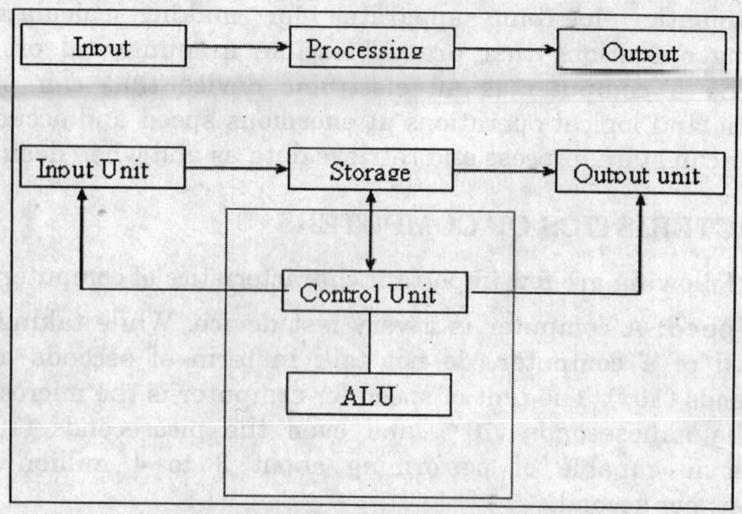

Structure of a Computer

A computer can process data, pictures, sound and graphics. They can solve highly complicated problems quickly and accurately.

Input Unit: Computers need to receive data and instruction in order to solve any problem. Therefore we need to input the data and instructions into the computers. The input unit consists of one or more input devices. Keyboard is the one of the most commonly used input device. Other commonly used input devices are the mouse, monitor (touch screen), scanner, digitizer, joy stick etc. All the input devices perform the following functions.

- Accept the data and instructions from the outside world.
- Convert it to a form that the computer can understand.
- Supply the converted data to the computer system for further processing.

Storage Unit: The storage unit of the computer holds data and instructions that are entered through the input unit, before they are processed. It preserves the intermediate and final results before these are sent to the output devices. It also saves the data for the later use. The various storage devices of a computer system are divided into two categories.

Primary Storage: Stores and provides very fast. This memory is generally used to hold the program being currently executed in the computer, the data being received from the input unit, the intermediate and final results of the program. The primary memory is temporary in nature. The data is lost, when the computer is switched off. In order to store the data permanently, the data has to be transferred to the secondary memory. The cost of the primary storage is more compared to the secondary storage. Therefore most computers have limited primary storage capacity. It is also called Random Access Memory (RAM).

Secondary Storage: Secondary storage is used like an archive. It stores several programs, documents, data bases etc. The programs that you run on the computer are first transferred to the primary memory before it is actually run. Whenever the results are saved, again they get stored in the secondary memory. The secondary memory is slower and cheaper than the primary memory. Some of the commonly used secondary memory devices are Hard disk, CD, Magnetic tape, Floppy, Pen drive, etc.

Memory Size: All digital computers use the binary system, i.e. 0's and 1's. Each character or a number is repre-sented by an 8 bit code. The set of 8 bits is called a byte. A character occupies 1 byte space. A numeric occupies 2 byte space. Byte is the space occupied in the memory.

The size of the primary storage is specified in KB (Kilobytes) or MB (Megabyte). One KB is equal to 1024 bytes and one MB is equal to 1000KB. One GB (Gigabyte) is equal to 1000MB. The size of the primary storage in a typical PC usually starts at 16MB. PCs having 32 MB, 48MB, 128 MB, 256MB, 1GB memory are quite common.

Output Unit: The output unit of a computer provides the information and results of a computation to outside world. Printers, Visual Display Unit (VDU) i.e. monitor and printer, plotter are the commonly used output devices.

Arithmetic Logical Unit: All calculations are performed in the Arithmetic Logic Unit (ALU) of the computer. It also does comparison and takes decision. The ALU can perform basic operations such as addition, subtraction, multiplication, division, etc and does logic operations viz, >, <, =, 'etc. Whenever calculations are required, the control unit transfers the data from storage unit to ALU once the computations are done, the results are transferred to the storage unit by the control unit and then it is send to the output unit for displaying results.

Control Unit: It controls all other units in the computer. The control unit instructs the input unit, where to store the data after receiving it from the user. It controls the flow of data and instructions from the storage unit to ALU. It also controls the flow of results from the ALU to the storage unit. The control unit is generally referred as the central nervous system of the computer that control and synchronizes its working.

Central Processing Unit: The control unit and ALU of the computer are together known as the Central Processing Unit (CPU). The CPU is like brain performs the following functions:

- It performs all calculations.
- It takes all decisions.
- It controls all units of the computer.

A PC may have CPU-IC such as Intel 8088, 80286, 80386, 80486, Celeron, Pentium, Pentium Pro, Pentium II, Pentium III, Pentium IV, Dual Core, and AMD etc.

FUNCTION OF COMPUTER

A Computer is a programmable, multipurpose Electr-onic machine that accepts data (e.g. raw data, facts and figures) and processes, or manipulates it into information we can use, such as summaries or totals.

E.g. An automatic teller machine (ATM) computes the deposits and withdrawals to give you the total money balance in your account.

Function

In programming, self-contained software is there that performs a routine task. Functions can do a large amount of processing or as little as adding two numbers and deriving a result. Values are passed to the function, and values may be returned, or, the function may just perform the operation and not return a resulting value. The concept of a function within a program is that, once written, it can be used over and over again without the programmer having to duplicate the same lines of code in the program each time that same processing is desired.

Standard and Programmer-Defined

Programming languages provide a set of standard functions as well as allow programmers to define their own functions. For example, the C and C++ programming languages are built entirely of functions and always contain a "main" function.

The Application Programming Interface (API)

Functions in one program can also be called for by other programs and shared. For example, operating systems (OS) can contain more than a thousand functions to display data, print, read and write discs and perform a myriad of tasks. Programmers write their applications to interact with the OS using these functions. This list of functions is called the "Application Programming Interface" (API).

GENERATIONS OF COMPUTER

The history of computer development is often referred to in reference to the different generations of computing devi-ces. Each generation of computer is characterized by a major technological development that fundamentally changed the way computers operates, resulting in increas-ingly smaller, cheaper, more powerful and more efficient and reliable devices.

Salient features about each generation and the develop-ments that led to the current devices that we use today are given below:

Mechanical Computers

Blaise Pascal made very first attempt towards automatic computing by inventing a device which consisted of lots of gears and chains and used to perform repeated addition and subtractions. This device was called pascaline. Later on the grandfather of modern computer Charles babbage designed two computers:

- The different engine
- The analytical engine

First Generation (1940-1956)

The first computers used vacuum tubes for circuitry and magnetic drums for memory, and were often enormous, taking up entire rooms. They were very expensive to operate and in addition to using a great deal of electricity, generated a lot of heat, which was often the cause of malfunctions. First generation computers relied on machine language, the lowest-level programming language understood by computers, to perform operations, and they could only solve one problem at a time. Use of ferrite-core main memory was started during this time. Input was based on punched cards and paper tape, and output was displayed on printouts.

Vaccum fubes and Magnetic drums used in First Generation Computer

The ENIAC (the Electronic Numerical Integrated and Calculator) was designed in 1945 at the University of Pennsylvania to calculate figures for thousand of gunnery tables required by US army for accuracy in artillery fire. The UNIVAC and ENIAC computers are examples of first-generation computing devices. The UNIVAC was the first commercial computer delivered to a business client, the U.S. Census Bureau in 1951.

Second Generation (1956-1963)

Transistors replaced vacuum tubes and ushered in the second generation of computers. The transistor was invented in 1947 and had launched the electronic revolution in the late 1950s. The transistor was far superior to the vacuum tube, allowing computers to become smaller, faster, cheaper, more energy-efficient and more reliable than their first-generation predecessors. Though the transistor still generated a great deal of heat that subjected the computer to damage, it was a vast improvement over the vacuum tube. Second-generation computers still relied on punched cards for input and printouts for output.

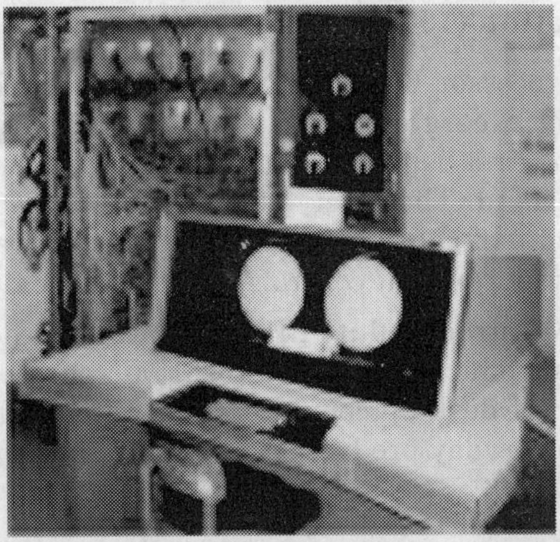

The first computers of this generation were developed for the atomic energy industry.

Second-generation computers moved from cryptic binary machine language to symbolic, or assembly languages, which allowed programmers to specify instructions in words. High-level programming languages were also being developed at this time, such as early versions of COBOL and FORTRAN. These were also the first computers that stored their instructions in their memory, which moved from a magnetic drum to magnetic core technology. One of the main computer series during this time was the IBM 700 series.

Third Generation (1964-1971)

The development of the integrated circuit was the hall-mark of the third generation of computers. Transistors were miniaturized and placed on silicon chips, called semiconductors, which drastically increased the speed and efficiency of computers.

Instead of punched cards and printouts, users interacted with third generation computers through keyboards and monitors and interfaced with an operating system, which allowed the device to run many different applications at one time with a central program that monitored the memory. Computers for the first time became accessible to a mass audience because they were smaller and cheaper than their predecessors.

An integrated circuit (IC) is a small electronic device made out of a semiconductor material. The first integrated circuit was developed in the 1950s by Jack Kilby of Texas Instruments and Robert Noyce of Fairchild Semiconductor.

Fourth Generation (1971-Present)

The microprocessor brought the fourth generation of computers, as thousands of integrated circuits were built onto a single silicon chip. What in the first generation filled an entire room could now fit in the palm of the hand. The Intel 4004 chip, developed in 1971, located all the components of the computer—from the central processing unit and memory to input/output controls—on a single chip.

In 1981 IBM introduced its first computer for the home user, and in 1984 Apple introduced the Macintosh. Microprocessors also moved out of the realm of desktop computers and into many areas of life as more and more everyday products began to use microprocessors.

A Layout of Fourth Generation Computer

As these small computers became more powerful, they could be linked together to form networks, which eventually led to the development of the Internet. Fourth generation computers also saw the development of GUIs, the mouse and handheld devices.

Fifth Generation (Present and Beyond)

Fifth generation computing devices, based on artificial intelligence, are still in development, though there are some applications, such as voice recognition, that are being used today. The use of parallel processing and superconductors is helping to make artificial intelligence a reality. Quantum computation and molecular and nanotechnology will radically change the face of computers in years to come. The goal of fifth-generation computing is to develop devices that respond to natural language input and are capable of learning and self-organization.

CLASSIFICATION OF COMPUTER

Computers are classified according to their data processing speed, amount of data that they can hold and price. Generally, a computer with high processing speed and large internal storage is called a big computer. Due to rapidly improving technology, we are always confused among the categories of computers. Depending upon their speed and memory size, computers are classified into following four main groups.

1. Supercomputer
2. Mainframe computer
3. Mini computer
4. Microcomputer

1. Supercomputer

Supercomputer is the most powerful and fastest, and also very expensive. It was developed in 1980s. It is used to process large amount of data and to solve the complicated scientific problems. It can perform more than one trillions calculations per second. It has large number of processors connected parallel. So parallel processing is done in this computer. In a single supercomputer thousands of users can be connected at the same time and the supercomputer handles the work of each user separately. Supercomputer is mainly used for:

- Weather forecasting.
- Nuclear energy research.
- Aircraft design.
- Automotive design.
- Online banking.
- To control industrial units.

The supercomputers are used in large organizations, research laboratory, aerospace centres, large industrial units etc. Nuclear scientists use super computers to create and analyse models of nuclear fission and fusion, predicting the action and reactions of millions of atoms as they interact. The examples of supercomputer are CRAY-1, CRYZ-2, Control Data CYBER 205 and ETA A-10. India has also announced its indigenous supercomputer Param.

2. Mainframe Computers

Mainframe computers are also large-scale computers but supercomputers are larger than mainframe. These are also very expensive. The mainframe computer specially requires a very large clean room with airconditioner. This makes it very expensive to buy and operate. It can support a large number of various equipments. It also has multiple processors. Large mainframe systems can handle the input and output requirements of several thousand of users. For example, IBM, S/390 Mainframe can support 50,000 users simultaneously. The users often access then mainframe with terminals or personal computers. There are basically two types of terminals used with mainframe systems. These are:

(i) Dumb Terminal: Dumb terminal does not have its own CPU and storage devices. This type of terminal uses the CPU and storage devices of mainframe system. Typically, a dumb terminal consists of monitor and a keyboard (or mouse).

(ii) Intelligent Terminal: Intelligent terminal has its own processor and can perform some processing operations. Usually, this type of terminal does not have its own storage. Typically, personal computers are used as intelligent terminals. A personal computer as an intelligent terminal gives facility to access data and other services from mainframe system. It also enables to store and process data locally.

The mainframe computers are specially used as servers on the World Wide Web. The mainframe computers are used in large organizations such as Banks, Airlines and Universities etc. where many people (users) need frequent access to the same data, which is usually organized into one or more huge databases. IBM is the major manufacturer of mainframe computers. The examples of mainframes are IBM S/390, Control Data CYBER 176 and Amdahl 580 etc.

3. Minicomputers

These are smaller in size, have lower processing speed and also have lower cost than mainframe. These computers are known as minicomputers because of their small size as compared to other computers at that time. The capabilities of a minicomputer are between mainframe and personal computer. These computers are also known as **midrange computers**.

The minicomputers are used in business, education and many other government departments. Although some minicomputers are designed for a single user but most are designed to handle multiple terminals. Minicomputers are commonly used as servers in network environment and hundreds of personal computers can be connected to the network with a minicomputer acting as server like mainframes, minicomputers are used as web servers. Single user minicomputers are used for sophisticated design tasks.

The first minicomputer was introduced in the mid-1960s by Digital Equipment Corporation (DEC). After this IBM Corporation (AS/400 computers) Data General Corporation and Prime Computer also designed the mini computers.

4. Microcomputer

The microcomputers are also known as personal computers or simply PCs. Microprocessor is used in this type of computer. These are very small in size and cost. The IBM's first microcomputer was designed in 1981 and was named as IBM-PC. After this many computer hardware companies copied the design of IBM-PC. The term "PC-compatible" refers any personal computer based on the original IBM personal computer design.

The most popular types of personal computers are the PC and the Apple. PC and PC-compatible computers have processors with different architectures than processors in Apple computers. These two types of computers also use different operating systems. PC and PC-compatible computers use the Windows operating system while Apple computers use the Macintosh operating system (MacOS). The majority of microcomputers sold today are part of IBM-compatible. However the Apple computer is neither an IBM nor a compatible. It is another family of computers made by Apple computer.

A desktop personal computer is most popular model of personal computer. The system unit of the desktop personal computer can lie flat on the desk or table. In desktop personal computer, the monitor is usually placed on the system unit.

Microcomputer is further divided into following categories.

1. Laptop computer
2. Workstation
3. Network computer
4. Handheld computer

1. Laptop computer

Laptop computer is also known as notebook computer. It is small size (85 inch x 11 inch) notebook computer and can fit inside a briefcase. The laptop computer is operated on a special battery and it does not have to be plugged in like desktop computer. The laptop computer is portable and fully functional microcomputer. It is mostly used during journey. It can be used on your lap in an airplane. It is because it is referred to as laptop computer.

The memory and storage capacity of laptop computer is almost equivalent to the PC or desktop computer. It also has the hard disk, floppy disk drive, Zip disk drive, CD-ROM drive, CD-writer etc. It has built-in keyboard and built-in trackball as pointing device. Laptop computer is also available with the same processing speed as the most powerful personal computer. It means that laptop computer has same features as personal computer. Laptop computers are more expensive than desktop computers. Normally these computers are frequently used by business and professional travellers.

2. Workstations

Workstations are special single user computers having the same features as personal computer but have the processing speed equivalent to minicomputer or mainframe computer. A workstation computer can be fitted on a desktop. Scientists, engineers, architects and graphic designers mostly use these computers.

Workstation computers are expensive and powerful computers. These have advanced processors, more RAM and storage capacity than personal computers. These are usually used as single-user applications but these are used as servers on computer network and web servers as well.

3. Network computers

Network computers are also version of personal computers having less processing power, memory and storage. These are specially designed as terminals for network environment. Some types of network computers have no storage. The network computers are designed for network, Internet or Intranet for data entry or to access data on the network. The network computers depend upon the network's server for data storage and to use software. These computers also use the network's server to perform some processing tasks.

In the mid-1990s the concept of network computers became popular among some PC manufacturers. As a result several variations of the network computers quickly became available. In business, variations of the network computer are Windows terminals, NetPCs and diskless workstations. Some network computers are designed to access only the Internet or an Intranet. These devices are sometimes called Internet PCs, Internet boxes etc. When used in home some network computers do not include monitor. These are connected to home television, which serves as the output devices. A popular example of a home-based network computer is Web TV, which enables the user to connect a television to the Internet. The Web TV has a special set-top box used to connect to the Internet and also provides a set of simple controls which enable the user to navigate the Internet, send and receive e-mails and to perform other tasks on the network while watching television. Network computers are cheaper to purchase and to maintain than personal computers.

4. Handheld computer

In the mid 1990s, many new types of small personal computing devices have been introduced and these are referred to as handheld computers. These computers are also referred to as Palmtop Computers. The handheld computers sometimes called Mini-Notebook Computers. The type of computer is named as handheld computer because it can fit in one hand while you can operate it with the other hand. Because of its reduced size, the screen of handheld computer is quite small. Similarly it also has small keyboard. The handheld computers are preferred by business traveller. Some handheld computers have a specialized keyboard. These computers are used by mobile employees, such as meter readers and parcel delivery people, whose jobs require them to move from place to place. The examples of handheld computers are:

1. Personal Digital Assistance
2. Cellular telephones
3. H/PC Pro devices

1. Personal Digital Assistance (PDAs)

The PDA is one of the more popular lightweight mobile devices in use today. A PDA provides special functions such as taking notes, organizing telephone numbers and addre-sses. Most PDAs also offer a variety of other application software such as word processing, spreadsheet and games etc. Some PDAs include electronic books that enable users to read a book on the PDA's screen.

Many PDAs are web-based and users can send/receive e-mails and access the Internet. Similarly, some PDAs also provide telephone capabilities. The primary input device of a PDA is the stylus. A stylus is an electronic pen and looks like a small ballpoint pen. This input device is used to write notes and store in the PDA by touching the screen. Some PDAs also support voice input.

2. Cellular phones

A cellular phone is a web-based telephone having features of analog and digital devices. It is also referred to as Smart Phone. In addition to basic phone capabilities, a cellular phone also provides the functions to receive and send e-mails and faxes and to access the Internet.

3. H/PC Pro Devices

H/PC Pro dive is new development in handheld techno-logy. These systems are larger than PDAs but they are not quite as large as typical notebook PCs. These devices have features between PDAs and notebook PCs. The H/PC Pro device includes a full-size keyboard but it does not include disk. These systems also have RAM with very low storage capacity and slow speed of processor.

CHARACTERISTICS ADVANTAGES AND LIMITATIONS OF COMPUTER

Computers have affected every aspect of our day-to-day life. The present global age is the consequence of the computer age. A computer is an electronic device that stores and processes data, according to a list of instructions. It allows a user to manipulate data easily. The speed of performance of a computer is incomparable. The computer and Internet have influenced our way of working, communicating, playing and also writing. In fact, computers are used in every aspect of life today.

Advantages of Computers

Because of the many advantages of a computer, it has become an important household item. A computer operated by an individual without any specific computer operator is called as a personal computer (PC). A PC can be a desktop or a laptop computer and can be used at home or at office. As per the requirement of the user, softwares are installed in a PC. Let's discuss the advantages of computers.

One can write more effectively by means of a computer. There are tools like spelling and grammar checker, thesaurus and dictionary, installed in the computer. Thus, it takes less time to proof read a written document and also, there is no need to open up a dictionary book to look for meanings of words. Typing is much faster than writing on a paper. If there is a need for reorganizing the sentences or paragraphs, one can cut and paste and make the necessary changes. Thus, overall a computer allows the user to create documents, edit, print, and store them so that they can be retrieved later.

Using a computer, one can remain connected to the world through Internet. Internet is a network of computers that communicates via the Internet Protocol Suite (TCP/IP). The World Wide Web (WWW) or simply web is a huge resource of information that can be accessed via the Internet. To mention a few of the resources, there are electronic mail (e-mail), file transferring and sharing, online chat and games. The Internet allows people from around the world to share knowledge, ideas and experiences in any field.

E-mail is a method of communication used globally and is provided with a system of creating, storing and forwarding mails. It may consist of text messages with attachments of audio-visual clips. One can also download or upload files using the Internet. There are also facilities like online chatting available on the Internet. As compared to telephonic conversation, both e-mail and online chat are cost saving. Online game is another important resource of the WWW. Many online games are available, which are of common interest for any age group. In addition, one can read current news, check weather conditions, plan vacations and make hotel and travel reservations, find out about diseases and treatment methods, conduct transactions, learn about specific countries and their cultures, seek jobs, buy products, etc via the Internet.

Nowadays, computers are widely used for education and training purposes. In schools, computer education has been made compulsory to spread awareness about computers. As a matter of fact, computers have become a learning tool for children. Also, there are many universities that provide online degrees, which is very advantageous for those people staying in the remote areas and for the disabled. In fact, online education is one of the most flexible and convenient forms of learning. One can take the benefit of such online degree programs staying at home without the need of relocation. Computers are also used for training purposes. Many companies use them to train their staffs.

However, in spite of the many advantages of computers, there are some disadvantages that cannot be ignored. The easy access to information via Internet has made students lazy in terms of their education since they are able to download information without exploring their topic of research. They also use computers for mathematical tables and calculations without actually solving the problems. Also, it is important for parents to keep a check on the browsing habits of their children as some websites are not meant for their viewing. Other disadvantages include identity theft and virus threat. Computers viruses are harmful to the systems and can be transferred from one computer system to another.

Limitations of computer

The computer can outperform human beings in speed, memory and accuracy but still the computer has limitations. There are following limitations of a computer.

Programmed by human: Though computer is programmed to work efficiently, fast and accurately but it is programmed by human beings to do so. Without a program, computer is nothing. A program is a set of instructions. Computer only follows these instructions. If the instructions are not accurate the working of computer will not accurate.

Thinking: The computer cannot think itself. The concept of artificial intelligence shows that the computer can think. But still this concept is dependent on set of instructions provided by the human beings.

Self Care: A Computer cannot care itself like a human. A computer is dependent still to human beings for this purpose.

Retrieval of memory: A computer can retrieve data very fast but this technique is linear. A human being's mind does not follow this rule. A human mind can think randomly which a computer machine cannot.

Feelings: One of the main limits in the computer is of feeling. A computer can not feel like human beings. A computer cannot match human being in respect of relations.

Human can feel, think and care but a computer machine itself cannot. A computer cannot take place of human because computer is always dependent of human being.

GIGO: The Input, Process and Output stages of computer are working on lay man principle of Garbage In and Garbage Out.

CENTRAL PROCESSING UNIT (CPU)

Pronounced as separate letters i.e. CPU it is the abbreviation for **c**entral **p**rocessing **u**nit. The CPU is the brain of a computer. Sometimes referred to simply as the central processor, but more commonly called processor, the CPU is where most calculations take place. In terms of computing power, the CPU is the most important element of a computer system.

On large machines, CPUs require one or more printed circuit boards. On personal computers and small workstations, the CPU is housed in a single chip called a micro-processor. Since the 1970's the microprocessor class of CPUs has almost completely overtaken all other CPU implementations.

The CPU itself is an internal component of the computer. Modern CPUs are small and square and contain multiple metallic connectors or pins on the underside. The CPU is inserted directly into a CPU socket, pin side down, on the motherboard. Each motherboard will support only a specific type or range of CPU so the motherboard manufacturer's specifications must be checked before attempting to replace or upgrade a CPU. Modern CPUs also have an attached heat sink and small fan that go directly on top of the CPU to help dissipate heat. Two typical components of a CPU are the following:

- The arithmetic logic unit (ALU), which performs arithmetic and logical operations.
- The control unit (CU), which extracts instructions from memory and decodes and executes them, calling on the ALU when necessary.

Integrated Chips

The Central Processing Unit (CPU) is the brain of the computer--it is the 'compute' in computer. Modern CPU's are what are called 'integrated chips'. The idea of an integrated chip is that several processing components are integrated into a single piece of silicon. Without the CPU, you have no computer. The CPU is composed of thousands (and soon billions) of transistors.

Intel Chip

Each transistor is a set of inputs and one output. When one or more of the inputs receive electricity, the combined charge changes the state of the transistor internally and you get a result out the other side. This simple effect of the transistor is what makes it possible for the computer to count and perform logical operations, all of which we call *processing.*

A modern computer's CPU usually contains an execution core with two or more instruction pipelines, a data and address bus, a dedicated arithmetic logic unit (ALU, also called the math co-processor), and in some cases special high-speed memory for caching program instructions from RAM.

The CPU's in most PC's and servers are general purpose integrated chips composed of several smaller dedicated purpose components which together create the processing capabilities of the modern computer. For example, Intel makes a Pentium, while AMD makes the Athlon, and Duron (no cache memory).

CPU Components

A lot of components go into building a modern computer processor and just what goes in changes with every generation as engineers and scientists find new, more efficient ways to do various tasks.

- Execution Core(s)
- Data Bus
- Address Bus

- Math Co-processor
- Instruction sets / Microcode
- Multimedia extensions
- Registers
- Flags
- Pipelining
- Memory Controller
- Cache Memory (L1, L2 and L3)

CPU Speed Measurements

The main measurement quoted by manufacturers as a supposed indication of processing speed, is the clock speed of the chip measured in hertz. The theory goes that the higher the number of mega or gigahertz, the faster the processor.

However, comparing raw speeds is not always a good comparison between chips. Counting how many instructions are processed per second (MIPS, BIPS, TIPS for millions, billions and trillions of instructions per second) is a better measurement. Still others use the number of mathematical calculations per second to rate the speed of a processor.

Of course, what measurement is most important and most helpful to you depends on what you use a computer for. If you primarily do intensive math calculations, measuring the number of calculations per second is most important. If you are measuring how fast the computer runs an appli-cation, then instructions per second are most important.

Processor Manufacturers

- American Micro Devices (AMD)
- Intel
- IBM
- Motorola
- Cyrix
- Texas Instruments

AMD and Intel have pretty much dominated the market. AMD and Intel are for IBM compatible machines. Motorola chips are made for MacIntoshes. Cyrix (another IBM compatible chip maker) runs a distant fourth place in terms of number of chips sold.

Today all chip manufacturers produce chips whose input and output are identical, though the internal architecture may be different. This means that though they may not be built the same way, they all do run the same software.

The CPU is built using logic gates, and contains a small number of programs called 'microcode' built into the chip to perform certain basic processes (like reading data from the bus and writing to a device). Current chips use a 'reduced instruction set' or RISC architectures. Chips can also be measured in terms of instructions processed per second (MIPS).

COMPUTER MEMORY

In computing, **memory** refers to the state information of a computing system, as it is kept active in some physical structure. The term "memory" is used for the information in physical systems which are fast (ie. RAM), as a distinction from physical systems which are slow to access (ie. data storage). By design, the term "memory" refers to temporary state devices, whereas the term "storage" is reserved for permanent data. Advances in storage technology have blurred the distinction a bit —memory kept on what is conventionally a storage system is called "virtual memory." The cost versus access time anomaly has lead to a hierarchy of memory where we supplement fast memories with large, cheaper, slower memories. The memory hierarchy will be fruitful if the frequency of access to slower memories is significantly less than the faster memories.

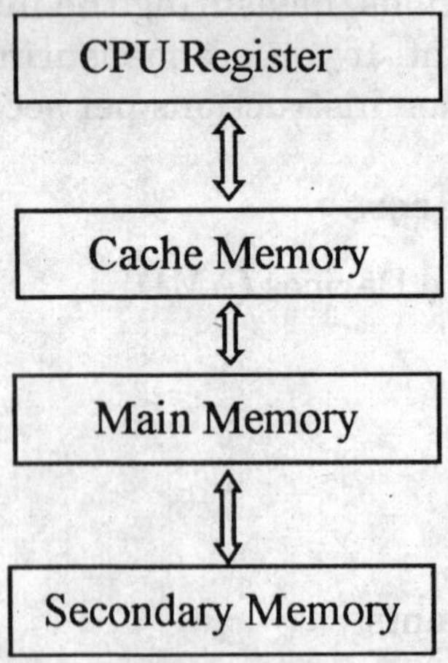

The Memory Hierorchy

Colloquially, **computer memory** refers to the physical devices used to store data or programs (sequences of instructions) on a temporary or permanent basis for use in an electronic digital computer. Computers represent information in binary code, written as sequences of 0s and 1s. Each binary digit (or "bit") may be stored by any physical system that can be in either of two stable states, to represent 0 and 1. Such a system is called bistable. This could be an on-off switch, an electrical capacitor that can store or lose a charge, a magnet with its polarity up or down, or a surface that can have a pit or not. Today, capacitors and transistors, functioning as tiny electrical switches, are used for temporary storage, and either disks or tape with a magnetic coating, or plastic discs with patterns of pits are used for long-term storage.

Computer memory is usually meant to refer to the semiconductor technology that is used to store information in electronic devices. Current primary computer memory makes use of integrated circuits consisting of silicon-based transistors. There are two main types of memory: volatile and non-volatile.

TYPE OF MEMORY

Modern electronic computers generally possess several distinct types of **memory**, each of which "holds" or stores information for subsequent use. The vast majority of computer memory can be placed into one of three categories:

Internal Processor Memories

These consist of small set of high speed registers which are internal to a processor and are used as temporary locations where actual processing done.

Primary memory

Primary memory, often called main memory, constitutes that device, or group of devices, that holds instructions and **data** for rapid and direct **access** by the computer's **central processing unit** (**CPU**). Primary memory is synonymous with **random-access memory (RAM)**. As a computer performs its calculations, it is continuously reading and writing (i.e., storing and retrieving) information to and from RAM. For instance, instructions and data are retrieved from RAM for processing by the CPU, and the results are returned to RAM. Modern RAM is made of **semiconductor** circuitry, which replaced the magnetic core memory widely used in computers in the 1960s. RAM is a volatile form of information storage, meaning that when electrical power is terminated any data that it contains is lost. There are other semiconductor memory devices accessed by the CPU that are generally considered as being distinct from primary memory (i.e., different from RAM). These memory units include cache memory, **read-only memory (ROM)**, and Programmable Read Only Memory (PROM).

Secondary memory

Secondary memory, also called auxiliary memory or mass storage, consists of devices not directly accessible by the CPU. Hard drives, floppy disks, tapes, and optical disks are widely used for secondary storage. The **input and output** of these devices is much slower than for the semiconductor devices that provide the computer's primary memory. Although access times (i.e., the time to read or write information) are slow as compared to that of primary memory, secondary memory devices have important features that are unmatched by primary memory. First, most secondary storage devices are capable of containing much more information than is feasible for primary memory (hence the use of the term "mass storage" as a synonym for secondary memory). A second, and essential, feature of secondary memory is that it is non-volatile. This means that data is stored with or without electrical power being supplied to the device, as opposed to RAM, which can retain its data only so long as electrical power is present.

Like primary memory, many secondary memory devices are capable of storing information, as well as retrieving it. Magnetic technology devices (such as hard drives, floppy disks, and tape) have this read-write capability, as do magneto-optical drives. However, some mass storage devices can only read data, as in the case of **CD-ROM** (Compact Disk-Read Only Memory) drives. CD-ROMs utilize optical technology; however, newer optical technologies, such as CD-RW (compact disk-rewriteable), can both read and write information like magnetic storage devices.

Cache memory: There is another kind of memory which is increasingly being used in modern computers, this is called Cache memory. It is logically positioned between the internal memory (registers) and main memory. It store or catches some of the content of the main memory which is currently in use of the processor.

Volatile memory: Volatile memory is computer memory that requires power to maintain the stored information. Current semiconductor volatile memory technology is usually either static RAM or dynamic RAM. Static RAM exhibits data remanence, but is still volatile, since all data is lost when memory is not powered. Whereas, dynamic RAM allows data to be leaked and disappear automatically without a refreshing. Upcoming volatile memory technologies that hope to replace or compete with SRAM and DRAM include Z-RAM, TTRAM and A-RAM.

Non-volatile memory: Non-volatile memory is computer memory that can retain the stored information even when not powered. Examples of non-volatile memory include read-only memory (ROM), flash memory, most types of magnetic computer storage devices (e.g. hard disks, floppy discs and magnetic tape), optical discs, and early computer storage methods such as paper tape and punched cards. Upcoming non-volatile memory technologies include FeRAM, CBRAM, PRAM, SONOS, RRAM, Racetrack memory, NRAM and Millipede.

TYPES OF DATA STORAGE DEVICES

A **data storage device** is a device for recording (storing) information (data). Recording can be done using virtually any form of energy, spanning from manual muscle power in handwriting, to acoustic vibrations in phonogra-phic recording, to electromagnetic energy modulating magnetic tape and optical discs.

A storage device may hold information, process information, or both. A device that only holds information is a recording medium. Devices that process information (data storage equipment) may either access a separate portable (removable) recording medium or a permanent component to store and retrieve information.

Electronic data storage is storage which requires electrical power to store and retrieve that data. Most storage devices that do not require vision and a brain to read data fall into this category. Electromagnetic data may be stored in either an analog or digital format on a variety of media. This type of data is considered to be electronically encoded data, whether or not it is electronically stored in a semiconductor device, for it is certain that a semiconductor device was used to record it on its medium. Most electronically processed data storage media (including some forms of computer data storage) are considered permanent (non-volatile) storage, that is, the data will remain stored when power is removed from the device. In contrast, most electronically stored information within most types of semiconductor (computer chips) microcircuits is volatile memory, for it vanishes if power is removed.

With the exception of barcodes and OCR data, electronic data storage is easier to revise and may be more cost effective than alternative methods due to smaller physical space requirements and the ease of replacing (rewriting) data on the same medium. However, the durability of methods such as printed data is still superior to that of most electronic storage media. The durability limitations may be overcome with the ease of duplicating (backing-up) electronic data.

From a few kilobytes a few years ago, data storage devices have come a long way to feature a storage capacity of over a 100 gigabytes. Let's have a look at some of the various types of computer data storage devices used earlier and today.

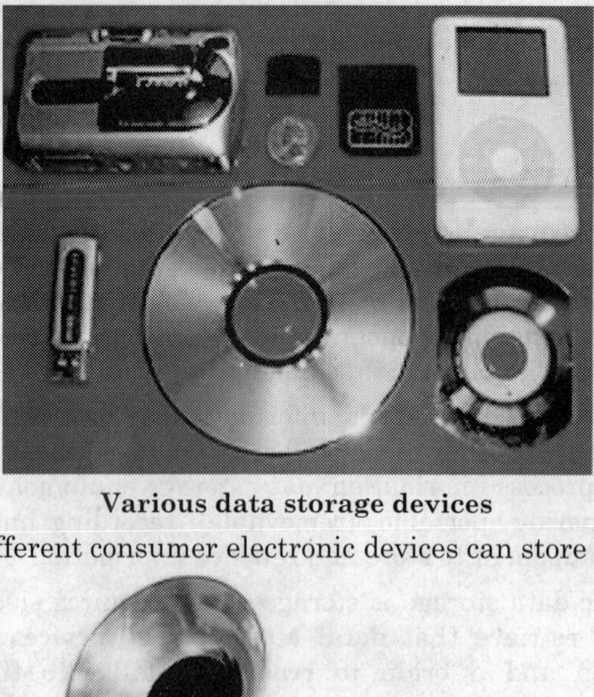

Various data storage devices

Many different consumer electronic devices can store data.

Phonogram

Edison cylinder phonograph 1899. The Phonograph cylinder is a storage medium. The phonograph may or may not be considered a storage device.

Magnetic Tape

A **reel-to-reel tape recorder (Sony TC-630)**. The magnetic tape is a data storage medium. The recorder is data storage equipment using a portable medium (tape reel) to store the data.

Computer data storage devices refers to computer components which can retain the data in digital format, to be used for computing at some point of time in the future. Data storage types commonly in use today include disk storage, flash memory, etc.

Disk Storage

Disk storage is a category of computer storage devices, wherein the data is recorded on a round and rotating surface, two-dimensional in nature. Disk drivers are used to record or retrieve information from these disks. Though these days, the term disk storage is mostly used to refer to a hard disk, it also refers to floppy disks and optical disks.

Floppy Disk

A floppy disk is a thin flexible medium of magnetic storage which is encased in a square plastic shell. A floppy disk is read and written by a floppy disk drive. This small storage device was invented by IBM in 1969. It comes in three sizes - 8-inch, 5¼-inch (1.2MB) and 3½-inch (1.44MB). Floppy disks enjoyed wide popularity from the 70s to the 90s, but post 90s they were overshadowed by devices which had more capacity and were faster. The use of floppies has almost ceased, though limited use can be still seen in some places.

Compact Disk

Compact disk, more commonly referred to as a CD, is an optical disk used to store digital data. After its introduction in the market in 1982, this technology was followed with the launch of CD-ROM, CD-R, CD-RW, VCD, SVCD and Enhanced CD. CD-ROM and CD-R are widely used in the field of computers. A standard CD having a diameter of 120 mm can hold up to 700 MB data. An estimated 300 billion CDs were sold all over the world by the year 2009.

Digital Versatile Disk

Digital versatile disk, more commonly referred to as DVD, is an optical storage device used for data storage in computer technology. Although they share the same dimensions as the CDs, DVDs have the capacity to store six times more data than the compact disks. DVD-video is used to store video content while DVD-audio is used to store audio content. The original DVD is more often referred to as Standard Definition DVD (SD-DVD). High-definition DVDs may be discontinued after the Blu-ray optical disk will be introduced into the market.

Pen Drive

Pen drives are classified as NAND style data storage devices. Equipped with a large amount of memory capacity, the pen drive is considered to be an improvement on both the older floppy drive disks and the more modern compact disks that are often used to copy data and reload the files on a different hard drive. Even a pen drive with a relatively low storage capacity tends to provide plenty of space for a number of files. The types of files that can be loaded onto a pen drive are all the common types that can be housed on any hard drive. This makes it possible for persons to copy photos, spreadsheets, word processing documents, movie clips, music tracks, and just about any other type of file.

Pen Drive

Utilizing a pen drive is a simple task. One end of the drive is equipped with a USB connector at one end. The connector is inserted into the USB port on a desktop or laptop and activated. Once the pen drive is in place, it is possible to drop and drag files into the memory of the drive, or forward the files to the drive. The process is no more difficult than attaching files to an email or copying files onto a disk.

Because there are several different operating systems in common use today, there are various types of levels of the pen drive that are configured to work with each system. Even persons who are using an older operating system can usually find a pen drive that is compatible. As long as the desktop or laptop is constructed with a USB port, and the pen drive is compatible with the operating system, the pen drive will provide practical and easy transmission of data from one hard drive to another one in a matter of minutes. The various storage capacity of pen drives of different companies in market with price variation are 1GB, 2GB, 4GB, 8GB, 16GB, 32GB etc.

Blu-Ray Disks

Blu-ray disks, also referred to as BD, are optical disks manufactured by Sony for the storage of digital data. It is most commonly used in gaming, high definition video storing, etc. Though it is of the same size as a CD or DVD, it can store up to 50 GB data. This technology uses a blue-violet laser to read the data, and hence is referred to as blu-ray disk. These optical disks have overshadowed other optical storage devices due to their high storage capacity.

Hard Disk Drive

A hard disk drive is a non-volatile storage device used to store digitally encoded data on rotating platters having magnetic surfaces. Being non-volatile means it can retain the data stored on it even when it is not powered. Hard disk drives were invented by an IBM team, led by Rey Johnson on 14th December, 1954. Earlier, hard disk drives were a removable form of data storage, but today it has become a sealed unit with fixed media. The first hard disk had a capacity to store 5 MB data on fifty 24 inch platters. Today, the capacity has risen to more than a 100 gigabytes, and is still increasing by the day.

Flash Memory

Flash memory is a non-volatile memory in computer technology which can be electrically programmed or erased. Flash memory devices commonly used today include USB flash drives and memory cards.

USB Flash Drive

USB flash drive is a type of memory storage device that consists of NAND-type flash memory, integrated with Universal Serial Bus (USB) interface. The USB flash drives are removable as well as rewritable. Although they are smaller than a floppy disk, their storage capacity ranges from 64 MB to 128 GB. Some USB drives allow as many as 1 million erases and write cycles, while some have a 10 year data retention capacity.

Memory Cards

Flash memory cards are solid electronic flash memory devices used to store data in digital format. These cards are often used in hand-held as well as mobile computers. They are rewritable and non-volatile in nature. Though small, they have a high capacity and can store data of around 8 GB or more. With the increasing use of technology, usage of digital data has increased to no limits. In order to store this enormous amount of data, we need more powerful and secured data storage devices. Development teams all over the world are working around the clock to make better devices which would be small and inexpensive, but at the same time having more capacity and security.

Flash drives come in various, sometimes bulky or novelty, shapes and sizes

INPUT DEVICES

Input device means any machine that feeds data into a computer. For example, a keyboard is an input device, whereas a display monitor is an output device but touch screen monitor is being used as input device also. Input devices other than the keyboard are sometimes called alternate input devices. Mice, trackballs, and light pens are all alternate input devices.

An **input device** is any peripheral (piece of computer hardware equipment) used to provide data and control signals to an information processing system (such as a computer). Input and output devices make up the hardware interface between a computer as a scanner. Many input devices can be classified according to:

- modality of input (e.g. mechanical motion, audio, visual, etc.)
- the input is discrete (e.g. keypresses) or continuous (e.g. a mouse's position, though digitized into a discrete quantity, is fast enough to be considered continuous)
- the number of degrees of freedom involved (e.g. two-dimensional traditional mice, or three-dimensional navigators designed for CAD applications)

Pointing devices, which are input devices used to specify a position in space, can further be classified according to:

- Whether the input is direct or indirect. With direct input, the input space coincides with the display space, i.e. pointing is done in the space where visual feedback or the cursor appears. Touchscreens and light pens involve direct input. Examples involving indirect input include the mouse and trackball.
- Whether the positional information is absolute (e.g. on a touch screen) or relative (e.g. with a mouse that can be lifted and repositioned)

Note that direct input is almost necessarily absolute, but indirect input may be either absolute or relative. For example, digitizing Graphics tablets that do not have an embedded screen involve indirect input and sense absolute positions and are often run in an absolute input mode, but they may also be setup to simulate a relative input mode where the stylus or puck can be lifted and repositioned.

Keyboard

A 'keyboard' is a human interface device which is repre-sented as a layout of buttons. Each button, or key, can be used to either input a linguistic character to a computer, or to call upon a particular function of the computer. Traditional keyboards use spring-based buttons, though newer variations employ virtual keys, or even projected keyboards.

Examples of types of keyboards include:

- Computer keyboard
- Keyer
- Chorded keyboard
- LPFK

Mouse

In computing, a **mouse** is a pointing device that functions by detecting two-dimensional motion relative to its supporting surface. Physically, a mouse consists of an object held under one of the user's hands, with one or more buttons. (Although traditionally a button is typically round or square, modern mice have spring-loaded regions of their top surface that operate switches when pressed down lightly.) It sometimes features other elements, such as "wheels", which allow the user to perform various system-dependent operations, or extra buttons or features that can add more control or dimensional input. The mouse's motion typically translates into the motion of a cursor on a display, which allows for fine control of a graphical user interface.

The name mouse originated at the Stanford Research Institute and derives from the resemblance of early models which had a cord attached to the rear part of the device (suggesting the idea of a tail) to the common mouse.

The first marketed integrated mouse, shipped as a part of a computer and intended for personal computer navigation, came with the Xerox 8010 Star Information System in 1981. However, the mouse remained relatively obscure until the appearance of the Apple Macintosh. The use of mice with desktop computers is now ubiquitous and they are widely available for separate purchase.

A computer mouse -two buttons and a scroll wheel, which can also act as a third button

Scanner

In computing, a **scanner** is a device that optically scans images, printed text, handwriting, or an object, and converts it to a digital image. Common examples found in offices are variations of the desktop (or flatbed) scanner where the document is placed on a glass window for scanning. Handheld scanners, where the device is moved by hand, have evolved from text scanning "wands" to 3D scanners used for industrial design, reverse engineering, test and measurement, orthotics, gaming and other applications. Mechanically driven scanners that move the document are typically used for large-format documents, where a flatbed design would be impractical.

Modern scanners typically use a charge-coupled device (CCD) or a Contact Image Sensor (CIS) as the image sensor, whereas older drum scanners use a photomultiplier tube as the image sensor. A rotary scanner, used for high-speed document scanning, is another type of drum scanner, using a CCD array instead of a photomultiplier. Other types of scanners are planetary scanners, which take photographs of books and documents, and 3D scanners, for producing three-dimensional models of objects.

Another category of scanner is digital camera scanners, which are based on the concept of reprographic cameras. Due to increasing resolution and new features such as anti-shake, digital cameras have become an attractive alternative to regular scanners. While still having disadvantages compared to traditional scanners (such as distortion, reflections, shadows, low contrast), digital cameras offer advantages such as speed, portability and gentle digitizing of thick documents without damaging the book spine. New scanning technologies are combining 3D scanners with digital cameras to create full-color, photo-realistic 3D models of objects.

Scanner

A **pointing device** is any human interface device that allows a user to input spatial data to a computer. In the case of mice and touch screens, this is usually achieved by detecting movement across a physical surface. Analog devices, such as 3D mice, joysticks, or pointing sticks, function by reporting their angle of deflection. Movements of the pointing device are echoed on the screen by movements of the cursor, creating a simple, intuitive way to navigate a computer's GUI.

Input devices, such as buttons and joysticks, can be combined on a single physical device that could be thought of as a composite device. Many gaming devices have controllers like this. Technically mice are composite devices, as they both track movement and provide buttons for clicking, but composite devices are generally considered to have more than two different forms of input.

- Game controller
- Gamepad (or joypad)
- Paddle (game controller)
- Wii Remote

Imaging and Video input devices

Video input devices are used to digitize images or video from the outside world into the computer. The information can be stored in a multitude of formats depending on the user's requirement.

- digital camera
- Webcam
- Image scanner
- Fingerprint scanner
- Barcode reader
- 3D scanner
- Laser rangefinder

Medical Imaging

- Computed tomography
- Magnetic resonance imaging
- Positron emission tomography
- Medical ultrasonography

Audio input devices

In the fashion of video devices, audio devices are used to either capture or create sound. In some cases, an audio output device can be used as an input device, in order to capture produced sound.

- Microphone
- MIDI keyboard or other digital musical instrument

Touch Screen

CRT touch screen having raster-generated light patterns at the viewing screen borders of a conventional CRT. Reflective surfaces proximal to the screen borders reflect the light patterns across the CRT surface to external photodetectors. Modulating the horizontal blanking signal or employing periodic non-reflective patterns on the reflective surfaces effects raster-generated light patterns having a unique time frequency higher than the vertical synch frequency, but lower than the horizontal synch frequency. A screen pointer blocks the lights patterns reflecting across the screen to two or more of the photodetectors. The blocking is time-relative to the CRT's horizontal and vertical synch signals. The photodetector outputs are bandpass filtered at the unique pattern frequency to suppress electromagnetic interference from the CRT's horizontal raster synch, the CRT's vertical synch and other electromagnetic and optical sources. The screen pointer's position is calculated based on which photodetectors' received patterns are blocked, and the times of the blocking relative to the horizontal and vertical synch.

Bar Code Reader

A **barcode reader** (or **barcode scanner**) is an electronic device for reading printed barcodes. Like a flatbed scanner, it consists of a light source, a lens and a light sensor translating optical impulses into electrical ones. Additionally, nearly all barcode readers contain decoder circuitry analyzing the barcode's image data provided by the sensor and sending the barcode's content to the scanner's output port.

Scanning methods are distinguished by the amount of operator manipulation required:

- Pen or wand-type readers: requires the operator to swipe the pen over the code.
- Semi-automatic handheld readers: The operator need not swipe, but must at least position the reader near the label
- Fix-mount readers for automatic reading: The reading is performed laterally passing the label over the reader. No

operator is required, but the position of the code target must coincide with the imaging capability of the reader.

- Reader gates for automatic scanning: The position of the code must be just under the gate for short time, enabling the scanner sweep to capture the code target successfully.

Barcode Reader

OUTPUT DEVICES

Output device means any machine that gives output. The various type of output devices are described below:

Monitor

A monitor or display (sometimes called a visual display unit) is an electronic visual display for computers. The monitor comprises the display device, circuitry, and an enclosure. The display device in modern monitors is typically a thin film transistor liquid crystal display (TFT-LCD), while older monitors use a cathode ray tube (CRT).

LCD Monitor

CRT

Pros:

- High dynamic range (up to around 15,000:1) excellent color, wide gamut and low black level.
- Can display natively in almost any resolution and refresh rate
- No input lag
- Sub-millisecond response times
- Near zero color, saturation, contrast or brightness distortion. Excellent viewing angle.
- Usually much cheaper than LCD or Plasma screens.

Cons:

- Large size and weight, especially for bigger screens (a 20-inch unit weighs about 50 lb (23 kg))
- High power consumption
- Geometric distortion caused by variable beam travel distances
- Older CRTs are prone to screen burn-in
- Produces noticeable flicker at low refresh rates

LCD

Pros:

- Very compact and light
- Low power consumption
- No geometric distortion
- Rugged
- Little or no flicker depending on backlight technology

Cons:

- Limited viewing angle, causing color, saturation, contrast and brightness to vary, even within the intended viewing angle, by variations in posture.
- Bleeding and uneven backlighting in some monitors, causing brightness distortion, especially toward the edges.
- Slow response times, which cause smearing and ghosting artifacts. Modern LCDs have response times of 8 ms or less.

- Only one native resolution. Displaying resolutions either requires a video scalar, lowering perceptual quality, or display at 1:1 pixel mapping, in which images will be physically too large or won't fill the whole screen.
- Fixed bit depth, many cheaper LCDs are incapable of true color.
- Input lag
- Dead pixels may occur either during manufacturing or through use.

Plasma

Pros:

- Compact and light.
- High contrast ratios (10,000:1 or greater), excellent color, wide gamut and low black level.
- High speed response.
- Near zero color, saturation, contrast or brightness distortion. Excellent viewing angle.
- No geometric distortion.
- Highly scalable, with less weight gain per increase in size (from less than 30 in (760 mm) wide to the world's largest at 150 in (3,800 mm)).

Cons:

- Large pixel pitch, meaning either low resolution or a large screen.
- Noticeable flicker when viewed at close range
- High operating temperature and power consumption
- Only has one native resolution. Displaying other resolutions requires a video scaler, which degrades image quality at lower resolutions.
- Fixed bit depth
- Input lag
- Older PDPs are prone to burn-in
- Dead pixels are possible during manufacturing

Printers and its functions

In computing, a **printer** is a peripheral which produces a hard copy (permanent readable text and/or graphics) of documents stored in electronic form, usually on physical print media such as paper or transparencies. Many printers are primarily used as local peripherals, and are attached by a printer cable or, in most newer printers, a USB cable to a computer which serves as a document source. Some printers, commonly known as network printers, have built-in network interfaces, typically wireless and/or Ethernet based, and can serve as a hard copy device for any user on the network. Individual printers are often designed to support both local and network connected users at the same time. In addition, a few modern printers can directly interface to electronic media such as memory cards, or to image capture devices such as digital cameras, scanners; some printers are combined with a scanners and/or fax machines in a single unit, and can function as photocopiers. Printers that include non-printing features are sometimes called multifunction printers (MFP), multi-function devices (MFD), or all-in-one (AIO) printers. Most MFPs include printing, scanning, and copying among their features.

Consumer and some commercial printers are designed for low-volume, short-turnaround print jobs; requiring virtually no setup time to achieve a hard copy of a given document. However, printers are generally slow devices (30 pages per minute is considered fast; and many inexpensive consumer printers are far slower than that), and the cost per page is actually relatively high. However, this is offset by the on-demand convenience and project management costs being more controllable compared to an out-sourced solution. The printing press remains the machine of choice for high-volume, professional publishing. However, as printers have improved in quality and performance, many jobs which used to be done by professional print shops are now done by users on local printers; see desktop publishing. The world's first computer printer was a 19th century mechanically driven apparatus invented by Charles Babbage for his Difference Engine.

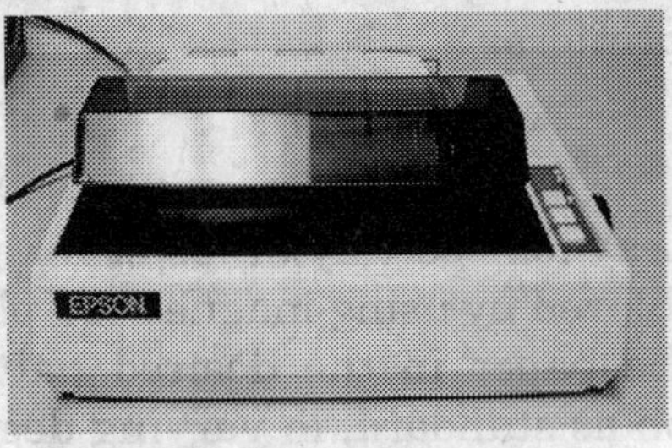

Dotmatrix Printer

Laser printer

A virtual printer is a piece of computer software whose user interface and API resemble that of a printer driver, but which is not connected with a physical computer printer.

Classification of Printer

Printers are used for producing output on paper. There are a large verity of printing devices which can be classified according to the print quality and the printing speeds. Current estimates indicate that about 1500 types of printers are commercially available conforming to about 15 different printing technologies. The following categories of printers are generally used.

Printer Technology- impact printers vs non-impact printers

Impact printers use variations of standards typewriter printing mechanism where a hammer strikes paper through inked ribbon. Non-impact printer uses chemical, heat or electrical signals to etch or induce symbol on paper. Many of these require special coated or treated paper.

Chemical forms-fully formed characters vs dot matrix

Fully formed characters are constructed from solid lines and curves like the characters of typewriter whereas a dot matrix character is made up from a carefully arranged sequence of dots packed very close to each other. Obviously print quality of a dot matrix printer will be poorer compared to that from fully formed characters.

Printer sequence-serial vs line vs page

This indicates the amount of information of printer can within a single cycle of operation. Serial printing is done character by character whereas line printing forms an entire line and prints a line at a time whereas a page printer outputs a whole page of character and images simultaneously during one cycle. Clearly the speed of output will depend upon the printing sequence incorporated in the printing device. We will now look at popular printers:

Ink-jets Printer

Ink-jets (bubble-jets) printers spray ionized tiny drops of ink onto a page to create an image. This is achieved by using magnetized plates which direct the ink's path onto the paper in the desired pattern. Almost all ink-jets offer a color option as standard, in varying degrees of resolution. Ink-jet printers are capable of producing high quality print which almost matches the quality of a laser printer. A standard ink-jet printer has a resolution of 300 dots per inch, although newer models have improved on that. As a rule color link-jet printers can also be used as a regular black and white printer.

Laser printer

Laser printers operate by shining a laser beam to produce an image on a drum. The drum is then rolled through a pool, or reservoir, or toner, and the electrically charged portions of the drum pick up ink. Finally, using a combination of heat and pressure, the ink on the drum is transferred onto the page. Laser printers print very fast, and the supply cartridges work a long time. Color laser printers use the same toner-based printing process as black and white (B/W) laser printers, except that they combine four different toner colors. Color laser printers can also be used as a regular black and white laser printer.

LED/LCD Printer

LED/LCD printers are types of electro photographic printers that are identical to laser printers in most ways. Both LCD (liquid crystal display) and LED (light-emitting diode) printers use a light source instead of a laser to create an image on a drum. In most contexts, "laser printer" covers LCD and LED printers as well. The print process is almost identical, but LED printers use Light Emitting Diodes to charge the drum, and the other uses Liquid Crystals. These printers produce a very high quality text and graphics print out.

Dot-matrix Printer

Impact (Dot-matrix) printers use a set of closely spaced pins and a ribbon to print letters or other characters on a page. These printers actually impact the page to print a character, much like a typewriter. Dot-matrix printers vary in terms of speed and the number of pins they have. They can run at a speed anywhere between 50 and 500 CPS (Characters Per Second). The number of pins, which can vary between 9 to 24, determines the quality of the print job. Dot matrix printers are commonly used for printing invoices, purchase orders, shipping forms, labels, and other multi-part forms. Dot matrix printers can print through multi-part forms in a single pass, allowing them to produce more pages than even high-speed laser printers.

Solid Ink printers

They are page printers that use solid wax ink sticks in a "phase-change" process. They work by liquefying wax ink sticks into reservoirs, and then squirting the ink onto a transfer drum, from where it is cold-fused onto the paper in a single pass. Solid-ink printers offer better color consistency than do most technologies, with little variation caused by changes in temperature, humidity, or type of paper. Solid ink machines have better reliability, because they have fewer components in comparison, for example with color laser printers.

Dye Sublimation printers

This is professional device widely used in demanding graphic arts and photographic applications. True these printers work by heating the ink so that it turns from a solid into a gas. The heating element can be set to different temperatures, thus controlling the amount of ink laid down in one spot. In practice, this means that color is applied as a continuous tone, rather than in dots, as with an inkjet. One color is laid over the whole of one sheet at a time, starting with yellow and ending with black. The ink is on large rolls of film which contain sheets of each color, so for an A4 print it will have an A4-size sheet of yellow, followed by a sheet of cyan, and so on. Dye sublimation requires particularly expensive special paper, as the dyes are designed to diffuse into the paper surface, mixing to create precise color shades.

Portable Printers

Portable printers are usually fairly lightweight and sometimes carry the option of using a battery instead of drawing power from the computer. Usually they realize basic print resolutions suitable for plain text printing. You can find on the market the following types of the portable printers: Thermal printer, Thermal transfer printer and Ink-Jet printer. The main advantage of thermal and thermal transfer printers is that they can be very small. The smallest thermal and thermal transfer printers weigh approximately one pound. Usually the ink-jet portable printer weighs more than 2 pounds. Thermal printers require a special type of paper.

Digital Photo Printers

Many middle range printers are now able to print photo quality images. Usually an option with color printers, specialist photo print heads allow a greater resolution to be achieved to improve photo image quality. Photo ink jet printers expand their gamuts by adding additional ink colors, usually light cyan and light magenta.

Network Printer

It is a printer that provides output capabilities to all network users.

Multifunction Printers

Combine top-quality color ink-jet or laser printing with plain-paper and PC faxing, color copying and color scanning, telephoning-all in one convenient, space-saving machine. If you work from home or have a small office a multifunctional device may be ideal.

The Bravo AutoPrinter is the worlds first automated CD/DVD printing system that can truly be called innovative. It combines automatic, robotic-based CD or DVD printing along with full-color, 2400 dpi disc printing all in one compact, desktop unit.

Printers for banking: these printers realize innovative technology and functionality to increase productivity, and reduce costs.

EZ CD/DVD Printers: provide a low cost way to create professional printed CD-Rs and DVD-Rs. Instead of writing on the CD or applying labels, you can print directly on the CD surface. With high speed capabilities, a full color image can be printed directly on the top surface of your CDs in less than 1 minute.

Label Printers are the smartest way to print labels one at a time. The printers allow easy installation. You can get high-quality, professional results every time.

VersaLaser™ (Universal Laser Systems Inc.) is peripheral tool, that can transform images or drawings on your computer screen into real items made out of an amazing variety of materials... wood, plastic, fabric, paper, glass, leather, stone, ceramic, rubber... and it's as easy to use as your printer. Two models of VersaLaser have 16"x12" (VL-200) and 24"x12" (VL-300) work areas.

3D Printers (Z corporation). The ZPrinter 310 System creates physical models directly from computer-aided design system ("CAD") and other digital data in hours instead of days. The printer is fast, versatile and simple, allowing engineers to produce a range of concept models and functional test parts quickly and inexpensively. The system is ideal for an office environment or educational institution, providing product developers easy access to a 3D Printer.

Plotters

Plotters are large-scale printers that are very accurate at reproducing line drawings. They are commonly used for technical drawings such as engineering drawings or architectural blueprints. The two basic types of plotters are called flatbed plotters and drum plotters. Flatbed plotters are horizontally aligned with a flat surface to which a piece of paper is attached. The paper remains stationary and the printer moves pens across the paper to draw the image. Drum plotters, also called upright plotters, are vertically positioned. They have a drum that the paper rolls on. Drum plotters usually make more noise and are more compact than flatbed plotters.

Printers and Printing

Printers are an essential resource for creating a hard copy — a physical reproduction using paper — of documents and collateral for business, academic, and home users. It has become an indispensable peripheral in all levels of business and institutional computing.

Types of Printers

Like any other computer peripheral, there are several types of printers available for use. Some printers employ technologies that mimic manual typewriter-style functionality, while others use sprayed organic ink or electrically-charged powder medium. Printer hardware interfaces with a PC or network using parallel, serial, or data networking protocols. There are several factors to consider when evaluating printers for procurement and deployment in your computing environment.

Printing Considerations

There are several aspects to factor into printer evaluations. The following specifies some of the most common criteria when evaluating your printing needs.

Function

Evaluating organizational needs and how a printer services those needs is the essential criteria in determining the right type of printer for your environment. The most important question to ask is "What do we need?". Since there are specialized printers for either text, images, or any variation thereof, you should be certain that you procure the right tool for your purposes.

For example, if your requirements call for high-quality color images on professional-grade glossy paper, it is recommended to use a dye-sublimation or thermal wax transfer color printer than a laser or impact printer.

Conversely, a laser or inkjet printers are well-suited for printing rough drafts or documents intended for internal distribution (such high-volume printers are usually called workgroup printers). Determining the needs of the everyday user allows administrators to determine the right printer for the job.

Other factors to consider are features such as duplexing — the ability of the printer to print on both sides of a piece of paper. Traditionally, printers could only print on one side of the page (called simplex printing). Most printer models today do not have this feature by default (or it may be able to simulate a manual duplexing method which forces the user to flip the paper themselves). Some models offer add-on hardware for duplexing; however, such add-ons can drive one-time costs up considerably. However duplex printing may reduce costs over time by reducing the amount of paper used to print documents, thus reducing recurring consumables costs.

Another factor to consider is paper size. Most printers are capable of handling letter (8 1/2" x 11") and legal (8 1/2" x 14") sized paper. If certain departments (such as marketing or design) have specialized needs such as creating posters or banners, there are large-format printers which can handle tabloid (11" x 17") sizes or larger.

Additionally, high-end features such as network modules for workgroup and remote site printing should also be considered during evaluation. More information about networked printing can be found in the Section called Networked Versus Local Printers.

Cost

Cost is another factor to consider when evaluating printers. However, simply determining the one-time cost associated with the purchase of the printer itself is not enough of a determinant. There are other costs to consider, such as consumables, parts and maintenance, and printer add-ons.

Consumables is a general term for printing supplies. Ink and paper are the two most common printing consumables. Ink is the material that the printer projects onto the medium (the paper).

Ink is, itself, a generalized term, as not all printers function using standard, water-based inks. Laser printers use powder, while impact printers use ribbons. There are specialized printers that heat the ink before it is transferred onto paper, while others spray the ink in small drops onto the printing surface. Ink replacement costs vary widely and depend on whether the ink can be recharged (refilled) by hand or if it requires a full replacement of the ink cartridge (the ink housing).

A comparative study based on printer technologies is given below:

Some Printer Technologies

Style of Print head	Character per second	Print quality
Dot matrix	40-400	Low quality but being steadily improved. Very useful for high-volume work because of great speeds. Lack of descenders on letters and the inability to response well on a photocopier are major problem
Impact printers have the ability to produce multiple copies of documents		
Ink-jet	Upto 92	High –quality character sets: choice of type set is controlled by program; print quality is not equal to the daisy-wheel low cost.
Laser	100-2000	Very high quality print at speeds unapproachable by other technologies.
Non impact printers cannot produce multiple copies at one running		

HARDWARE AND SOWTWARE

Hardware is a general term for the physical artifacts of a technology. It may also mean the physical components of a computer system, in the form of computer hardware.

Hardware historically meant the metal parts and fittings that were used to make wooden products stronger, more functional, longer lasting and easier to fabricate or assemble.

Modern hardware stores typically sell equipment such as keys, locks, hinges, latches, corners, handles, wire, chains, plumbing supplies, tools, utensils, cutlery and machine parts, especially when they are made of metal.

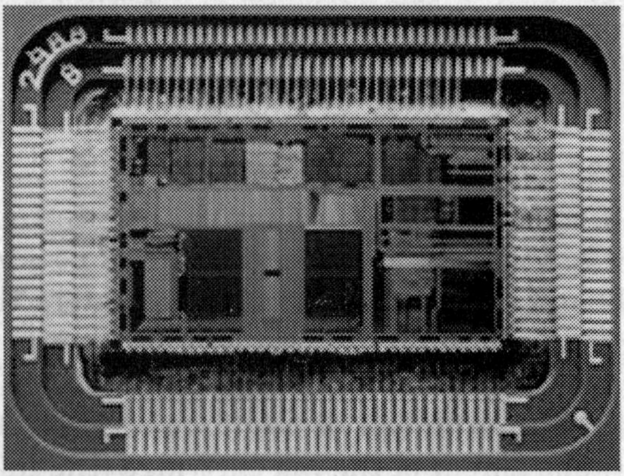

CPU is a piece of computer hardware

Computer software, or just **software**, is the collection of computer programs and related data that provide the instructions telling a computer what to do. The term was coined to contrast to the old term hardware (meaning physical devices). In contrast to hardware, software is intangible, meaning it "cannot be touched". Software is also sometimes used in a more narrow sense, meaning application software only. Sometimes the term includes data that has not traditionally been associated with computers, such as film, tapes and records. Examples of computer software include:

- Application software includes end-user applications of computers such as word processors or Video games, and ERP software for groups of users.
- Middleware controls and co-ordinates distributed systems.
- Programming languages define the syntax and sematics of computer programs. For example, many mature banking applications were written in the COBOL language, originally invented in 1959. Newer applications are often written in more modern programming languages.
- System software includes operating systems, which govern computing resources. Today large applications running on remote machines such as Websites are considered to be system software, because the end-user interface is generally through a Graphical user interface (GUI), such as a web browser.
- Testware is software for testing hardware or a software package.
- Firmware is low-level software often stored on electrically programmable memory devices. Firmware is given its name because it is treated like hardware and run ("executed") by other software programs.
- Device drivers control parts of computers such as disk drives, printers, CD drives, or computer monitors.
- Programming tools help conduct computing tasks in any category listed above. For programmers, these could be tools for debugging, or reverse engineering older legacy systems in order to check source code compatibility.

Application software

Application software, also known as **applications**, is computer software designed to help the user to perform singular or multiple related specific tasks. Examples include Enterprise software, Accounting software, Office suites, Graphics software and media players.

Application software is contrasted with system software and middleware, which manage and integrate a computer's capabilities, but typically do not directly apply them in the performance of tasks that benefit the user. A simple, if imperfect analogy in the world of hardware would be the relationship of an electric light bulb (an application) to an electric power generation plant (a system). The power plant merely generates electricity, not itself of any real use until harnessed to an application like the electric light that performs a service that benefits the user. OpenOffice.org is a popular example of open source application software. There are two categories of application software:

- Pre-written software package, and
- User application program.

A number of powerful application software packages, which does not require significant programming knowledge, have been developed and few are:

- Data Base Management Software
- Spreadsheet Software
- Word Processing Desktop Publishing (DTP) and Presentation Software
- Graphic Software
- Data Communication Software
- Statistical and Operational Research Software.

System software

System software is computer software designed to operate the computer hardware and to provide and maintain a platform for running application software.

The most important types of system software are:

- The computer BIOS and device firmware, which provide basic functionality to operate and control the hardware connected to or built into the computer.
- The operating system (prominent examples being Microsoft Windows, Mac OS X and Linux), which allows the parts of a computer to work together by performing tasks like transferring data between memory and disks or rendering

output onto a display device. It also provides a platform to run high-level system software and application software.

- Utility software, which helps to analyze, configure, optimize and maintain the computer.

In some publications, the term system software is also used to designate software development tools (like a compiler, linker or debugger).

System software is usually not what a user would buy a computer for - instead, it can be seen as the basics of a computer which come built-in or pre-installed. In contrast to system software, software that allows users to do things like create text documents, play games, listen to music, or surf the web is called application software.

Special Purpose Software: Special purpose programs are those which extended the capability of operating system to provide specialised services to application programs. A few example are:

- Spreadsheet software like LOTUS, VISICALC etc.
- Data management software like dBASE, Unify etc.

Types of system software programs

System software helps use the operating system and computer system. It includes diagnostic tools, compilers, servers, windowing systems, utilities, language translator, data communication programs, data management programs and more. The purpose of system software is to insulate the applications programmer as much as possible from the details of the particular computer complex being used, especially memory and other hardware features, and such accessory devices as communications, printers, readers, displays, keyboards, etc.

Specific kinds of system software include:

- Loaders
- Linkers
- Utility software
- Desktop environment / Graphical user interface
- Shells
- BIOS
- Hypervisors
- Boot loaders

If system software is stored on non-volatile memory such as integrated circuits, it is usually termed firmware

TYPE OF LANGUAGES

The term computer language includes a wide variety of languages used to communicate with computers. It is broader than the more commonly-used term programming language. Programming languages are a subset of computer languages. For example, HTML is a markup language and a computer language, but it is not traditionally considered a programming language. Machine code is a computer language. It can technically be used for programming, and has been (e.g. the original bootstrapper for Altair BASIC), though most would not consider it a programming language.

Computer languages can be divided into two groups: high-level languages and low-level languages. High-level languages are designed to be easier to use, more abstract, and more portable than low-level languages. Syntactically correct programs in some languages are then compiled to low-level language and executed by the computer. Most modern software is written in a high-level language, compiled into object code, and then translated into machine instructions.

Computer languages could also be grouped based on other criteria. Another distinction could be made between human-readable and non-human-readable languages. Human-readable languages are designed to be used directly by humans to communicate with the computer. Non-human-readable languages, though they can often be partially understandable, are designed to be more compact and easily processed, sacrificing readability to meet these ends.

Machine Language

Machine code or **machine language** is a system of instructions and data executed directly by a computer's central processing unit. Machine code may be regarded as a primitive (and cumbersome) programming language or as the lowest-level representation of a compiled and/or assembled computer program. Programs in interpreted languages are not represented by machine code however, although their interpreter (which may be seen as a processor executing the higher level program) often is. Machine code is sometimes called native code when referring to platform-dependent parts of language features or libraries. Machine code should not be confused with so called "bytecode", which is executed by an interpreter.

Programming Language

A **programming language** is an artificial language designed to express computations that can be performed by a machine, particularly a computer. Programming languages can be used to create programs that control the behavior of a machine, to express algorithms precisely, or as a mode of human communication.

Many programming languages have some form of written specification of their syntax (form) and semantics (meaning). Some languages are defined by a specification document. For example, the C programming language is specified by an ISO Standard. Other languages, such as Perl, have a dominant implementation that is used as a reference.

The earliest programming languages predate the invention of the computer, and were used to direct the behavior of machines such as Jacquard looms and player pianos. Thousands of different programming languages have been created, mainly in the computer field, with many more being created every year. Most programming languages describe computation in an imperative style, i.e., as a sequence of commands, although some languages, such as those that support functional programming or logic programming, use alternative forms of description.

Advantage of Machine Language: It is faster execution since the computer directly starts executing it.

Disadvantage of Machine Language: It is difficult to understand and develop a program using machine language. Anybody going through this program for checking will have a difficult task understanding what will be achieved when this program is executed.

Assembly Language

Assembly languages are a type of low-level languages for programming computers, microprocessors, microcontrollers, and other (usually) integrated circuits. They implement a symbolic representation of the numeric machine codes and other constants needed to program a particular CPU architecture. This representation is usually defined by the hardware manufacturer, and is based on abbreviations (called mnemonics) that help the programmer remember individual instructions, registers, etc. An assembly language family is thus specific to a certain physical (or virtual) computer architecture. This is in contrast to most high-level languages, which are (ideally) portable.

A utility program called an **assembler** is used to translate assembly language statements into the target computer's machine code. The assembler performs a more or less isomorphic translation (a one-to-one mapping) from mne-monic statements into machine instructions and data. This is in contrast with high-level languages, in which a single statement generally results in many machine instructions.

An assembly language program cannot be executed by a machine directly as it is not in binary form. An assembler is needed in order to translate as assembly language program into the object code executed by machine. This is illustrated below:

Assembly Language Programe ⟹ [Assembler] ⟹ Object Code in machine language

Many sophisticated assemblers offer additional mechanisms to facilitate program development, control the assembly process, and aid debugging. In particular, most modern assemblers include a macro facility (described below), and are called **macro assemblers**.

Advantage of Assembly Language: Writing a program in assembly language is more convenient than in machine language. Instead of binary sequence, as in machine language, it is written in the form of symbolic instruction. Therefore, it gives a little more readability.

Disadvantage of Assembly Language: Assembly lang-uage (program) is specific to particular machine architecture. Assembly languages are designed for specific mark and model of a microprocessor. That is why it is not portable. Assembly language program is not as fast as machine language. It has to be first translated into machine language.

High level Programming Language

A **high-level programming language** is a program-ming language with strong abstraction from the details of the computer. In comparison to low-level programming languages, it may use natural language elements, be easier to use, or be more portable across platforms. Such languages hide the details of CPU operations such as memory access models and management of scope.

This greater abstraction and hiding of details is generally intended to make the language user-friendly, as it includes concepts from the problem domain instead of those of the machine used. A high-level language isolates the execution semantics of a computer architecture from the specification of the program, making the process of developing a program simpler and more understandable with respect to a low-level language. The amount of abstraction provided defines how "high-level" a programming language is.

The first high-level programming language to be designed for a computer was Plankalkül, created by Konrad Zuse. However, it was not implemented in his time and his original contributions were isolated from other develop-ments.

Since a high level source program must be translated first into the form the machine can understand, this is done by software called Complier which takes the source code as input and produces as output the machine language code of the machine on which it is to be executed. This is illustrated below:

Source Program in High level Language ⟹ [Complier] ⟹ Object Code

Advantage of High level Programming Language: There are four main advantages of High level Programming Language. These are:

- Readability
- Portability
- Easy debugging
- Easy Software development

High level Programming Languages are also called Third generation languages.

Fourth Generation Language

The fourth generation of programming language is not as clearly defined as are the other earlier generations. Most people feel that a fourth generation language, commonly referred to as 4GL is a high level language that requires significantly fewer instructions to accomplish a particular task than a third generation language does. Thus, a programmer should be able to write a program faster in 4GL than in third generation language. Forth generation language are mostly machine independent. Usually they can be used on more than one type of computer. They are mostly used office automation or business application, but not for scientific program. Some fourth generation languages are designed to be easily learnt and used by end users.

COMPILER AND INTERPRETER

Compiler

A **compiler** is a special program that processes statements written in a particular programming language and converts them into **machine language**, a "binary program" or "code," that a computer processor uses. A compiler works with what are sometimes called 3GL and higher-level languages (3rd-generation languages, such as Java, C, and PL/1). Typically, a programmer writes language statements in a language such as C, Pascal, or C++ one line at a time using a tool called an editor. The "edited" file contains the source statements. The progra-mmer then runs the appropriate language compiler (there may be several compilers for each language), specifying the name of the file that contains the source statements.

When executing the file, the compiler first parses or analyzes all of the language statements syntactically in a sequential manner and then, in one or more successive passes, builds the output **code**, ensuring that statements that refer to other statements are referenced correctly in the final code. The code is linked to various libraries, which are common code sections found in many programs. The use of libraries helps keep redundant coding to a minimum. The compilation output is sometimes referred to as **object** code or an object module. (Note that the term "object" as used in this instance is not related to **object-oriented programming**. The object code as used here refers to **machine code** that the processor executes one instruction at a time.)

High-level languages are usually compiled and are not limited to any particular **computer architecture**. High-level languages are much easier to read than **assembly language**. Compiled languages are preferred by many developers because, once compiled, the program runs faster than if it were interpreted. Once a program has been compiled, it cannot easily be changed, so there's an element of security built in to compiled programs.

The Java programming language has taken code compilation one step further. Java, which is used in object-oriented programming, has introduced the idea of compiling output that can run on any computer system platform for which a Java bytecode interpreter (called a Java Virtual Machine) is provided to convert the bytecode into instructions that can be executed by the actual **hardware** processor. Using this virtual machine, the bytecode can be recompiled at the execution platform by a "just-in-time" compiler. What all this means is that the bytecode is platform-independent code that can be sent to any platform (**Windows**, MAC, **Unix**) and run on that platform. This is one of the principal advantages of Java: write once, compile once.

A **compiler** is a computer program (or set of programs) that transforms source code written in a programming language (the source language) into another computer language (the target language, often having a binary form known as object code). The most common reason for wanting to transform source code is to create an executable program.

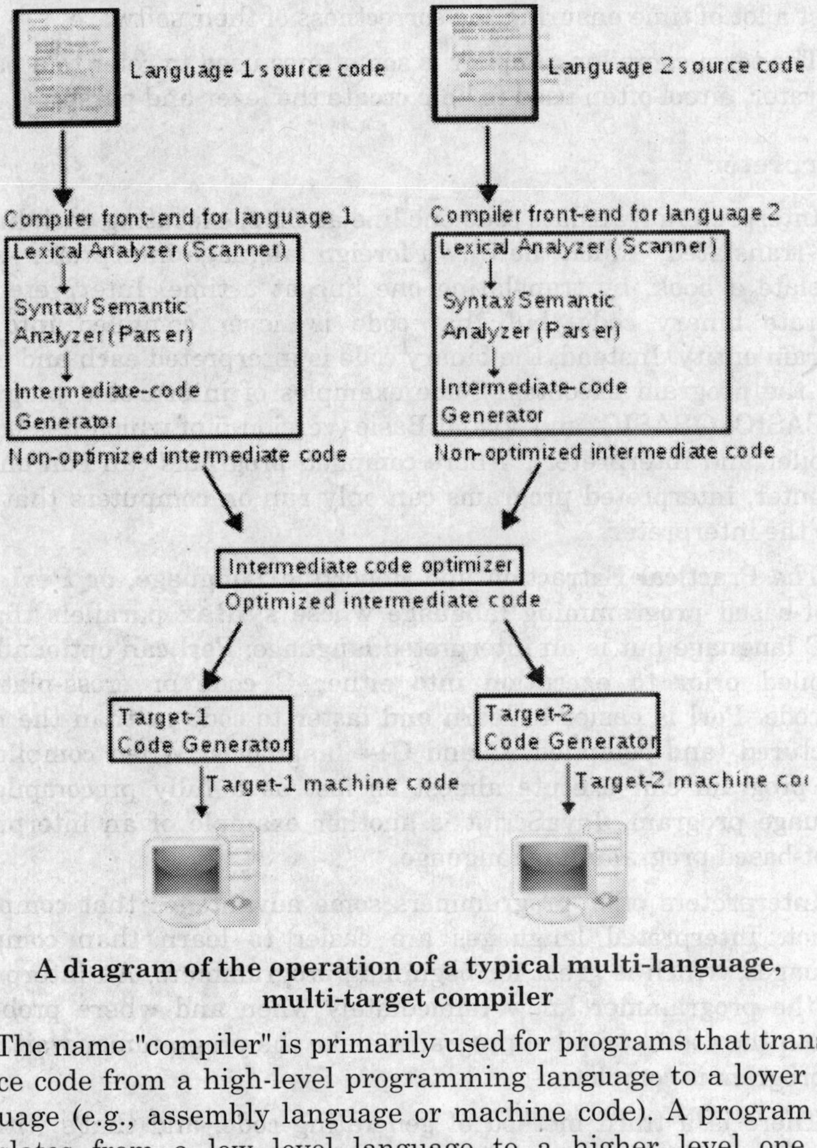

A diagram of the operation of a typical multi-language, multi-target compiler

The name "compiler" is primarily used for programs that translate source code from a high-level programming language to a lower level language (e.g., assembly language or machine code). A program that translates from a low level language to a higher level one is a decompiler. A program that translates between high-level languages is usually called a language translator, source to source translator, or language converter. A language rewriter is usually a program that translates the form of expressions without a change of language.

A compiler is likely to perform many or all of the following operations: lexical analysis, preprocessing, parsing, semantic analysis, code generation, and code optimization.

Program faults caused by incorrect compiler behavior can be very difficult to track down and work around and compiler implementors invest a lot of time ensuring the correctness of their software.

The term compiler-compiler is sometimes used to refer to a parser generator, a tool often used to help create the lexer and parser.

Interpreter

Interpreters translate code one line at time, executing each line as it is "translated," much the way a foreign language interpreter would translate a book, by translating one line at a time. Interpreters do generate binary code, but that code is never compiled into one program entity. Instead, the binary code is interpreted each and every time the program executes. Some examples of interpreted programs are BASIC, QBASIC, and Visual Basic (version 5 of which has both a compiler and interpreter). Where compiled programs can run on any computer, interpreted programs can only run on computers that also have the interpreter.

The Practical Extraction and Reporting Language, or **Perl**, is a script-based programming language whose **syntax** parallels that of the C language but is an interpreted language; Perl can optionally be compiled prior to execution into either C code or cross-platform bytecode. Perl is easier to learn and faster to code in than the more structured (and compiled) C and C++ languages. When compiled, a Perl program can execute almost as fast as a fully precompiled C language program. JavaScript is another example of an interpreted script-based programming language.

Interpreters offer programmers some advantages that compilers do not. Interpreted languages are easier to learn than compiled languages, which is great for beginning programmers. An interpreter lets the programmer know immediately when and where problems exist in the code; compiled programs make the programmer wait until the program is complete.

There is a third method of generating code, and that's with an assembler, which is used in Assembly language. The assembler translates Assembly language into machine language. In computer science, an **interpreter** normally means a computer program that executes, i.e. performs, instructions written in a programming language. An interpreter may be a program that either

1. executes the source code directly
2. translates source code into some efficient intermediate representation (code) and immediately executes this
3. explicitly executes stored precompiled code made by a compiler which is part of the interpreter system

Perl, Python, MATLAB, and Ruby are examples of type 2, while UCSD Pascal and Java are type 3: Source programs are compiled ahead of time and stored as machine independent code, which is then linked at run-time and executed by an interpreter and/or compiler (for JIT systems). Some systems, such as Smalltalk, BASIC and others, may also combine 2 and 3.

While interpretation and compilation are the two principal means by which programming languages are implemented, these are not fully distinct categories, one of the reasons being that most interpreting systems also perform some translation work, just like compilers. The terms "interpreted language" or "compiled language" merely mean that the canonical implementation of that language is an interpreter or a compiler; a high level language is basically an abstraction which is (ideally) independent of particular implementations.

Interpreter Vs. Compiler

Programming languages can be divided into two major categories: low level and high level. "Assembly language" and "machine language" are called low-level languages because they more than others "speak" the language the computer understands. On the other hand, **C**, **C++**, **Pascal**, **BASIC**, Visual Basic, **Java** and **COBOL** are high-level languages because they require more manipulation by the computer, a process called compiling.

An interpreter translates some form of source code into a target representation that it can immediately execute and evaluate. The structure of the interpreter is similar to that of a compiler, but the amount of time it takes to produce the executable representation will vary as will the amount of optimization. The following diagram shows one representation of the differences.

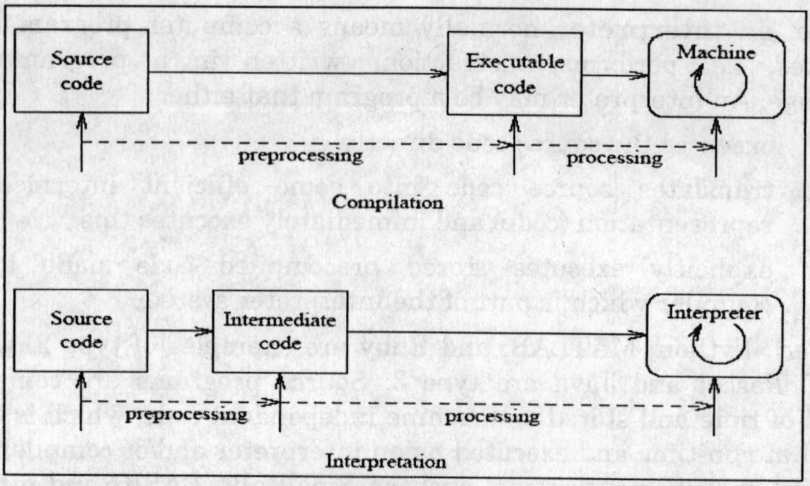

- *Compiler* -- spends some time evaluating the entire program and then translates all the programming statements of a program into a machine language program, which is then executed at once.
- *Interpreter* -- translates interactively each programming statement into an immediately usable machine language instruction. Although an interpreter slows down the execution speed of a program somewhat, it does not require extra steps to compile and link like a compiler.
- In a production environment where throughput is more critical, a compiled language is preferred.
- Any high-level language can either be interpreted or compiled.
- These are programs which translate computer programs from high-level languages such as Pascal, C++, Java or JavaScript into the raw 1s and 0s which the computer can understand, but the human programmers cannot:

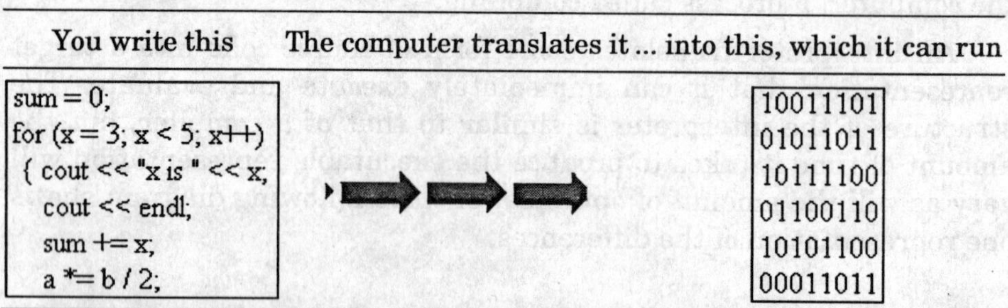

Computer translate programs from High level language to machine language

Compiler characteristics

- spends a lot of time analyzing and processing the program
- the resulting executable is some form of machine-specific binary code
- the computer hardware interprets (executes) the resulting code
- program execution is fast
- Compilers were the first sort of translator program to be written. The idea is simple: You write the program, then hand it to the compiler which translates it. Then you run the result.
- The compiler takes the file that you have written and produces another file from it. In the case of Pascal programs, for instance, you might write a program called myProg.pas and the Pascal compiler would translate it into the file myProg.exe which you could then run. If you tried to examine the contents of myProg.exe using, say, a text editor, then it would just appear as gobbledy-gook.
- The compiler has another task apart from translating your program. It also checks it to make sure that it is grammatically correct. Only when it is sure that there are no grammatical errors does it do the translation. Any errors that the compiler detects are called compile-time errors or syntax errors. If it finds so much as one syntax error, it stops compiling and reports the error to you. Here is an example of the C++ compiler reporting a whole list of errors:
- Most "serious" languages are compiled, including Pascal, C++ and Ada.

Interpreter characteristics:

- relatively little time is spent analyzing and processing the program
- the resulting code is some sort of intermediate code
- the resulting code is interpreted by another program
- program execution is relatively slow

The above characteristics are typical. There are well-known cases that are somewhere in between, such as Java with it's JVM

An interpreter is also a program that translates a high-level language into a low-level one, but it does it at the moment the program is run. You write the program using a text editor or something similar, and then instruct the interpreter to run the program. It takes the program, one line at a time, and translates each line before running it: It translates the first line and runs it, then translates the second line and runs it etc. The interpreter has no "memory" for the translated lines, so if it comes across lines of the program within a loop, it must translate them afresh every time that particular line runs. Consider this simple Basic program:

```
10 FOR COUNT = 1 TO 1000
20   PRINT COUNT * COUNT
30 NEXT COUNT
```

Line 20 of the program displays the square of the value stored in COUNT and this line has to be carried out 1000 times. The interpreter must also translate that line 1000 times, which is clearly an inefficient process. However, interpreted languages do have their uses, as we will see in a later section. Examples of interpreted languages are BASIC, JavaScript and LISP.

The Compiler and Interpreter have different approaches to translate. The following table lists the differences between a Complier and an Interpreter.

Complier	**Interpreter**
(1) Scan the entire program first and then translates it into code.	Translate the program line by line.
(2) Converts the entire program to machine code; when all the syntax errors are removed execution takes place.	Each time the program executed, every line is checked for syntax error and then converted to equivalent machine code.
(3) Slow for debugging (removal of mistakes from program)	Good for fast debugging.
(4) Execution time is less.	Execution time is more.

So which is better?

Well, that depends on how you want to write and run your program. The main advantages of compilers are as follows:

- They produce programs which run quickly.
- They can spot syntax errors while the program is being compiled (i.e. you are informed of any grammatical errors before you try to run the program). However, this does not means that a program that compiles correctly is error-free!

The main advantages of interpreters are as follows:

- There is no lengthy "compile time", i.e. you do not have to wait between writing a program and running it, for it to compile. As soon as you have written a program, you can run it.
- They tend to be more "portable", which means that they will run on a greater variety of machines. This is because each machine can have its own interpreter for that language. For instance, the version of the BASIC interpreter for the PDP series computers is different from the QBasic program for personal computers, as they run on different pieces of hardware, but programs written in BASIC are identical from the user's point of view.

CHAPTER-II

WINDOWS OPERATING SYSTEM

INTRODUCTION

Microsoft Windows is a series of software operating systems and graphical user interfaces produced by Microsoft. Microsoft first introduced an operating environment named Windows in November 1985 as an add-on to MS-DOS in response to the growing interest in graphical user interfaces (GUIs). Microsoft Windows came to dominate the world's personal computer market, overtaking Mac OS, which had been introduced previously. As of October 2009, Windows had approximately 91% of the market share of the client operating systems for usage on the Internet. The most recent client version of Windows is Windows 7.

Operating Systems (OS)

General

It allows to use computer without any knowledge of coding. Without an operating system, hardware would not work at all, until user wrote own code for the hardware to do what you want. An OS takes care for all input and output in a computer system. It manages users, processes, memory management, printing, telecommunication, networking etc. It sends data to a disk, the printer, the screen and other peripherals connected to the computer. And because every machine is build different, commands for in or output will have to be treated differently too. In almost all cases an Operating System is not one large big behemoth but consists of many small system programs governed by the core or kernel of the OS. Because of the compactness of these small supporting programs it is easier to rewrite parts or packages of the OS than to redesign an entire program. In general programmers only have to make a "call" to the system to make things happen.

This not only makes their live less miserable but the production time becomes shorter. As well as that programs can run on different types of machines with the same family of CPU's without changing anything in the program. This is what makes a standard Operating System so important. In fact any form of standardization is important for production and compatibility.

Functions and Structure

At first operating systems were designed to help applications interact with the computer hardware. While this is still the case, the importance of the operating system has grown to the point where (at least in the minds of many users) the operating system defines the machine. The operating system provides a layer of abstraction between the user and the bare machine. Users and applications do not see the hardware directly, but view it through the operating system. This abstraction can be used to hide certain hardware details from users and applications. Thus, changes in the hardware are not seen by the user (even though the OS must accommodate them).

This is particularly advantageous for venders that want offer a consistent OS interface across an entire line of hardware platforms. For example, certain operations such as interaction with 3D graphics hardware can be controlled by the operating system. When an instruction pertaining to the hardware is executed and if the hardware is present then all is fine. However, if the hardware is not present then a trap is generated by the illegal instruction. In this case the OS can emulate the desired instruction in software.

Another way that abstraction can be used is to make related devices appear the same from the user point of view. For example, hard disks, floppy disks, CD-ROMs, and even tape are all very different media, but in many operating systems they appear the same to the user.

An operating system is providing four basic interfaces. Each of these interfaces provides the appropriate view for different groups of individuals:

- **interface to the underlying hardware**- hardware developers who want their hardware to be supported by a particular operating system are primarily interested in the OS-hardware interface.
- **interface to application programs**- application programmers are primarily interested in the OS-application interface.
- **interface to the user**- ordinary users are interested in the user interface. Many books that purport to be about a

particular operating system in fact mainly discuss the user interface.

- **interface to the system manager-** system managers are obviously interested in the system management interface.

Most operating systems in use today are composed of two distinct parts: the kernel and the system programs. The kernel is primarily responsible for the first two of the interfaces described above, and the system programs are primarily responsible for the last two.

Resource Allocation

Modern operating systems often provide users and applications with a virtual machine, an interface to the underlying hardware that makes it appear as though the user is the only user of the machine and it's hardware.

CPU

Whether the computer has one CPU or several CPUs, it is usually the case that there are more processes than CPUs. Thus, the operating system is responsible for scheduling the processes on the CPU(s).

Memory

There is a finite amount of memory that must be shared among the processes. The way this is done varies between different operating systems, but a commonly used mechanism is that of virtual memory.

Input Output (IO) devices

Several different processes may be trying to access a single IO device and the operating system must manage these accesses. Note that this is a different issue than processes scheduling since often IO is being performed for processes that are not currently executing. Some devices (e.g. disks) have resources that can be shared among users and/or user processes. The operating system is responsible for managing and protecting these resources.

Support Services. Another important operating system task is providing support services for processes. These include:

- Support for IO operations.
- File system management.
- Networking
- Protection.

Operating System Design Principles

Operating system design is a complex task. One of the driving forces behind software engineering was the complexity of OS design.

System design goals

User interface: should the interface be easy to learn by a novice user, or should it be designed for the convenience of an experienced user? (multiple user interfaces?)

Efficient system resource management: Unfortunately, the more complete the resource management, the more overhead.

Security: Once again, the more secure a system is the less efficient it is.

Flexibility: Most operating systems come preconfigured for many different devices. Part of the process of setting up a particular machine is to construct a version of the operating system that is tuned for the local installation. This tuning often involves setting certain limits, such as the maximum number of processes. It also involves specifying the attached hardware so that only the necessary drivers will be loaded. Some operating systems can load and unload drivers automatically at run-time.

Portability: Will the operating system be portable to widely varying types of hardware, or just different models of a particular class of hardware?

Backwards compatibility and emulation: Is it important that software that ran under previous operating system versions or under different operating systems be supported?

Layered design

Operating system consists of multiple layers. Each layer depends on the layer(s) beneath it.

Advantages:	improved security, since only layers close to hardware need to operate in kernel mode. improved portability since only small part of operating system interfaces with the hardware. makes maintenance of operating system code easier.
Disadvantages:	Selecting proper functionality to put in each layer can be difficult. This is because there are some

	interdependencies that would violate the layering model leading to decreased efficiency.

Stacked Job Batch Systems (mid 1950s - mid 1960s)

A batch system is one in which jobs are bundled together with the instructions necessary to allow them to be processed without intervention.

The basic physical layout of the memory of a batch job computer is shown below:

Monitor (permanently resident)

User Space
(compilers, programs, data, etc.)

The monitor is system software that is responsible for interpreting and carrying out the instructions in the batch jobs. When the monitor starts a job, the entire computer is dedicated to the job, which then controls the computer until it finishes.

A sample of several batch jobs might look like this:

$JOB user_spec;	identify the user for accounting purposes
$FORTRAN;	load the FORTRAN compiler
	source program cards
$LOAD ;	load the compiled program
$RUN;	run the program data cards
$EOJ ;	end of job
$JOB	user_spec; identify a new user
$LOAD;	application
$RUN;	data
$EOJ	

Advantages of batch systems - move much of the work of the operator to the computer increased performance since it was possible for job to start as soon as the previous job finished.

Disadvantages - turn-around time can be large from user standpoint more difficult to debug program due to lack of protection scheme, one batch job can affect pending jobs (read too many cards, etc.) a job could corrupt the monitor, thus affecting pending jobs a job could enter an infinite loop.

One of the major shortcomings of early batch systems is that there's no protection scheme to prevent one job from adversely affecting other jobs.

The solution to this brought a simple protection scheme, where certain memory (e.g. where the monitor resides) were made off-limits to user programs. This prevented user programs from corrupting the monitor.

To keep user programs from reading too many (or not enough) cards, the hardware is changed to allow the computer to operate in one of two modes: one for the monitor and one for the user programs. IO can only be performed in monitor mode, so that IO requests from the user programs are passed to the monitor. In this way, the monitor can keep a job from reading past it's on $EOJ card.

To prevent an infinite loop, a timer is added to the system and the $JOB card is modified so that a maximum execution time for the job is passed to the monitor. The computer will interrupt the job and return control to the monitor when this time is exceeded.

Spooling Batch Systems (mid 1960s - late 1970s)

One difficulty with simple batch systems is that the computer still needs to read the the deck of cards before it can begin to execute the job. This means that the CPU is idle (or nearly so) during these relatively slow operations.

Since it is faster to read from a magnetic tape than from a deck of cards, it became common for computer centers to have one or more less powerful computers in addition to there main computer. The smaller computers were used to read a decks of cards onto a tape, so that the tape would contain many batch jobs. This tape was then loaded on the main computer and the jobs on the tape were executed. The output from the jobs would be written to another tape which would then be removed and loaded on a less powerful computer to produce any hardcopy or other desired output.

It was a logical extension of the timer idea described above to have a timer that would only let jobs execute for a short time before interrupting them so that the monitor could start an IO operation. Since the IO operation could proceed while the CPU was crunching on a user program, little degradation in performance was noticed.

Since the computer can now perform IO in parallel with computation, it became possible to have the computer read a deck of cards to a tape, drum or disk and to write out to a tape printer while it was computing. This process is called Spooling (Simultaneous

Peripheral Operation On Line). Spooling batch systems were the first and are the simplest of the multiprogramming systems.

One advantage of spooling batch systems was that the output from jobs was available as soon as the job completed, rather than only after all jobs in the current cycle were finished.

Multiprogramming Systems (1960s - present)

As machines with more and more memory became available, it was possible to extend the idea of multiprogra-mming (or multiprocessing) as used in spooling batch systems to create systems that would load several jobs into memory at once and cycle through them in some order, working on each one for a specified period of time.

Monitor (more like an operating system)
User program 1
User program 2
User porgram 3
User program 4

At this point the monitor is growing to the point where it begins to resemble a modern operating system. It is responsible for:

- starting user jobs
- spooling operations
- IO for user jobs
- switching between user jobs
- ensuring proper protection while doing the above

As a simple, yet common example, consider a machine that can run two jobs at once. Further, suppose that one job is IO intensive and that the other is CPU intensive. One way for the monitor to allocate CPU time between these jobs would be to divide time equally between them. However, the CPU would be idle much of the time the IO bound process was executing.

A good solution in this case is to allow the CPU bound process (the background job) to execute until the IO bound process (the foreground job) needs some CPU time, at which point the monitor permits it to run. Presumably it will soon need to do some IO and the monitor can return the CPU to the background job.

Timesharing Systems (1970s - present)

Back in the days of the "bare" computers without any operating system to speak of, the programmer had complete access to the machine. As hardware and software was developed to create monitors, simple and spooling batch systems and finally multiprogrammed systems, the separation between the user and the computer became more and more pronounced.

Users, and programmers in particular, longed to be able to "get to the machine" without having to go through the batch process. In the 1970s and especially in the 1980s this became possible two different ways.

The first involved timesharing or timeslicing. The idea of multiprogramming was extended to allow for multiple terminals to be connected to the computer, with each in-use terminal being associated with one or more jobs on the computer. The operating system is responsible for switching between the jobs, now often called processes, in such a way that favored user interaction. If the context-switches occurred quickly enough, the user had the impression that he or she had direct access to the computer.

Interactive processes are given a higher priority so that when IO is requested (e.g. a key is pressed), the associated process is quickly given control of the CPU so that it can process it. This is usually done through the use of an interrupt that causes the computer to realize that an IO event has occurred.

There are several different types of time sharing systems. One type is represented by computers like VAX/ VMS computers and UNIX workstations. In these computers entire processes are in memory (albeit virtual memory) and the computer switches between executing code in each of them. In other types of systems, such as airline reservation systems, a single application may actually do much of the timesharing between terminals. This way there does not need to be a different running program associated with each terminal.

Operating system ABCs

An operating system, or OS, is a software program that enables the computer hardware to communicate and operate with the computer software. Without a computer operating system, a computer would be useless.

Operating system types

As computers have progressed and developed so have the types of operating systems. Below is a basic list of the different types of operating systems and a few examples of operating systems that fall into each of the categories. Many computer operating systems will fall into more than one of the below categories.

GUI - Short for Graphical User Interface, a GUI Operating System contains graphics and icons and is commonly navigated by using a computer mouse. Examples of GUI Operating Systems are System 7.x, Windows 98, Windows CE.

Multi-user - A multi-user operating system allows for multiple users to use the same computer at the same time and/or different times. Examples of multi-user operating systems are Linux, Unix, Windows 2000.

Multiprocessing - An operating system capable of supporting and utilizing more than one computer processor. Examples of multiprocessing operating systems are Linux, Unix, Windows 2000.

Multitasking - An operating system that is capable of allowing multiple software processes to run at the same time. Examples of multitasking operating systems are Unix, Windows 2000.

Multithreading - Operating systems that allow different parts of a software program to run concurrently. Operating systems that would fall into this category are Linux, Unix, Windows 2000.

BENEFITS OF WINDOWS OPERATING SYSTEM

Windows is a hugely popular OS and not without reason. While some versions are perhaps not as popular as others, they're all extremely good systems capable of managing system resources, multitasking and much more.

Why Choose Windows?

XP, Vista, Window 7 – they're all examples of the Windows operating system, the almost ubiquitous user interface across the majority of offices, banks and other major businesses throughout North America, Europe, Asia and Australia.

There are other OS – such as the Apple OS X or any of the Linux variations (or "distros"). Each of these three popular operating systems can multitask, and they are all adept at managing system resources (such as processing time and memory).

Hardware Support

The Windows operating system is designed to be compatible with the largest combination of PC hardware. This have vast compatibility, motherboards, processors, memory chips, expansion cards and USB devices, other devices and standards yet to be designed can all be configured to run under Windows.

By offering such a large degree of compatibility, Microsoft has made Windows, the number one operating system for the majority of computing tasks. While basic standards are in place for motherboards and CPUs that go all the way back to the first PCs from IBM, it wouldn't be possible to home build a computer without this hardware support – one of the key advantages of the Windows OS.

Software Support

Windows offers a huge user base to any manufacturer of software – as such the vast majority of software available to purchase is designed to run primarily with Windows.

While some applications and software can be installed on both Windows and Apple OS X (for instance Football Manager 2010, or any of the Adobe Air applications), the majority of releases are designed for one operating system.

The Windows brand is so recognized that now games and software alike prominently feature the Windows logo on all packaging in order avoid confusion and to reinforce that the product is safe to use.

User Familiarity

Although the early Apple computers pioneered the concept of a mouse driven user interface in office and home computers, the standard was popularized by Microsoft Windows in the 1990s. With the arrival of the Internet and email in the same decade and the subsequent proliferation of home PCs, Windows became the brand associated with home computing.

As a result of this, the Windows desktop and its simple user interface has become synonymous with computing; while the various Linux operating systems offer a similar mouse driven interface and the Apple Mac continues to pioneer with its single button mouse, Windows remains the most popular and the most recognizable simply by virtue of its earlier successes and the work done by each release of the operating system to maintain this user familiarity.

APPLICATIONS OF WINDOWS OPERATING SYSTEM

An **operating system (OS)** is a set of system software programs in a computer that regulate the ways application software programs use the computer hardware and the ways that users control the computer. For hardware functions such as input/output and memory space allocation, operating system programs act as an intermediary between application programs and the computer hardware, although application programs are usually executed directly by the hardware. Operating Systems is also a field of study within Applied Computer Science. Operating systems are found on almost any device that contains a computer with multiple programs—from cellular phones and video game consoles to supercomputers and web servers. Operating systems are two-sided platforms, bringing consumers (the first side) and program developers (the second side) together in a single market. Some popular modern operating systems for personal computers include Microsoft Windows, Mac OS X, and Linux.

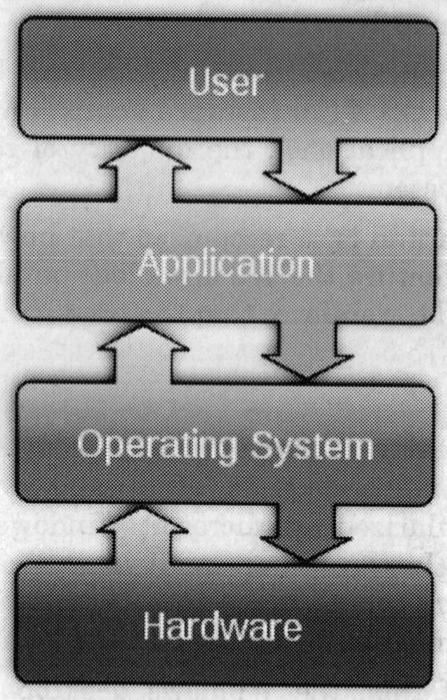

Component of Computer

The operating system is the core software component of computer. It performs many functions and is, in very basic terms, an interface between computer and the outside world. A computer is described as consisting of several component parts including monitor, keyboard, mouse, and other parts. The operating system provides an interface to these parts using what is referred to as "drivers".

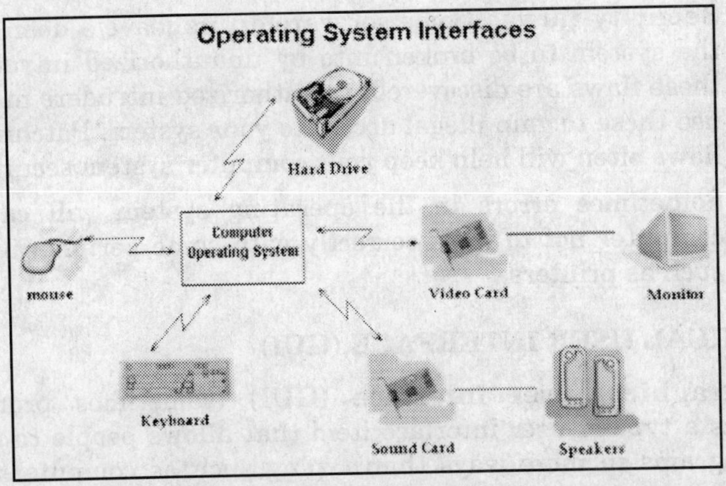

The operating system provides for several other applications including:

- System tools (programs) used to monitor computer performance, debug problems, or maintain parts of the system.
- A set of libraries or functions which programs may use to perform specific tasks especially relating to interfacing with computer system components.

The operating system makes these interfacing functions along with its other functions operate smoothly and these functions are mostly transparent to the user.

Operating System Concerns

As mentioned previously, an operating system is a computer program. Operating systems are written by human programmers who may make mistakes. Therefore there can be errors in the code even though there may be some testing before the product is released. Some companies have better software quality control and testing than others so it may be noticed that varying levels of quality from operating system to operating system. Errors in operating systems cause three main types of problems:

- **System crashes and instabilities** - These can happen due to a software bug typically in the operating system, although computer programs being run on the operating system can make the system more unstable or may even crash the system by themselves. This varies depending on the type of operating system. A system crash is the act of a system freezing and becoming unresponsive which would cause the user to need to reboot.

- **Security flaws** - Some software errors leave a door open for the system to be broken into by unauthorized intruders. As these flaws are discovered, unauthorized intruders may try to use these to gain illegal access to your system. Patching these flaws often will help keep your computer system secure.
- Sometimes errors in the operating system will cause the computer not to work correctly with some peripheral devices such as printers.

GRAPHICAL USER INTERFACE (GUI)

A **graphical user interface (GUI)** (sometimes pronounced **gooey**) is a type of user interface item that allows people to interact with programs in more ways than typing such as computers; hand-held devices such as MP3 players, portable media players or gaming devices; household appliances and office equipment with images rather than text commands. A GUI offers graphical icons, and visual indicators, as opposed to text-based interfaces, typed command labels or text navigation to fully represent the information and actions available to a user. The actions are usually performed through direct manipulation of the graphical elements.

The term GUI is historically restricted to the scope of two-dimensional display screens with display resolutions capable of describing generic information, in the tradition of the computer science research at the Palo Alto Research Center (PARC). The term GUI earlier might have been applicable to other high-resolution types of interfaces that are non-generic, such as videogames, or not restricted to flat screens, like volumetric displays.

STARTING APPLICATIONS

The various application of Windows operating system is described below:

Creating a Shortcut to a Program or File

To create a shortcut on the desktop to a program or file, there are two possible methods to choose from.

First Method

1. Right-click an open area on the desktop, point to **New**, and then click **Shortcut**.
2. Click **Browse**.

3. Locate the program or file to which you want to create a shortcut, click the program or file, click **Open**, and then click **Next**.
4. Type a name for the shortcut. If a **Finish** button appears at the bottom of the dialog box, click it. If a **Next** button appears at the bottom of the dialog box, click it, click the icon you want to use for the shortcut, and then click **Finish**.

Second Method

1. Click **Start**, point to **Programs**, and then right-click the program you want to create the shortcut to.
2. Click **Create Shortcut**.
3. The shortcut is now at the end of the Programs list. For example, if you created a shortcut to Microsoft Word, to find that program, click **Start**, and then point to **Programs**. You will find the shortcut, named "Microsoft Word (2)" (without the quotation marks), at the bottom of the Program list.
4. Drag the shortcut to the Desktop.

Creating a Shortcut to a Printer or Dial-Up Networking Connection

To create a shortcut on the desktop to a printer or Dial-Up Networking connection, follow these steps:

1. To create a shortcut to a printer, click **Start**, point to **Settings**, and then click **Printers**. To create a shortcut to a Dial-Up Networking connection, click **Start**, point to **Programs**, point to **Accessories**, and then click **Dial-Up Networking**.
2. Right-click the printer or **Dial-Up Networking** connection icon, drag it to an open area on the desktop, and then click **Create Shortcut(s) Here**

Creating Shortcuts to Other Objects

To create a shortcut on the desktop to other objects (such as a folder or computer), follow these steps:

1. Use **My Computer** or **Windows Explorer** to locate the object to which you want to create a shortcut.
2. Right-click the object, and then click **Create Shortcut**.

3. Drag the new shortcut to an open area on the desktop.

Helpful Tips

- To modify settings for a shortcut, right-click the shortcut, and then click **Properties**. Settings that can be modified include the key combination used to start the shortcut and whether the program starts minimized, maximized, or normally.
- To delete a shortcut, right-click the shortcut, and then click **Delete**. Or, you may drag the shortcut to the **Recycle Bin**. When you delete a shortcut to an object, the original object is not deleted.
- After you create a shortcut to a printer, you can print documents by dragging the documents to the printer shortcut. The program used to print the document will open briefly and then close.

One way to use Windows XP better and more efficiently is to have a quick path to your most common tasks. Here's how to create useful shortcuts.

The icons placed on the desktop, are the shortcuts to open programs. These shortcuts can be placed in the taskbar. However, the average PC user is often unfamiliar with the various methods that exist for creating shortcuts, not just to programs but also for other functions. There are a number of methods for creating new shortcuts:

- Drag and drop
- The right-click "Send To" function
- The right-click "New" function

A discussion of each approach to creating shortcuts is given in the sections below. Examples of useful shortcuts are discussed here.

Drag and drop

The drag and drop method can be used in several ways. Either the left or the right mouse button can be used for drag and drop with somewhat different behaviour. The right- click method will be the basis for the rest of the discussion. Dragging with the right-click brings up the context menu shown in the figure. One way to employ drag and drop is to use the menu entry "Copy Here" to make a copy of an existing shortcut in a different location. For example, an entry in the Start-All Programs menu can be dragged to the desktop or to the Quick Launch bar to place a copy of a shortcut in a more readily available spot. Shortcuts can also be made from files or folders by using the menu entry "Create Shortcuts Here". Open the folder containing the object whose shortcut is desired, hold down the right-click, and drag to the desired destination, such as another folder or the desktop.

The right-click "Send To" function

For making shortcuts specifically on the desktop, the Send to function of the right-click can be used (figure on the left). Simply right-click on the desired file or folder and select "Desktop (create shortcut)" from the "Send To" menu.

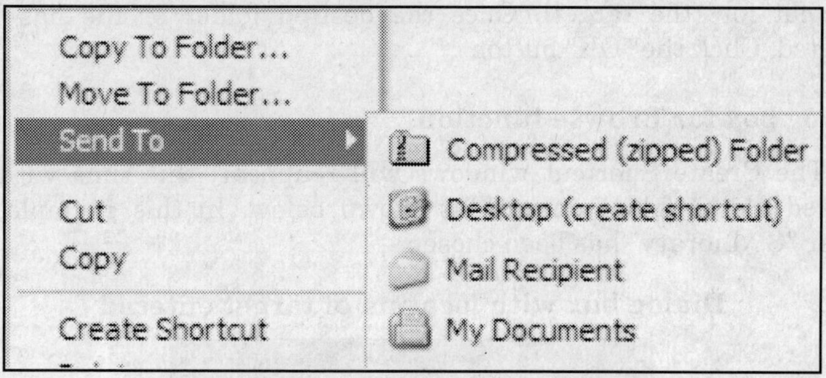

The right-click "New" function

The most general method for creating shortcuts uses the "New" function of the context menu that appears when a vacant spot within a folder windows or on the desktop is right-clicked (figure on the left). Right-click in the folder where the shortcut is to be placed and select the entry "Shortcut" from the menu. The dialog box shown below will open. The location of the target item can be entered or the "Browse" function can be used to locate it.

First dialog box for creating new shortcut

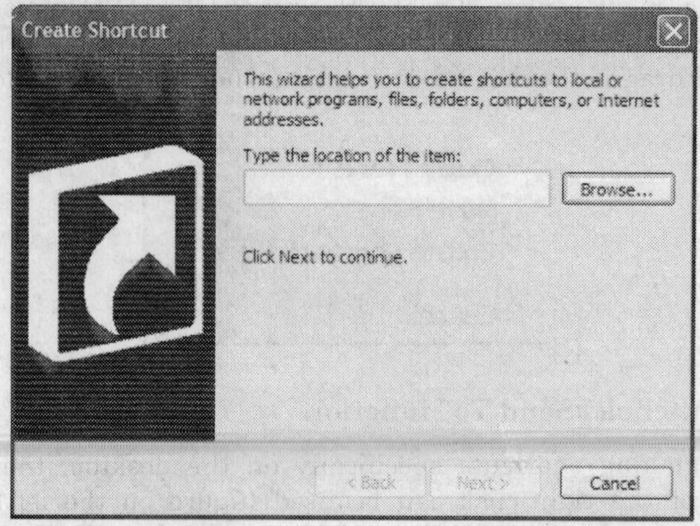

If the "Browse" button is selected, the dialog shown below will open. Here you can select the file or folder that you wish to create a shortcut for (the target). Once the desired folder or file has been selected, Click the "OK" button

Dialog box for Browse function

The Create Shortcut windows will reappear, this time with the desired file or folder entered as shown below. In this example, the folder "C:\Library" has been chosen

Dialog box with location of target entered

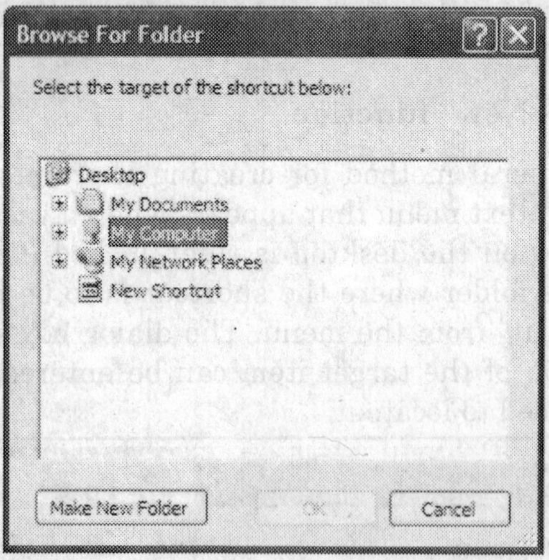

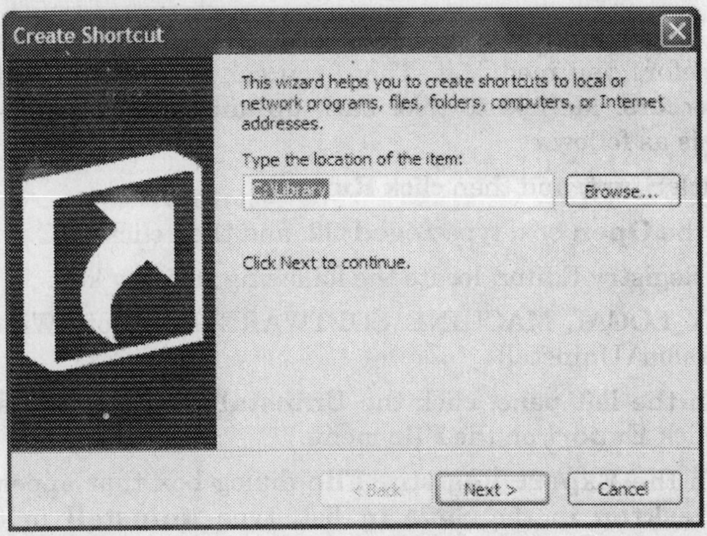

Click "Next" and a window where the shortcut can be named appears. After entering a name or accepting the default, click "Finish

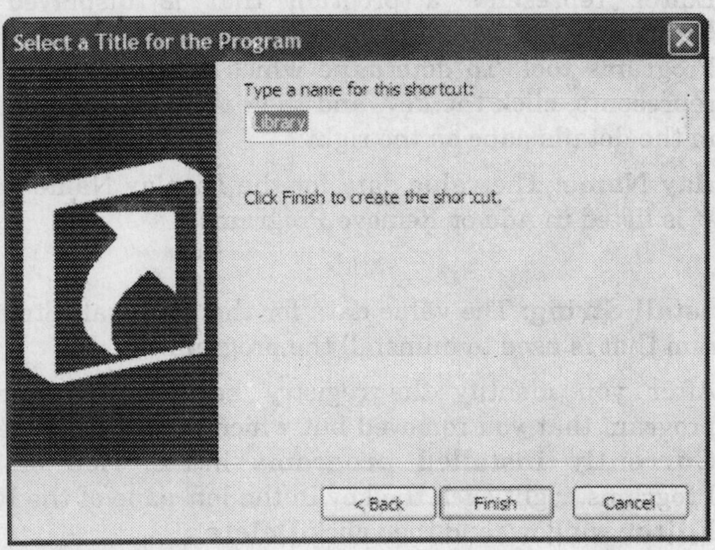

Naming the shortcut

The **Currently installed programs** list in the Add or Remove Programs tool lists all of the Windows-compatible programs that have an uninstall program or feature. Occasionally, a program may not be removed completely, and the registry key that is used to display the program in the **Currently installed programs** list remains. In this situation, you may need to remove the program manually from the **Currently installed programs** list in Add or Remove Programs. To do this, follow these steps.

It is important that for added protection, take back up of the registry before you modify it. Then, you can restore the registry if a problem occurs. Method to take back up and restore the registry in Windows is as follows:

1. Click **Start**, and then click **Run**.
2. In the **Open** box, type **regedt32**, and then click **OK**.
3. In Registry Editor, locate the following registry key:

HKEY_LOCAL_MACHINE\SOFTWARE\Microsoft\Windows\CurrentVersion\Uninstall

1. In the left pane, click the **Uninstall** registry key, and then click **Export** on the **File** menu.
2. In the **Export Registry File** dialog box that appears, click **Desktop** in the **Save in** list, type **uninstall** in the **File name** box, and then click **Save**.
3. Each key listed under **Uninstall** in the left pane of Registry Editor represents a program that is displayed in the **Currently installed programs** list of the Add or Remove Programs tool. To determine which program that each key represents, click the key, and then view the following values in the details pane on the right:

Display Name: The value data for the Display Name key is the name that is listed in Add or Remove Programs.

-and-

Uninstall String: The value data for the Uninstall String key is the program that is used to uninstall the program.

1. After you identify the registry key that represents the program that you removed but which is still displayed in the **Currently installed programs** list of Add or Remove Programs, right-click the key in the left pane of the **Registry Editor** window, and then click **Delete**.
2. Click **Yes** in response to the "Are you sure you want to delete this key and all of its subkeys?" message.
3. On the **File** menu, click **Exit** to quit Registry Editor.
4. Click **Start**, click **Control Panel**, and then click **Add or Remove Programs**. In the **Currently installed programs** list, verify that the program whose registry key you deleted is no longer listed.
5. Do one of the following:

- If the program list is not correct in Add or Remove Programs, double-click the **Uninstall.reg** file that you saved to your desktop in step 5 to restore the original list of programs in the registry.

-or-

- If the program list is correct in Add or Remove Programs, right-click the **Uninstall.reg** file on your desktop, and then click **Delete**.

Creating Folders

Folders (or directories) are containers for files that enable you to organize your data. This tutorial will show you how to create your own folders. There are a number of techniques to create a folder, all of which achieve the same effect.

First Method

1. Right click on an open area of desktop, or in an open area of Windows Explorer.
2. Then left click New
3. Then left click Folder.

Once a new folder appears either on desktop or in Windows Explorer you will notice that the folder name is highlighted. This is giving you the opportunity to name the folder. It is always best to give your folder a very memorable name that accurately describes its contents.

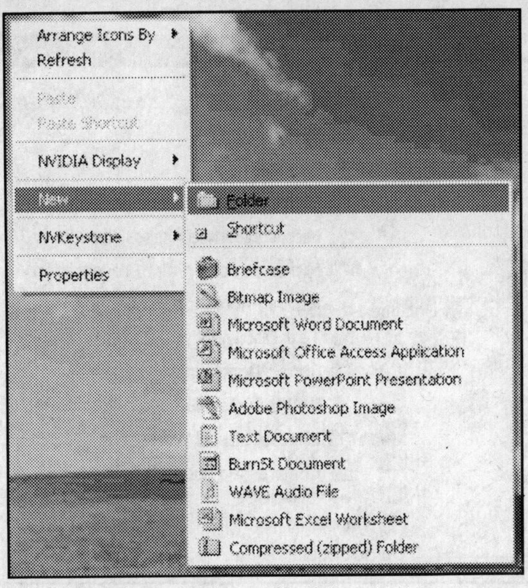

4. Type in the name you want to give to newly created folder, and then hit Enter to complete the process.

Second Method

This method is for use in Windows Explorer only.

1. Open up Windows Explorer ((Hold down the Windows Key and press E) or left click Start/Programs/Accessories/Windows Explorer)
2. Navigate to the place you where you want your new folder to be created.
3. Then from the top toolbar click File
4. Then left click New
5. Then left click Folder

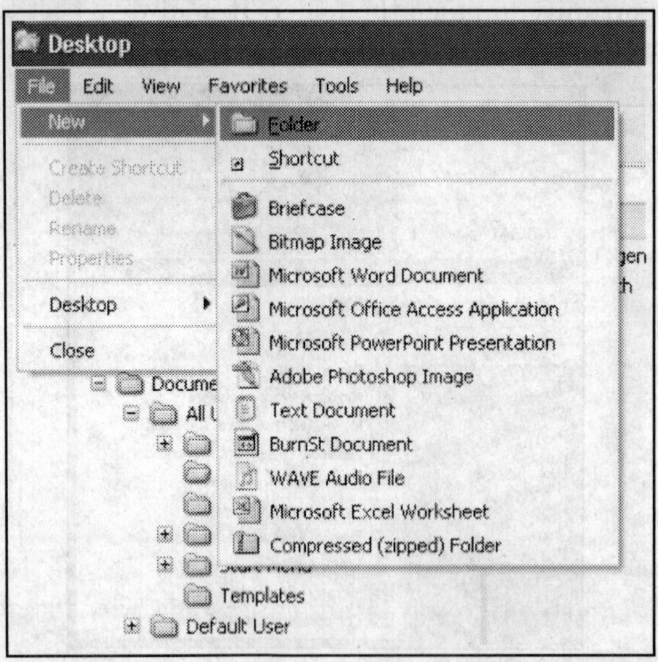

Once new folder appears in Windows Explorer you will notice that the folder name is highlighted. Give a name to the folder that describes its contents.

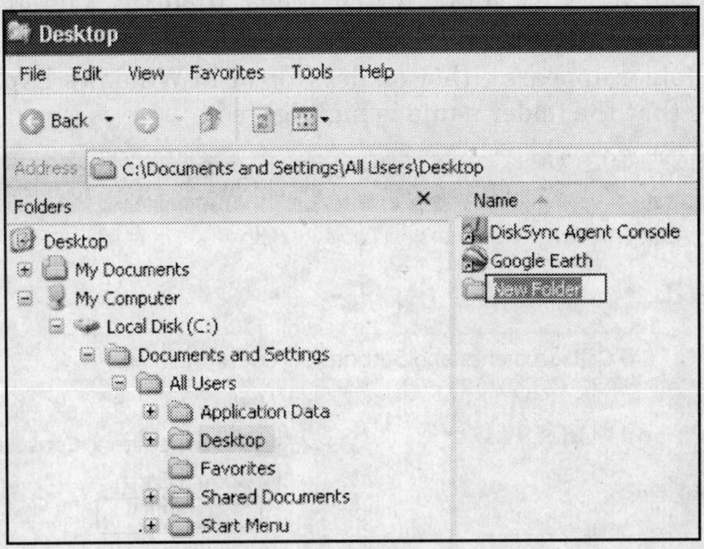

1. Type in the name you want to give to your newly created folder, and then hit Enter to complete the process.

Third Method

This method can only be used by Windows XP, and Windows 2003 users.

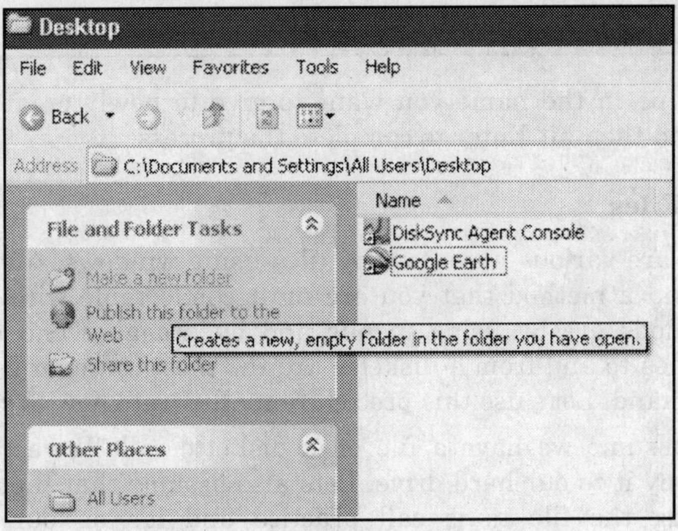

1. Open My Computer ((Left click Start/My Computer) or double click the My Computer icon on desktop)

2. Navigate to the place where you want new folder to be created.
3. Then left click Make a new folder from the File and Folder Tasks menu in Common Tasks toolbar.

Once folder appears either on desktop or in Windows Explorer you will notice that the folder name is highlighted.

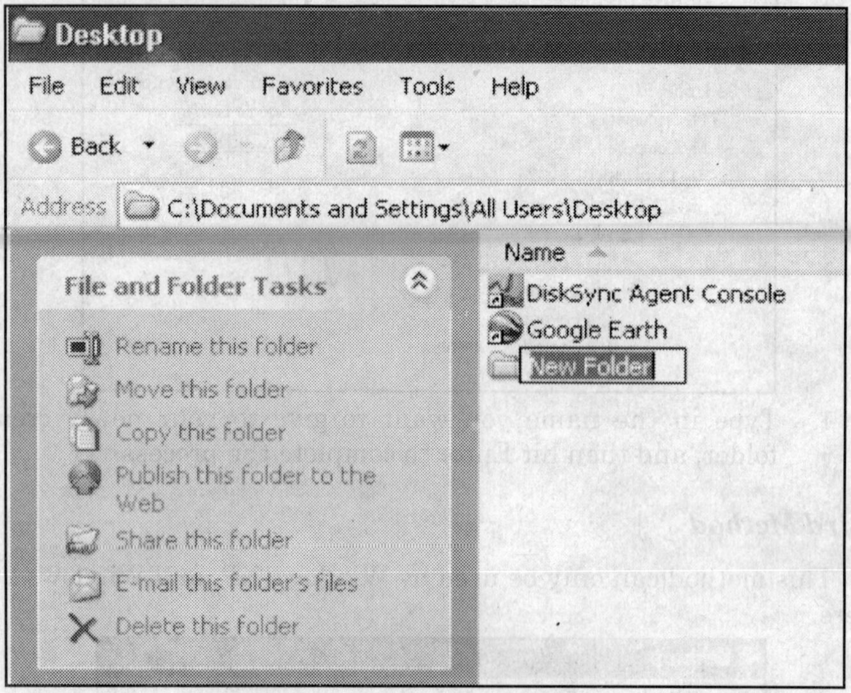

4. Type in the name you want to give to newly created folder, and then hit Enter to complete the process.

Copying Files

There are various ways to copy files using windows. All you need to do is find a method that you are most comfortable with. The two basic methods are by using menus and by dragging and dropping. Copying files to and from a diskette are the most common uses of the Copy command. Let's use this procedure to illustrate how to copy files.

Lets assume we have a file on a diskette call "Project" and we want to copy it to our hard drive. Lets also assume that the folder we are copying the file to is call practice and it's on our C drive. Therefore, PROJECT is our source file and PRACTICE is our destination folder

Menu Method

Step 1: Inset diskette into Computer

Step 2: Open My Computer or Windows Explorer

Shortcut: Hold down the **Windows Key** and press **E** to open Windows Explorer. (The windows key is next to the left **CTRL** key. It has the Windows logo on it. However, if your do not own a Windows keyboard, you will not see this key.)

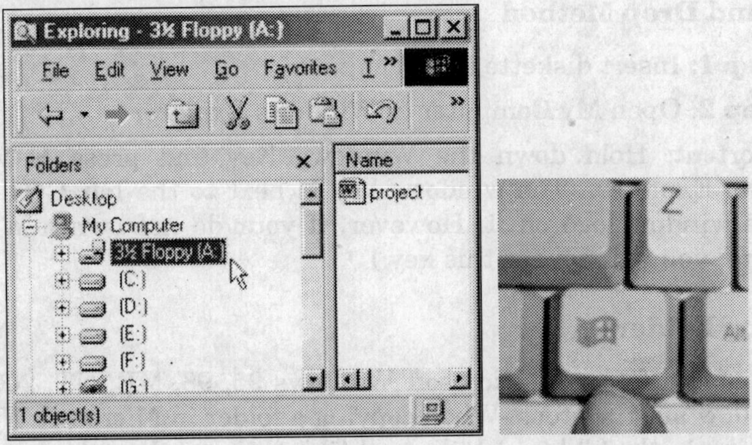

Windows Explorer

Step 3: View contents of disk by double clicking the floppy disk icon.

Step 4: Select the file you want to copy. In our example, select project

Step 5: Select the Edit menu and click Copy

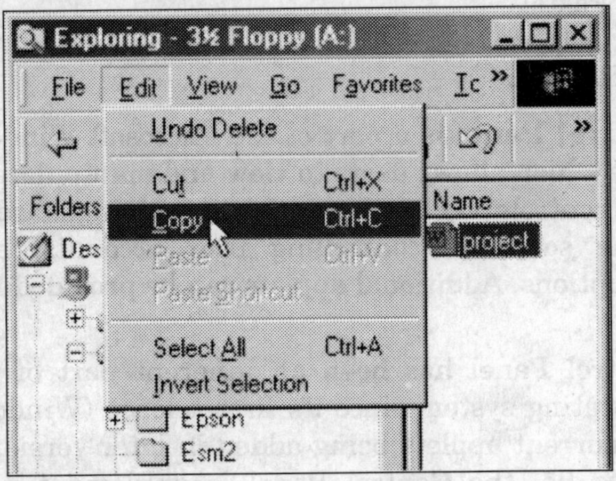

The Edit Menu

Tip. You can also right mouse click on the file and choose copy from the menu.

Step 6: Open to the destination folder. In our example, double click Practice.

Step 7: Select the Edit menu and click Paste.

Tip. You can also right mouse click on the file and choose paste from the menu

Drag and Drop Method

Step 1: Insert diskette into Computer

Step 2: Open My Computer or Windows Explorer

Shortcut: Hold down the Windows Key and press **E** to open Windows Explorer. (The windows key is next to the left **Ctrl** key. It has the window logo on it. However, if your do not own a Windows keyboard, you will not see this key.)

Copying Folders

To copy a folder in Microsoft Windows 95, 98, ME, NT, 2000, XP, 2003 follow are the steps. When copying a folder in Microsoft Windows everything in the folder including all **files** and **subdirectories** will be copied.

1. Locate and highlight the folder you wish to copy.
2. Right-click the folder and click Copy or click Edit and then Copy.
3. Move to the location you wish to place the folder and all its contents and click Edit and then Paste or right-click and then click Paste.

CONTROL PANEL

The **Control Panel** is a part of the Microsoft Windows graphical user interface which allows users to view and manipulate basic system settings and controls via applets, such as adding hardware, adding and removing software, controlling user accounts, and changing accessibility options. Additional applets can be provided by third party software.

The Control Panel has been an inherent part of the Microsoft Windows operating system since its first release (Windows 1.0), with many of the current applets being added in later versions. Beginning with Windows 95, the Control Panel is implemented as a special folder, i.e. the folder does not physically exist, but only contains shortcuts to various applets such as Add or Remove Programs and Internet Options. Physically, these applets are stored as .cpl files. For example, the Add or Remove Programs applet is stored under the name appwiz.cpl in the SYSTEM32 folder.

In recent versions of Windows, the Control Panel has two views, Classic View and Category View, and it is possible to switch between these through an option that appears on the left side of the window.

Many of the individual Control Panel applets can be accessed in other ways. For instance, Display Properties can be accessed by right-clicking on an empty area of the desktop and choosing Properties.

The classic view consists of shortcuts to the various control panel applets, usually without any description (other than the name). The categories are seen if the user use "Details" view.

The category view consists of categories, which when clicked on display the control panel applets related to the category. In Windows Vista, the category displays links to the most commonly used applets below the name of the category.

Change an installed program

These features can be used to modify all programs.

You can use this feature to change the installation of Windows Installer-based programs such as Microsoft Office XP. Windows Installer-based programs include a Maintenance Mode option. With this option, you can add or remove features, change the installation state of the program or of individual components, or repair and restore the installation.

To change a program, follow these steps:

1. Click **Start**, click **Control Panel**, and then double-click **Add or Remove Programs**.
2. In the **Currently installed programs** box, click the program that you want to remove, and then click **Change** or **Change/Remove**.
3. Follow the instructions that appear on the screen to make the changes that you want.

Remove an installed program

To remove a program that is installed on your computer, follow these steps:

1. Click **Start**, click **Control Panel**, and then double-click **Add or Remove Programs**.
2. In the **Currently installed programs** box, click the program that you want to remove, and then click **Remove**.
3. If you are prompted to confirm the removal of the program, click **Yes**.

Troubleshooting

- Make sure that the program that you click in the Add or Remove Programs tool is the program that you want to remove from your computer. Some programs may not prompt you to confirm the removal before the program is removed from the computer.
- You can only remove a program with the Add or Remove Programs tool if the program is written for Windows. If you do not see the program that you want to remove in the **Currently installed programs** box, view the program documentation for instructions about how to remove it.

Setting the date / time through Microsoft Windows 95, 98, ME, NT 4.0, 2000, and XP

1. Right-click on the time. This is commonly in the bottom right hand of your screen.
2. Click the **Adjust Date/Time** menu item.
3. This will open the Date/Time Properties window. In this window you can adjust the time, date, and time zone. If you wish to change how the computer handles daylight savings, click the **Time Zone** tab and check or uncheck the 'Automatically adjust clock for daylight saving changes' option.
4. Once the proper date and/or time has been set, click Apply and then Ok.
5. Setting the date / time through MS-DOS
6. Setting the date through MS-DOS can be done by using the date command. Additional information and help with this command can be found on our date command page.
7. To adjust the time whiles in MS-DOS use the time command. Additional information about this command can be found on our time command page.
8. Setting the date through Linux / Unix

9. Use the date command to set the date and/or time. See our date command page for additional information and examples of how to do this.

Windows Date/Time Utility

This is where you set the date and time, this is very important, if incorrect you will have problems. This in the Windows Control Panel, It would set to automatically update the time. Many programs need the clock set to the correct time for them to run without errors. If you notice computer programs are running strangely check to make sure the time and date are set correctly.

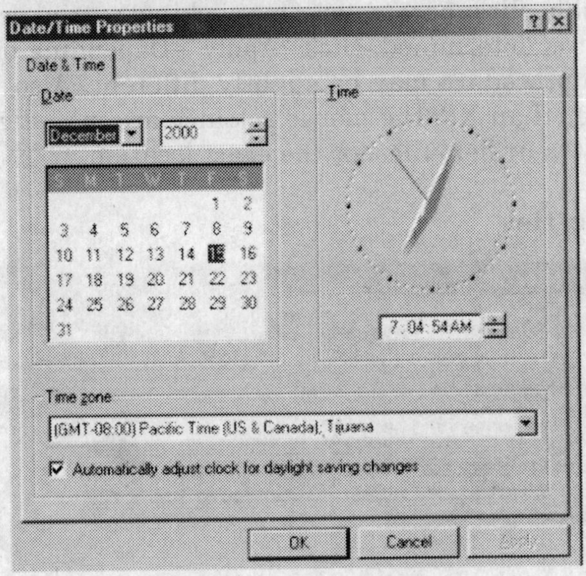

Date/Time Properties

Double-click made easier

The double-click can be especially troublesome since it involves precise timing between clicks as well as accurate and steady placement of the mouse pointer. It is suggested to replace the double-click with one of the two following alternatives.

- Instead of double-clicking an icon, file, or other object of interest, highlight or select the object with a single left-click. The object will turn blue or become darkened indicating that it has been selected for further action. Then press the "Enter" key on the keyboard. The net result will be the same as double-clicking. This method works for files listed in Explorer as well as for icons.

- Another method for opening programs or folders is to use the right mouse button instead of the left. Right-click once on an icon. A menu will open, listing a group of possible actions. Click once more (right or left) on the entry in the menu that says "Open" and the net result is the equivalent of a double-click with the left mouse button.

The parameters of the double-click can also be adjusted to conform to an individual's patterns. Open the "Mouse Properties" dialog box by going to **Control Panel-Printers and Other Hardware-Mouse**. Under the "Buttons "tab is a dialog box with an entry "Double-click speed" with a slider that allows the user to test different double-click parameters by clicking a trial icon. Once the desired speed is determined, click "Apply". Depending on your mouse software, the procedure may be slightly different. Also in versions of Windows older than XP, the mouse settings are in a slightly different place. Consult your help files for the exact location.

Mouse properties

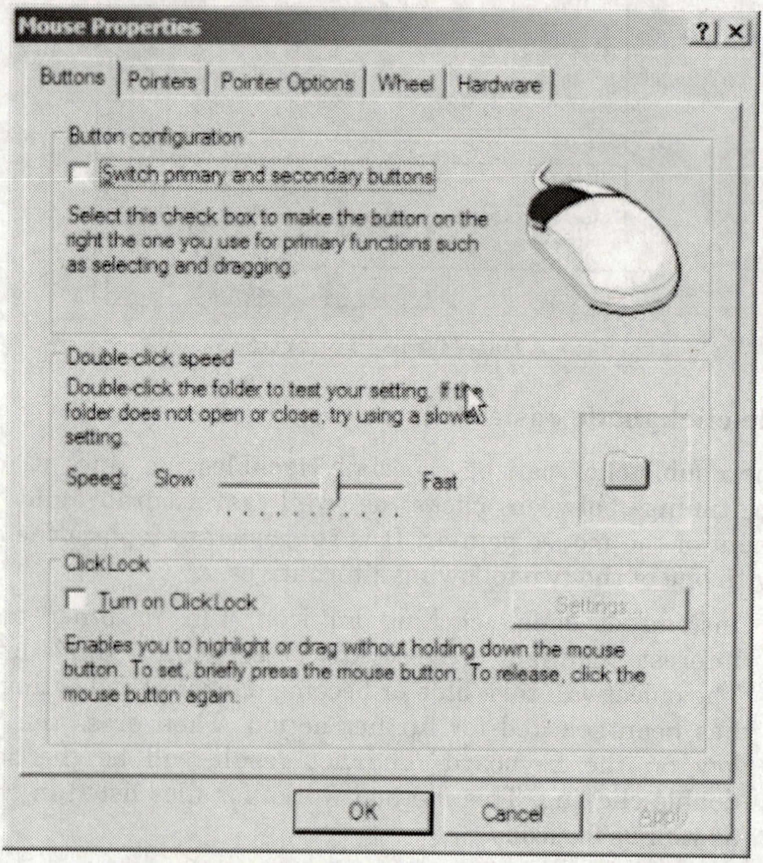

For Lefties

Those who are left-handed and who wish to switch the right- and left-click buttons have the option in the Properties dialog box. In the top portion of Figure is an area "Button configuration." Putting a check by "Switch primary and secondary buttons" will reverse the usual configuration. Removing the check will return the default button assignment.

Turn off the double-click

It is also possible to dispense entirely with the necessity of the double-click and to configure the system to behave like a Web page. Open "My Computer" or any folder and click on the "Tools" menu and choose "Folder Options". (For Windows 98, go to "View-Folder Options-Settings".) In the dialog box under "Click items as follows" choose the radio button by "Single-click to open an item..." You then have a choice to have icons titles appear underlined just like links on the Internet or to have the underlining appear only when the mouse pointer is over the icon. Click "Apply" for the settings to take effect.

Replacing the double-click

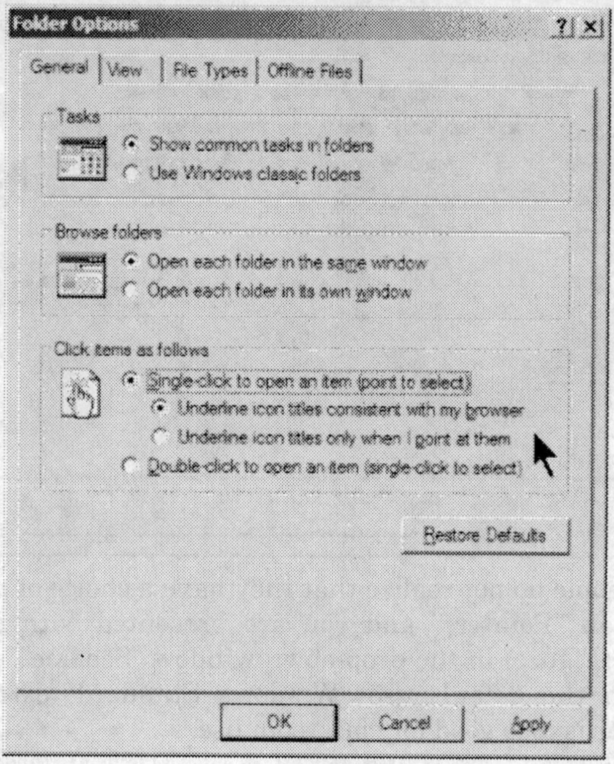

Adjust pointer speed and appearance

It is also possible to adjust a number of other characteristics of the mouse in the Mouse Properties dialog box. For example the speed at which the pointer moves can be adjusted by clicking on the "Pointer Options" tab (Figure). Use the slide bar in the section "Motion" to obtain the speed that you find most suitable. Sometimes can't find the mouse pointer on the screen, put a check in the box "Show location of pointer when I press the CTRL key."

Pointer options

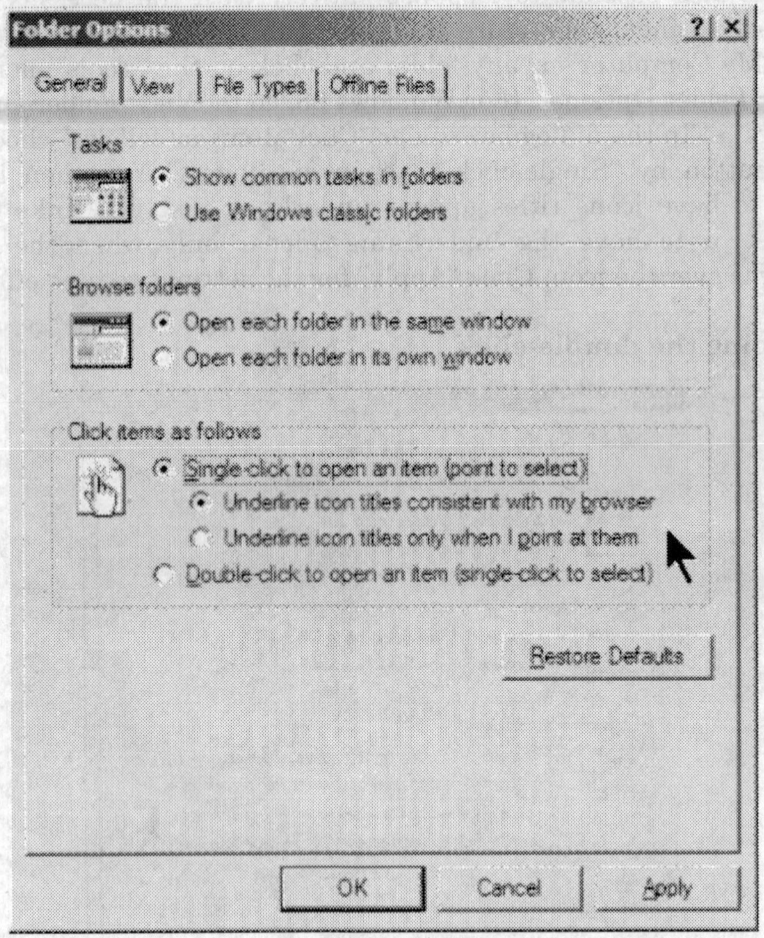

Many people do not realize that they have a choice of pointer type. Select the tab "Pointers" and you are presented with a variety of possibilities (Figure) in the drop-down window "Scheme". For a larger pointer than the default use "Windows Standard (extra large). A larger pointer is also good for classroom use.

Pointer choices

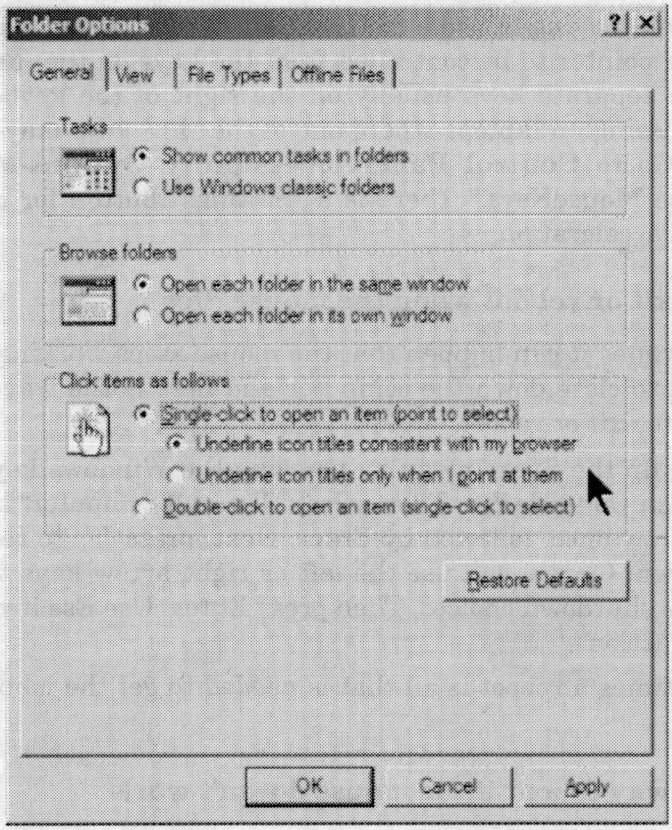

Finding a lost mouse pointer

Sometimes lose the pointer because it goes somewhere off the screen. The pointer can also get obscured when using certain graphics programs. The Pointer Options shown in Figure have a mouse locator setting that can be useful in these situations. At the bottom of Figure, there is an entry, "Show location of pointer when I press the CTRL key". Putting a check here will activate this feature. The only drawback is that using the CTRL key for other reasons may also flash the pointer location.

Shortcut to mouse properties

To open the mouse properties dialog box on a frequent basis, here is how to create a shortcut in Windows XP. Right-click on an empty spot on the Desktop or in any other folder where you want to place the shortcut. In the context menu, choose **New-Shortcut**. Enter the command exactly as given below into the line under "Type the location of the item." Click "Next," choose a name, and click "Finish."

Keyboard instead of the mouse

To avoid having to use a mouse at all, Windows has a setting that allows the pointer to be controlled from the keys on the numeric pad. These are separate keys usually on the right of the keyboard. They may be missing on laptops where one of the "Fn" keys may have to be invoked. Go to **Control Panel-Accessibility Options-Mouse** and check "Use MouseKeys." There is a "Settings" button for configuring speed and acceleration.

How to exit or reboot when the mouse dies

Sometimes it can happen that the mouse stops working. First you may want to close down the computer and here is the way to use the keyboard to exit or reboot.

Bring up the **Start** menu by pressing the Windows key or by the combination Control+Esc. Then select "Turn off computer" by pressing the Up arrow once, followed by Enter. Next, press "r"' to reboot or "u" to shutdown. Or you can use the left or right arrow keys to navigate among the shutdown choices. Then press Enter. Use Esc if you want to cancel an action.

Sometimes a reboot is all that is needed to get the mouse to work again.

Another way to exit if the mouse doesn't work

If there are no programs open, there is an even quicker keyboard shortcut. Press Alt+F4 (F4 is a function key) to bring up the Shutdown menu and then enter "u" (no quotes") to turn off the computer. To reboot enter "r" instead.

If programs are open, successive applications of Alt+F4 can be used.

Sounds

To enable sound recording (to convert flash movies with sound) in Windows Vista:

1. **Select** "sound" from the control panel (double click "Sound" icon to open sound options dialog):

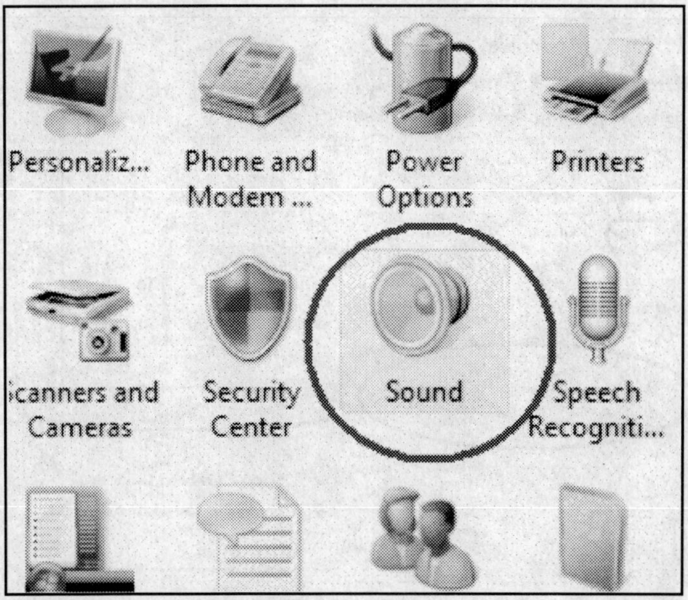

2. Select the recording tab
3. **Right-click** on the background of the tab and choose "Show Disabled Devices" and click to show disabled devices:

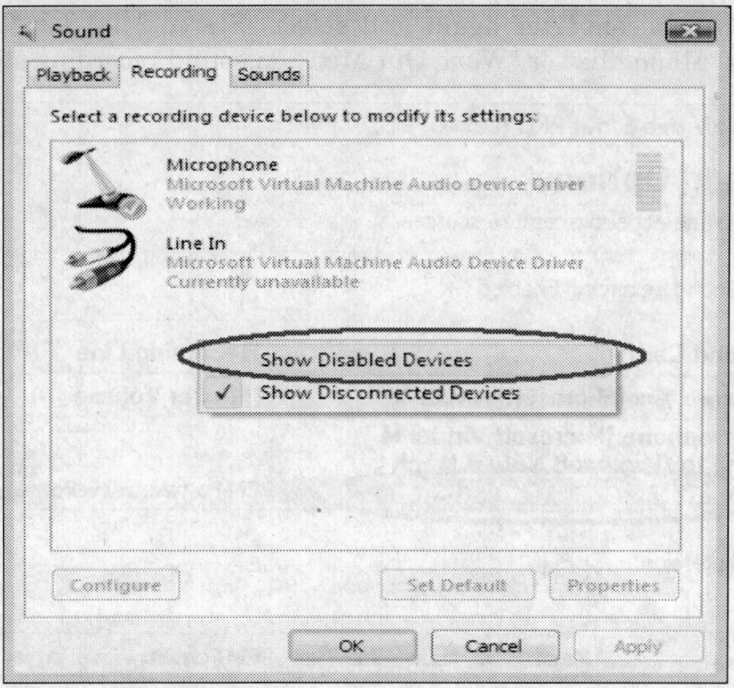

4. Disabled devices will be displayed. Right-click on "Stereo Mix" (or "Wave Out Mix" or "Mono Mix" or "What U Hear") and click "Enable" as shown below:

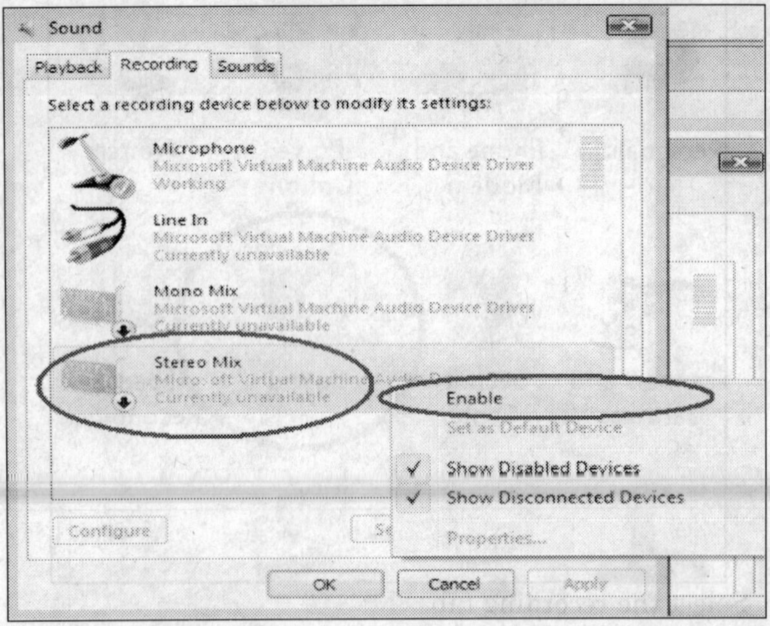

5. Now it should work the same way as Stereo Mix in Windows XP, allowing you to record any sound your computer makes.

Then run converter again and select "Stereo Mix" (or "What U Hear" or "Mono Mix" or "Wave Out Mix") on sound recording step:

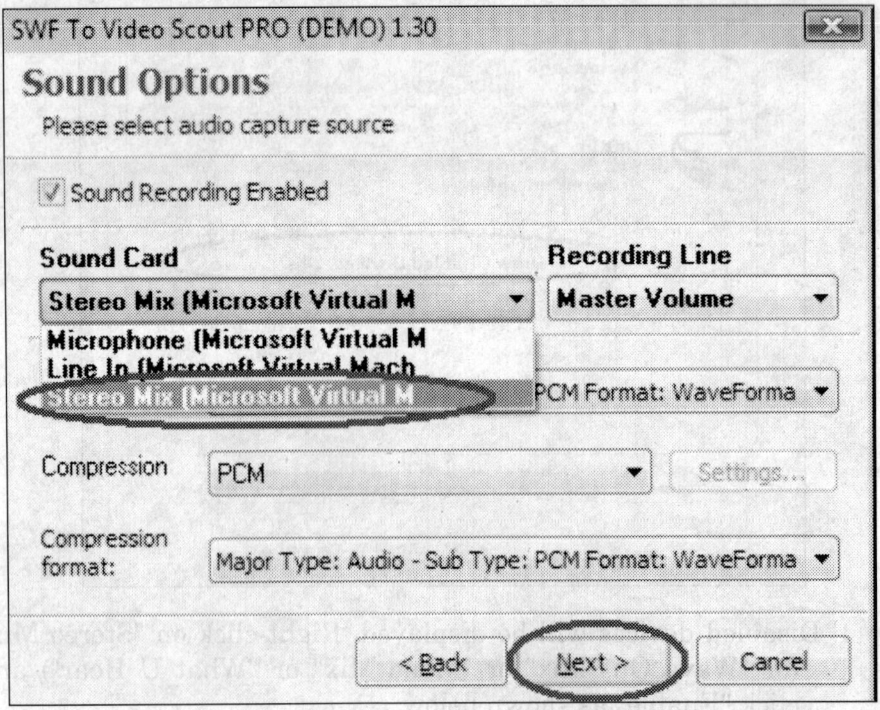

System

Windows pagefile sizes are set during installation, and normally do not have to be changed. However, if you add memory to system after initialization, you may need to increase the "initial pagefile size" on the primary boot drive. This is especially true if you're trying to get a kernel memory dump to diagnose a problem.

To change the Pagefile size:

1. Log in as a system administrator.
2. Open the system control panel, and double-click "System":

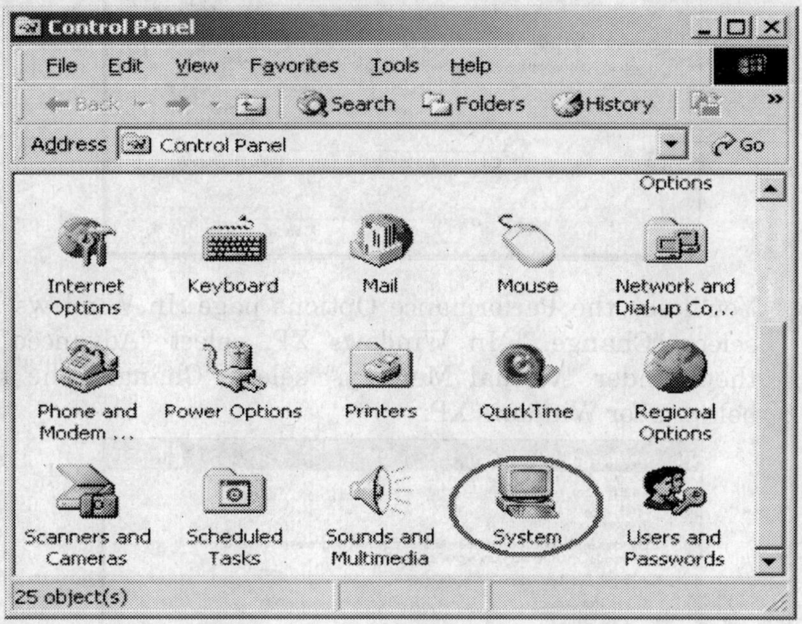

3. After a short pause, you'll see the general system properties page. Select the "Advanced tab"

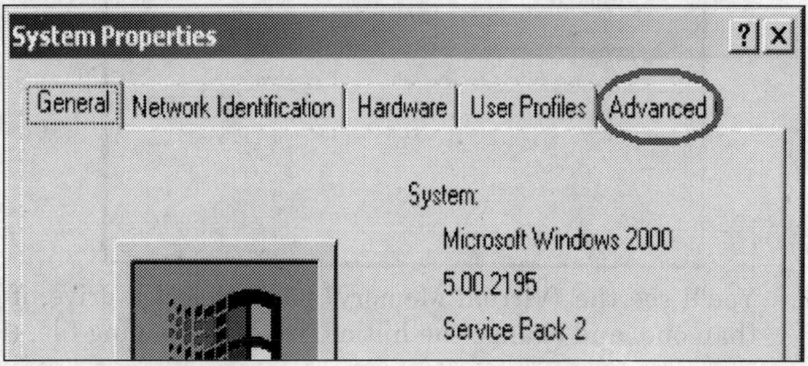

4. In Windows 2000, select "Performance Options". In Windows XP, select the "Settings" button under "Performance". The image below is for Windows XP:

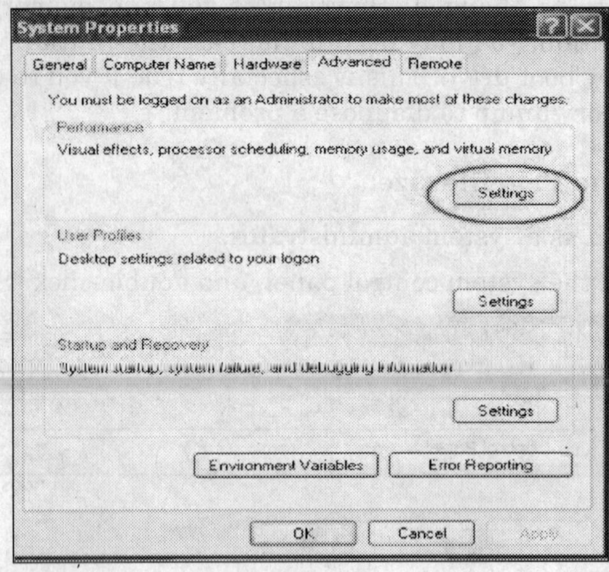

5. You'll see the Performance Options page. In Windows 2000, select "Change..." In Windows XP, select "Advanced" and then, under "Virtual Memory," select "Change. The image below is for Windows XP:

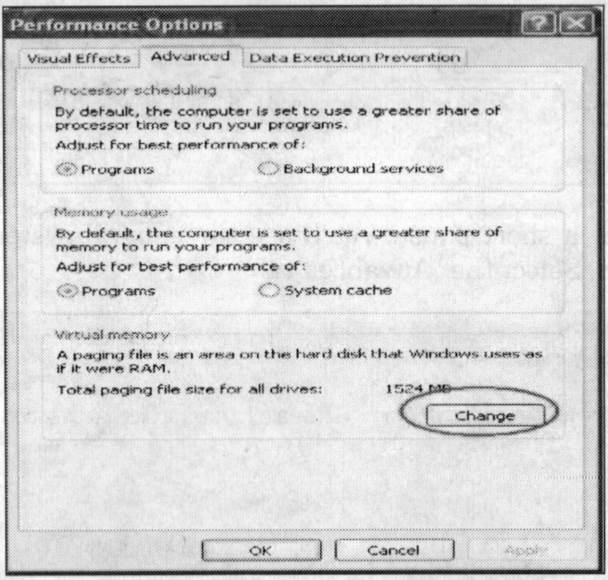

6. You'll see the "Virtual Memory" page. Select a drive, if more than one, and change the initial size of the paging file. (If you

are doing this because of a message from "How to Enable Kernel Memory Dumps in Windows 2000", be sure to select the drive mentioned in the alert box, and also set the initial size according to the alert box.) The image

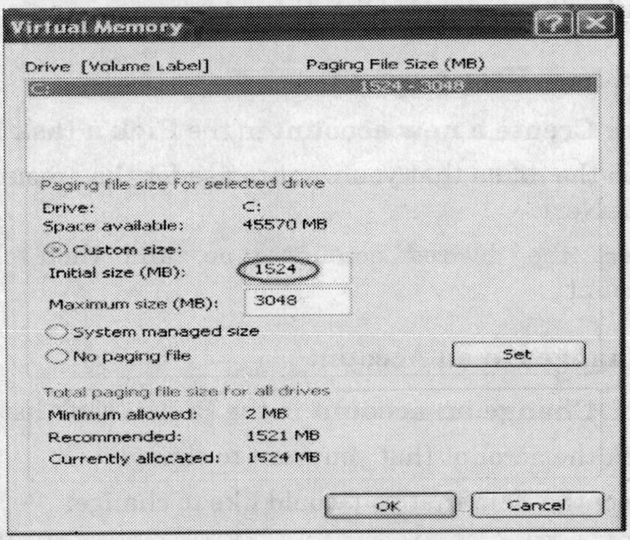

7. Press OK, and exit from the Performance Options (2K) or Virtual Memory (XP) page.
8. Restart the system.

User Accounts

A **user** is a person who uses a computer or Internet service. A user may have a **user account** that identifies the user by a **username** (also **user name**), **screen name** (also **screenname**), or "handle", which is derived from the identical Citizens Band radio term. To log in to an account, a user is typically required to authenticate himself/ herself/ itself with a password or other credentials for the purposes of accounting, security, logging, and resource management.

Users are also widely characterized as the class of people that use a system without complete technical expertise required to fully understand the system. In most hacker-related contexts, they are also divided into lusers and power users. Both are terms of degradation, but the latter connotes a "know-it-all" attitude. See also End-user and Nomadic User

Separate accounts for each person can be created who will be using the computer. This allows each user to have their own document folders and settings such as the wallpaper, **Start** menu, visual style, and so forth. You can create and configure user accounts with the User Accounts tool in Control Panel.

To open the User Accounts tool, open Control Panel from the **Start** menu, and then double click **User Accounts**.

To Create a New User Account

1. Click **Create a new account** in the **Pick a task** list box.
2. Type the name that you want to use for the account, and then click Next.
3. Select the desired account type, and then click Create Account.

To Make Changes to an Account

1. Click **Change an account** in the **Pick a task** list box.
2. Click the account that you want to change.
3. Select the item that you would like to change:
   - Click **Change the name** to change the name that appears on the Welcome screen for the account.
   - Click **Change the picture** to change the picture that is used to represent the user account. You can use any image file on the computer for the user's picture.
   - Click **Change the account type** to change the account type to increase or decrease the user's rights on the computer.
   - Click **Create/change the password** to create or change the password for the user and create or change the password hint.
   - Click **Delete the account** to delete the user account from the computer. When you delete the account, you are given the option to save the user's files on the computer.

Note: You cannot delete the account for a user that is currently logged on to the computer.

Requirements

- The Welcome screen must be available
- There must be only one user account on the computer
- The user account must not have a password

Make the Welcome Screen available

To make the Welcome screen available, follow these steps:

1. Click **Start**, click **Control Panel**, and then double-click **User Accounts**.
2. Click **Change the way users log on or off**.
3. Click to select the **Use the Welcome screen for fast and easy logon** check box.
4. Click **OK**.

Remove the password from a user account

To remove the password from a user account, follow these steps:

1. Click **Start**, click **Control Panel**, and then double-click **User Accounts**.
2. Click the user account.
3. Click **Remove my password**.
4. Type the password in the **Type your current password** box, and then click **Remove Password**.

Consent Prompt

The consent prompt is displayed to administrators in Admin Approval Mode when they attempt to perform an administrative task. This is the default user experience for administrators in Admin Approval Mode and can be configured in the local Security Policy Manager snap-in (secpol.msc) and with Group Policy.

The following figure is an example of a User Account Control consent prompt.

User Account Control consent prompt

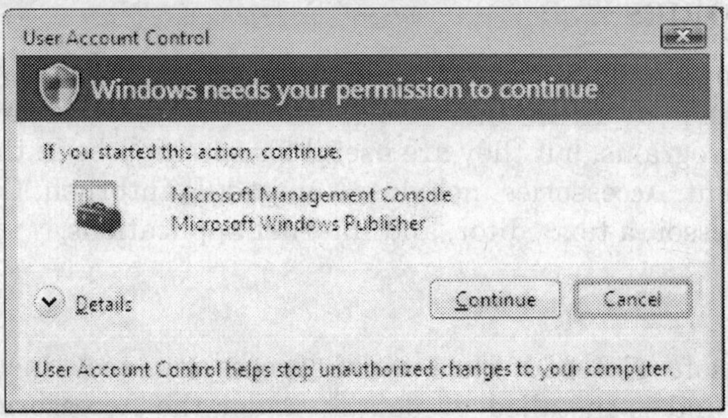

Credential Prompt

The credential prompt is displayed to standard users when they attempt to perform an administrative task. This is the default user experience for standard users and can be configured in the local Security Policy Manager snap-in (secpol.msc) and with Group Policy.

The following figure is an example of a User Account Control credential prompt.

User Account Control credential prompt

ACCESSORIES

Windows provides several accessories, or applications, that can be used to help users in their work. These accessories are not full-featured programs, but they are useful for specific jobs in the Windows environment. Accessories include a Notepad, Paintbrush, Calculator, a word processor, a text editor, and Internet applications.

Notepad

Microsoft Notepad is a word processing tool included with Windows and is installed by default under the Accessories program group. It can be used to create a log-type file that adds the current date and time each time the Notepad file is opened. How to create a log file with Notepad is described below:

To create a log file in Notepad:

1. Click **Start**, point to **Programs**, point to **Accessories**, and then click **Notepad**.
2. Type **.LOG** on the first line, and then press ENTER to move to the next line.
3. On the **File** menu, click **Save As**, type a descriptive name for file in the **File name** box, and then click **OK**. When you next open the file, note that the date and time have been appended to the end of the log, immediately preceding the place where new text can be added. This functionality can be used to automatically add the current date and time to each log entry.

Paintbrush

Paintbrush is a drawing program. Drawings created in this program can be used as wallpaper for computer. Similar to the picture on the refrigerator concept. It should be noted that this is a very rudimentary drawing program.

Starting Paintbrush

From the **Start** menu, choose **Accessories**, then **Paint**

If the program is on desktop, double click while pointing at the icon

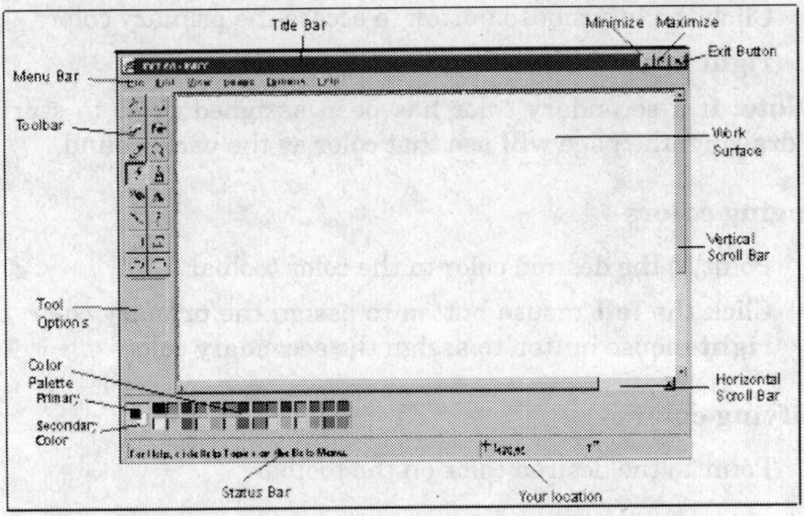

Visual of Microsoft Paint for Windows 98

The program will open, if it does not take up the entire area of screen, maximize it. Following are the default settings for this program.

- Paint will print using a standard letter size paper (8½" X 11") with margins set to 0.75". If anything other is required go to **File, Page Setup** to modify the size.
- Drawing surface, things to consider. What is the drawing going to be used for? *For example*: If you wanted to make a drawing that would fill up an entire page of printed material (allowing for the margins) you would want to set you drawing service to 6.97" wide by 9.43" long (we have discovered that Paint needs that extra couple of .02-3" to set the page properly)
- Should it be a picture for your desktop, the maximum you should make it would be the resolution size of your screen, (i.e. 800x600 pixels)
- The pencil tool is active (notice it looks as though it is depresses)
- The primary pencil color is Black
- The secondary pencil color is White.

Start drawing

- Select a tool from the toolbar, adjust the line thickness and color options
- Position your cursor on the work surface
- Click the **left** mouse button to access the primary color.
- **right** mouse button to access the secondary color

Note: If a secondary color has been assigned prior to starting a new drawing, the page will use that color as the background.

Changing colors

- Point to the desired color in the color toolbar
- Click the **left** mouse button to assign the primary color, or the **right** mouse button to assign the secondary color

Modifying colors

- Point to the desired color on the toolbar

- Double click the left mouse button, the edit color dialog box will open
- In the Edit color dialog box, slide the scroll markers to different position.
- Click OK or tap Enter

Restore the original color

- Point to the desired color on the toolbar
- Double click the left mouse button
- In the Edit color dialog box, click the Reset button
- Click OK or tap Enter

Zoom Command

To take a closer look at an area of work, zoom command is used. Almost every program has this feature.

- From the **View** menu, choose **zoom**
- Point to the area of the drawing you want to zoom on.
- The zoom will magnify the drawing by 1600%. Modify your drawing.
- To return to full size, repeat step 1

Using the toolbar

There are a variety of tools available to you. Following is the basic procedure to using them

- Select the desired tool
- Determine the conditions of the tool, the fill/line/etc
- Choose the color(s)
- Position the cursor in the work surface
- Click the left mouse and drag
- Release the mouse

Toolbar descriptions

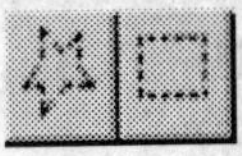	**Selecting tool**	Left = Odd shapes Right = Rectangular shapes **Used with Cut and Copy options, described later.**

	**Spray paint**	Drag the mouse pointer. Use the left mouse button to spray with the foreground color, or use the right mouse button to spray with the background color. The longer you leave your mouse stationary, the darker the color
	**Text tool**	Click in the work surface, type the text. To change the font style or size, select **Font** from the **Text** menu. If color is required, choose the color prior to typing.
	**Eraser**	Move you mouse indicator to work surface. Left mouse button = erases top color Right mouse button = erases all marks If the entire picture is to be erased, double click on the eraser tool
	**Fill tool**	Fills empty spaces with selected color. Ensure that the tip of the tool in positioned inside the area prior clicking.
	**Brush tool**	Freehand brush tool draws solid lines when mouse button is held and dragged. There are different brush shapes to choose from. To accomplish this From the **Options** menu, choose **Brush shapes** or double click on the brush tool button Select the desired shape Click OK or tap Enter
	**Line draw**	Right = Straight lines Left = Curved line (use as follows) Draw a straight line by dragging the mouse pointer. Click where you want one arc of the curve to be, and then drag the mouse pointer to adjust the curve. Each curve must have at least one arc but no more than two. Repeat this step for a second arc.
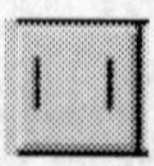	**Square boxes**	Select the type of box you desire (Unfilled or Filled box) prior to starting the shape

	**Rounded corner boxes**	Select the type of box you desire (Unfilled or Filled box) prior to starting the shape
	**Circles/ Ovals**	Select the type of box you desire (Unfilled or Filled circle) prior to starting the shape. If you want perfect circles, hold the **shift** key while dragging the mouse.
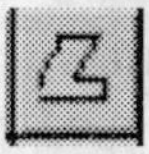	**Polygons**	Select the type of box you desire (Unfilled or Filled polygon) prior to starting the shape. To finish a polygon, double click at the last point of the polygon.

Saving a file

Use Save to save your document as a file.

- Do not use periods, slashes or unusual characters in the names as many of them have special meaning to computers.
- You should use Save periodically to avoid losing your work if a power or system failure occurs.
- Pictures created in Paintbrush can be used as wallpaper for your computer. Refer to the desktop section for instructions

Steps

From the **File** menu, choose **Save As** or (Shortcut) Hold **Ctrl** tap **S.** If this is a first time save, the **Save** dialog box will open

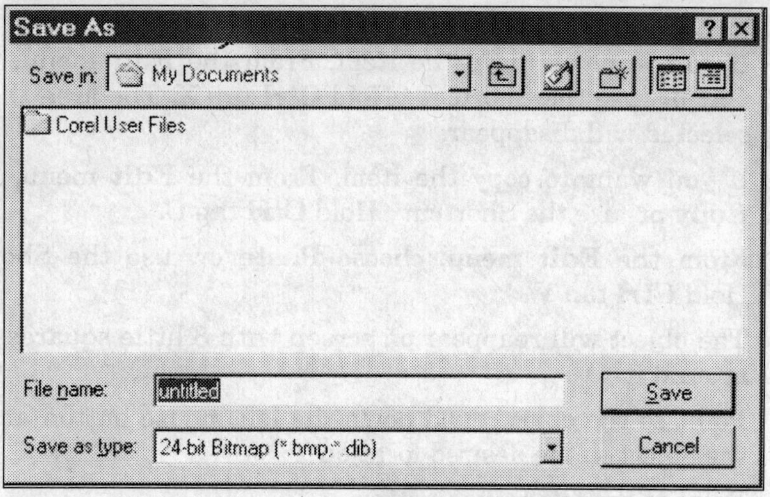

- Select the location where you want to save a new or renamed file from the **Save in:** drop down list.
- Select the type of file from the **Save as type:** drop down list.

- Give the file a name.
- Click on the **Save** button or tap the **Enter** key on your keyboard.

Start a new file

From the **File** menu, select **New** or (Shortcut) Hold **Ctrl** tap **N**

Note: If a secondary color has been chosen the new file background will use that color

Cut/Copy and Paste

There are often times when you want to move some-thing from its original position, or copy an item to some-where else. When those times happen use the following procedure.

Remember there are three questions that need to be asked first, "Do you want to cut something out and move it, or do you want a copy of something?

"What exactly do you want to copy or move?", and "Where do you want to put it?" Once the first question is addressed, go to the area of what you want to work with, then

- Choose one of the selecting tools
- Point to where you want to start the selection.
- Hold down the left mouse button, drag the mouse until the desired area is enclosed. You should notice a dashed line surrounding the selected area.
- If you want to move the item, From the **Edit** menu, choose **Cut** or use the Shortcut Hold **Ctrl** tap **X.** The area that was selected will disappear.
- If you want to copy the item, From the **Edit** menu, choose **Copy** or use the Shortcut Hold **Ctrl** tap C.
- From the **Edit** menu, choose **Paste** or use the Shortcut Hold **Ctrl** tap **V**
- The object will reappear on screen with 8 little squares visible around it.
- Point to the object, hold down the left mouse button and drag the object to the desired location.
- Release the left mouse button.

You can also re-size the object while the squares are visible. Point to one of them, notice the mouse indicator will change into a sizing arrow. Hold down your left mouse button and drag in the direction you want to size. Remember if you want to keep the proper proportions of the object, use the corners instead of the sides.

Undo last action

As with all humans, we make mistakes. Unlike drawing with pencils and paper, computers offer us this handy tool, so that we do not have to start a project over if we make a mistake. This operation is available in almost every program. Remember it, it is your best friend when dealing with computers.

From the Edit menu, choose under use the Shortcut Hold Ctrl tap Z

Calculator

An electronic hardware device or software capable of performing mathematical calculations such as addition, multiplication, subtraction, and/or division. To the right is an example of the Microsoft Windows Calculator included in every version of Microsoft Windows.

Running the calculator

Microsoft Windows users

Users running Microsoft Windows 95, Windows 98, Windows NT 4.0, Windows 2000, Windows XP, and above can access the Windows calculator by following either of the below steps.

1. Click Start, Programs, and then Accessories
2. Click Calculator

or

1. Click Start and then Run
2. Type: **calc** and pressing enter.

Windows Calculator Tips

Tip 1: By default Microsoft Windows Calculator is set to be displayed in basic mode, this can be changed by opening Calculator and clicking View and choosing Scientific. Scientific mode gives you a lot more options and abilities.

Tip 2: By default digit grouping is disabled. Enabling this feature will cause your long numbers to have commas. For example, instead of

10000000 it would display 10,000,000. To enable this feature click View and select Digit grouping.

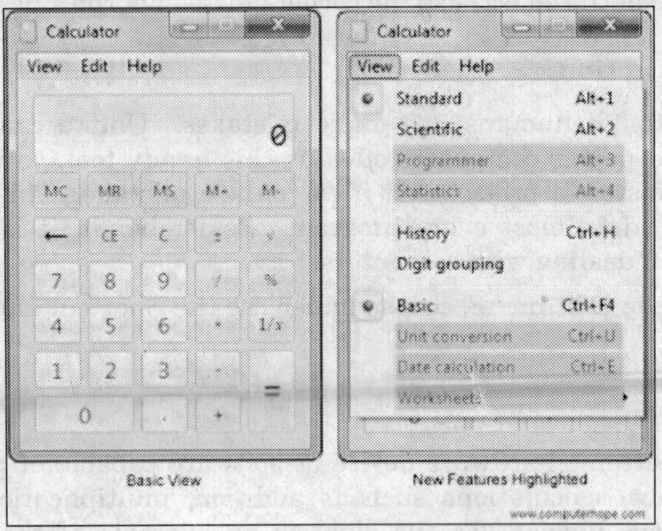

For Windows 7 and above users, Microsoft has included a much more sophisticated calculator. As can be seen in the picture to the right, there are several new features that have been highlighted that are not available in previous versions of Windows.

Windows 7 Calculator

The new Windows 7 Calculator now allows you to choose from 4 options:

1. **Standard** - Which is just the basic calculator function.
2. **Scientific** - Which allows you to do more advanced calculations, such as Sine, Cosine, and Tangents.
3. **Programmer** (New)- Which allows you to do more advanced computer programming functions such as boolean operations.
4. **Statistics** (New)- Which allows you to do Statistical calculations.

There are also new functions that allow you to do more specific tasks, such as figuring out a Mortgage payment. They are as follows:

1. **Unit Conversion** - Which allows you to convert units into different units? Such as, converting an angle from Degrees to Radian. Or, Quarts into Gallons.
2. **Date Calculation** - Which allows you to either calculate the difference between two dates, or, add or subtract days to a specified date.

3. **Worksheets** - Which allows you to choose from 4 options to calculate? Mortgage, Vehicle Lease, Fuel Economy (mpg), or Fuel Economy (l/100 km).

RECYCLE BIN

Microsoft introduced the Recycle Bin in the Windows 95 operating system. The Recycle Bin keeps some files that have been deleted, whether accidentally or intentionally. Whether a deleted file is put into the Recycle Bin depends on how it is deleted; typically only files deleted via the Explorer graphical interface (but not necessarily other Windows graphical interfaces such as file selection dialogs) will be put into the Recycle Bin; files deleted via the Command Prompt, or via operating system APIs are not. Users can review the contents of the Recycle Bin before deleting the items permanently. In previous Windows operating systems and in MS-DOS, undeletion was the only way to recover accidentally deleted files. The Recycle Bin holds data that not only lists deleted files, but also the date, time and the path of those files. The Recycle Bin is opened like an ordinary Windows Explorer folder and the files are viewed similarly. Deleted files may be removed from the Recycle Bin by restoring them with a command, or by deleting them permanently.

The Recycle Bin's icon indicates whether there are items in the Recycle Bin. If there are no files or folders in the Recycle Bin, then the icon resembles an empty wastepaper basket. Otherwise if there are files and/or folders the icon resembles a full wastepaper basket.

Prior to Windows Vista, the default configuration of the Recycle Bin was to hold 10% of the total capacity of the host hard disk drive. For example, on a hard drive with a capacity of 20 gigabytes, the Recycle Bin will hold up to 2 gigabytes. If the Recycle Bin fills up to maximum capacity, the oldest files will be deleted in order to accommodate the newly deleted files. If a file is too large for the Recycle Bin, the user will be prompted to permanently delete the file instead.

Physical storage locations

The actual location of the Recycle Bin depends on the type of operating system and file system. On older FAT file systems (typically Windows 98 and prior), it is located in Drive:\RECYCLED. In the NTFS file system (Windows 2000, XP, NT) it is Drive:\RECYCLER. On Windows Vista and Windows 7 it is Drive:\$Recycle.Bin folder.

The Recycle Bin can be accessed from the desktop or Windows Explorer. (It is the only icon shown by default on the Windows XP desktop.) When accessed from the desktop the Recycle Bin options and information are different to those of the physical Recycle Bin folders seen on each partition in Windows Explorer. With NTFS, users cannot see the contents of each others' Recycle Bins.

Prior to Windows Vista, a file in the Recycle Bin is stored in its physical location and renamed as D<original drive letter of file><#>.<original extension>. A hidden file called info2 (info in Windows 95 without the Internet Explorer 4 shell extension) stores the file's original path and name in binary format. Since Windows Vista, the "meta" information of each file is saved as $I<number>.<original extension> and the original file is renamed to $R<number>.<original extension>.

When the user views the Recycle Bin, the files are displayed with their original names. When the file is "Restored" from the Recycle Bin, it is returned to its original directory and name. When the file is "deleted" by emptying the Recycle Bin, the space on the disk used by the file is designated as "free" without any changes being made to the file data itself. Future files will overwrite the data when they are saved on the disk. In other words, the data is not erased, but the address marking the data's existence is.

Deleting files

In Windows Explorer, files are moved to the Recycle Bin in a number of ways:

- By right-clicking on a file and selecting delete from the menu
- Selecting the file and pressing the delete key
- Selecting delete from the side menu in Windows XP
- Selecting the file and choosing delete from the File menu (in Windows XP Explorer)
- From a context menu command or some other function in a software application (usually configurable)

- By dragging and dropping a file into the Recycle Bin icon

It is also possible to bypass the Recycle Bin and directly delete a file by holding the SHIFT key while performing one of the above mentioned delete techniques.

Note that Windows is inconsistent about whether the Recycle Bin is used by other graphical interfaces that may appear similar to Explorer; in some cases, apparently identical interfaces may permanently delete a file.

Known issues

The Recycle Bin only stores files deleted from hard drives, not from removable media, such as memory cards and floppy disks. It also doesn't store files deleted from network drives.

Having a big disk and full Recycle Bin can considerably slow down deleting files. This can be resolved by emptying the Recycle Bin.

In versions prior to Windows Vista, the Recycle Bin icon cannot be deleted from the desktop like other icons. Deleting a registry key from the Windows Registry resolves this issue. The key varies with the version of the operating system.

In Windows Vista, it is not possible to view the cumulative size of multiple items in the Recycle Bin. Neither the status bar nor the Properties show the total size of items present in the Recycle Bin. To view total size of the Recycle Bin the user would have to make hidden system files and folders visible and then add the size of each $RECYCLE.BIN folder. Windows 7 has this issue fixed, the details pane (at the bottom of the window) showing the total size of selected deleted items.

MY DOCUMENTS

On Microsoft Windows computer operating systems (except for Windows NT), **My Documents** is the name of a special folder on the computer's hard drive that the system commonly uses to store a user's documents, music, pictures, downloads, and other files.

Overview

Microsoft first introduced the "My Documents" folder in Windows 95 OEM Service Release 2, as a standard location for storing user-created files. The folder - located under the root of the hard drive that Windows is installed on - is displayed (but not stored) directly on the user's desktop.

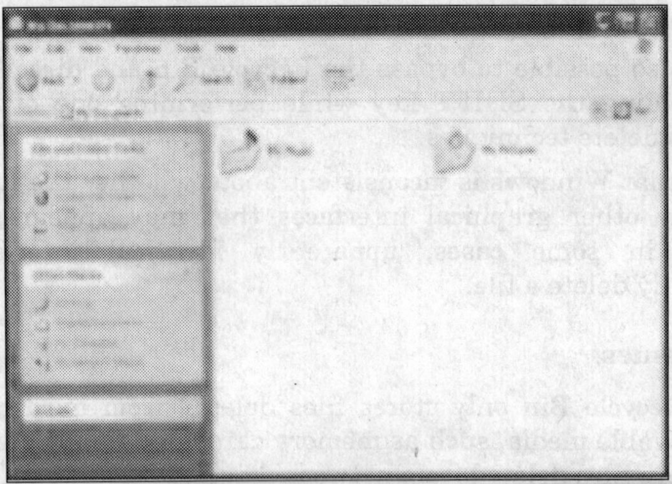

"My Documents" as it appears in Windows XP

In Windows 2000, Windows XP and Windows Server 2003 set up the "My Documents" folder (by default) in the user's profile directory, as Documents and Settings\[user name]\My Documents on the same hard drive that Windows is installed on. Note that "My Documents" in these operating systems is one of a number of Special Folders - a concept introduced in Windows 2000 to add a layer of abstraction between the user interface's presentation of the folder and its physical location and contents. As such, "My Documents" in file load/save dialogs (and in Windows Explorer) doesn't appear as an absolute path. A user can change the physical location of "My Documents" by right-clicking on the "My Documents" icon, selecting the Properties option, and entering a new folder location (path) in the Target tab.

Windows Vista renames "My Documents" as, simply, "Documents". "My Music", "My Pictures" and "My Videos" have also lost their prefix, and have moved to directly under the users profile directory (C:\Users\[user name]).

As of Windows 7, The "Documents", "Pictures", "Music" and "Videos" folders appear displayed in Windows Explorer with a "My" prefix but are actually still stored in the file system without the prefix (as in Windows Vista).

Other "My" folders

Windows 98 introduced two additional special folders with a "My" prefix: "My Music" and "My Pictures". In Windows XP, as with "My Documents", these folders can be pointed elsewhere by using Microsoft's TweakUI utility.

"My Music" and "My Pictures" are not present in Windows Server 2003 by default unless enabled using the start-menu customization.

Installing Windows Media Player 9 or 10 on Windows XP adds a "My Videos" folder which Windows Media Player uses to store video files that are shown in its media library.

Many other applications have adopted the "My" naming convention when placing folders in the user's "My Documents" directory:

- Windows Messenger and Windows Live Messenger create a "My Received Files" folder when used for the first time.
- As of 2010 "My Games" (or "Saved Games" since Windows Vista) is becoming an increasingly common place for games (especially those published by Microsoft Game Studios) to store a player's saved game and settings files. This practice aims to make it easier for users to keep their saved games if they uninstall a game, and if they eventually migrate their files to a newer computer (using the Files and Settings Transfer Wizard, for example). For networks with a shared "My Documents", computers that have copies of the same game installed often cannot run the same game at the same time. Microsoft's TweakUI does not include the ability to re-path the "My Games" folder.

Additionally, Windows XP and higher may add a prefix to "My Documents" et al. (for example, "My Music", "My Photos). The prefix is generally the user id of the owner for the particular folder at the time the folder was created. The value of the prefix is controlled by undocumented section in the desktop.ini file which stored in the former folder

MY COMPUTER

A section of Microsoft Windows that was introduced with the release of Microsoft Windows 95 and included with all versions of Windows after that. **My Computer** allows the user to explore the contents of their computer drives as well as manage their computer files. To the right, the top image is an example of the My Computer icon in Microsoft Windows XP. With the introduction of Windows Vista, Microsoft changed the traditional My Computer icon to **Computer**, the bottom image to the right is an example of what this icon looks like. Although the name has changed this icon still acts identical to the earlier My Computer.

How to open My computer

1. Get to the Windows Desktop.
2. Double-click the My Computer icon, this icon is almost always located on the top-left portion of the desktop and should look similar to the icon above. Below are two examples of what should appear when My Computer is open. Drive listing in My Computer

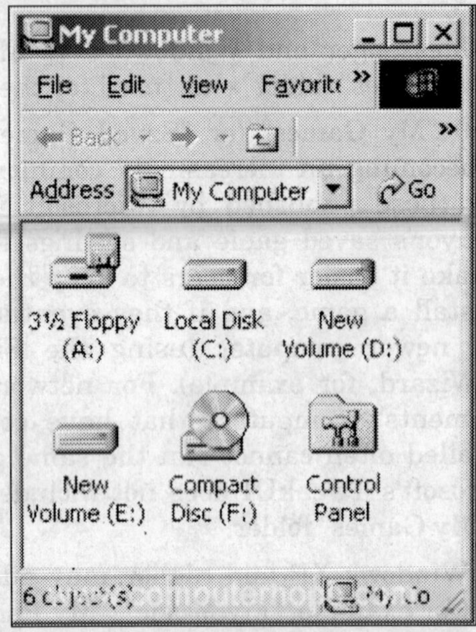

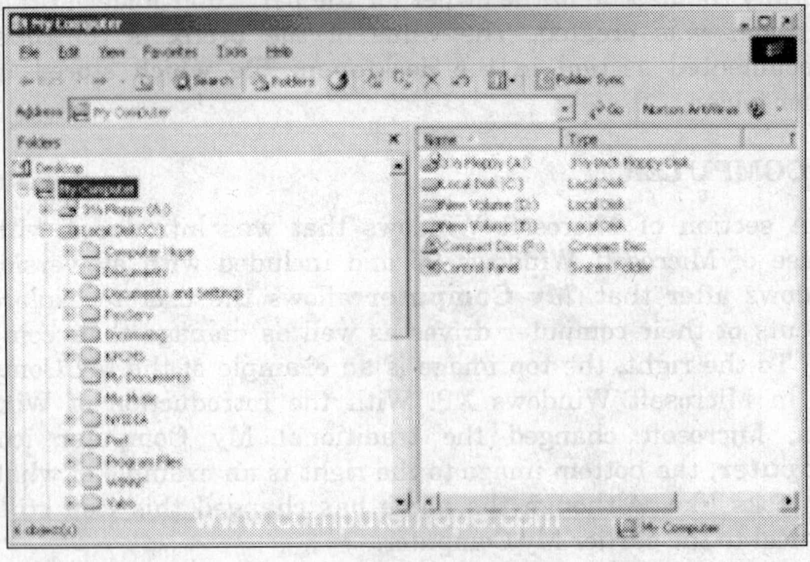

Browsing My Computer in Windows 2000

Using My Computer

Once My Computer is open you'll see all available drives on your computer. For most users you'll only be concerned with the Local Disc (C:) drive. This is your hard disk drive and what all your files are stored on. Double-click this drive icon to open it and view of its contents.

Tip: If you're looking for a document such as a word processor file you've created, music file, picture, or other personal file it's likely that it's contained in your documents folder. This folder is displayed in My computer as a folder and usually contains your name. For example, if your username was John, this folder would be named John's Documents.

Finding files in My Computer

If you're having trouble finding where one of your files is stored use the Windows find feature to quickly find the file. To do this from within My Computer either click on File and then Search or right-click on the C: drive or other folder you wish to search and click Search.

In the Search window type the name or part of the name of the file you're looking for.

Adjust system settings with your computer

If you wish to manage computer and/or view other settings and information about computer instead of double-clicking the My Computer icon to open it, right-click on the My Computer icon and click Properties. Performing these steps will open your System Properties (the same window accessible through the Control Panel).

WINDOWS EXPLORER

Windows Explorer is a file manager application that is included with releases of the Microsoft Windows operating system from Windows 95 onwards. It provides a graphical user interface for accessing the file systems. It is also the component of the operating system that presents many user interface items on the monitor such as the taskbar and desktop. Controlling the computer is possible without Windows Explorer running (for example, the File | Run command in Task Manager on NT-derived versions of Windows will function without it, as will commands typed in a command prompt window). It is sometimes referred to as the Windows Shell, explorer.exe, or simply "Explorer".

Windows Explorer is an application that provides detailed information about your files, folders, and drives. You can use it to see how your files are organized and to copy, move, and rename files, as well as perform other tasks pertaining to files, folders, and drives.

The simplest way to access Windows Explorer is to right-click the **Start** menu or the **My Computer** icon and selects **Explore**. If your keyboard has a Windows logo key, you can press Win-e to launch Windows Explorer. Alternatively, you can access it from the **Start** menu. In newer operating systems, it is under **Accessories**.

SYSTEM TOOLS

Desktop Central provides various system tools, such as Disk Cleaner, Disk Checker, and Disk Defragmenter, that can be run on the multiple computers simultaneously.

For a smooth performance of a system, periodic maintenance is necessary. Tools like Disk Check, Disk Defragmenter, etc., help in system maintenance. It is practically impossible for administrators to manually perform the maintenance on a regular basis.

Desktop Central provides an option to schedule these tasks at regular intervals to be executed on multiple computers simultaneously. It allows creating multiple tasks that can be created to execute various tools on different target computers at different intervals. Moreover, these tasks can also be done during off hours.

Check Disk

- Disk errors related to bad sectors, cross-linked files, directory errors, etc., create problems in I/O operations. The Check Disk tool creates a status report of the disk based on its file system. Desktop Central supports the following options to run the check disk tool:
- **Verbose:** Displays the name of each file in every directory as the disk is checked.
- **Quick Check:** This option is available only for the NTFS File system. Selecting this option will perform the check disk operation quickly by skipping the checking of cycles within the folder structure and by performing a less vigorous check of index entries.

Disk Cleanup

Disk Cleanup (cleanmgr.exe) is a computer mainte-nance utility included in Microsoft Windows designed to free up disk space on a computer's hard drive. The utility first searches and analyzes the hard drive for files that are no longer of any use, and then removes the unnecessary files. There are a number of different file categories that Disk Cleanup targets when performing the initial disk analysis:

- Compression of old files
- Temporary Internet files
- Temporary Windows file
- Downloaded Program files
- Recycle Bin
- Removal of unused applications or optional Windows components
- Setup Log files
- Offline files

The above list, however, is not exhaustive. For instance, 'Temporary Remote Desktop files' and 'Temporary Sync Files' may appear only under certain computer configura-tions, differences such as Windows Operating System and use of additional programs such as Remote Desktop. The option of removal hibernation data may not be ideal for some users as this may remove the hibernate option.

Aside from removing unnecessary files, users also have the option of compressing files that have not been accessed over a set period of time. This option provides a systematic compression scheme. Infrequently accessed files are compressed to free up disk space while leaving the frequently used files uncompressed for faster read/write access times. If after file compression, a user wishes to access a compressed file, the access times may be increased and vary from system to system. In addition to the categories that appear on the Disk Cleanup tab, the More Options tab offers additional options for freeing up hard drive space through removal of optional Windows components, installed programs, and all but the most recent System Restore point or Shadow Copy data in some versions of Microsoft Windows

Disk Defragmenter

Disk Defragmenter is a computer program included in Microsoft Windows designed to increase access speed by rearranging files stored on a disk to occupy contiguous storage locations, a technique commonly known as defragmenting. The purpose is to optimize the time it takes to read and write files to/from the disk by minimizing head travel time and maximizing the transfer rate. As of Windows XP, Disk Defragmenter is also used to improve system startup times.

Disk gets fragmented as users create and delete files and folders, download files from internet, or install/uninstall programs. When a file or a folder is deleted from the hard disk, the space that was occupied by it will be used to store any new files. When a file gets saved, it uses the first contiguous free space that is large enough for the file and the remaining part of the file is saved in the next available free space.

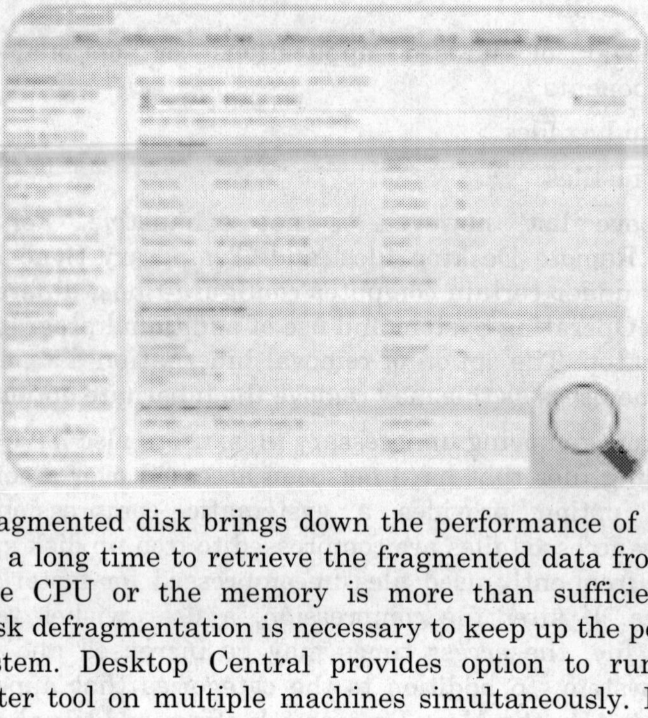

The fragmented disk brings down the performance of the system as it takes a long time to retrieve the fragmented data from the disk even if the CPU or the memory is more than sufficient. Hence, periodic disk defragmentation is necessary to keep up the performance of the system. Desktop Central provides option to run the disk defragmenter tool on multiple machines simultaneously. It supports the following options:

- Verbose: Displays the complete analysis and disk defragmentation reports
- Analyze: Analyzes the volume and displays a summary of the analysis report.
- Force Defragmentation: Forces disk defragmentation regardless of whether it needs to be defragmented

Scandisk

SCANDISK or **Scan Disk** is a utility in MS-DOS and Microsoft Windows systems which checks and repairs file systems and bad clusters on the hard drive. It was introduced in MS-DOS version 6.2.

Previous versions of MS-DOS supplied only the simpler, purely text-based program CHKDSK.

Scan Disk included a more user-friendly interface than MS-DOS CHKDSK, more command-line and other configuration options, and the ability to detect and sometimes recover from physical errors on the disk. Unlike CHKDSK, Scan Disk would also repair cross linked files.

In Windows 95 onwards, SCANDISK also had a graphical user interface, although the text interface continued to be available for use in single-tasking ("DOS") mode.

SCANDISK can't check NTFS disk drives and therefore isn't available for computers running NT based (including Windows 2000, Windows XP, etc.) versions of Windows: a newer CHKDSK is provided instead (not to be confused with the older MS-DOS CHKDSK).

Scan Disk is one of the most common maintenance tools bundled with an operating system such as Windows. This is an application that is used in checking the hard drive of your computer for errors and bad sectors. Once Scan Disk finds an error in the hard drive, it will attempt to fix it.

The errors found inside a hard drive are caused by a number of reasons. These include:

- frequent system crashes
- critical system applications that have been improperly closed
- existence of harmful programs such as viruses, trojans, etc

While Scan Disk is running, it will check the hard disk for defects in its platters (these are round flat steel plates in the hard drive on which data is stored). It will also check file systems (FAT, FAT32, NTFS etc). It will search as well as correct the lost and bad clusters that were created when a certain program was aborted.

Once Scan Disk finishes its task, it will provide a report that contains the errors it has found and the amount of disk space it has scanned. It is therefore important for users to use the Scan Disk application because it ensures that their data is safe from being corrupted. Aside from this, there is a guarantee that their computer will perform at optimum performance levels.

The earliest version of Scan Disk appeared in MS DOS 6.2. In Windows 95 and 98, Scan Disk was given a graphical user interface (GUI). In this graphical environment, the user can find:

- progress bars
- buttons

- information regarding the status of the scan and the errors (if any)

How to Run Scan Disk in Windows 2000 and Windows XP

- Press the **Start** button on desktop
- Double click on **My Computer**
- Highlight the disk which you want to scan for bad sector on the list of Hard Disk Drives.
- Open the **File** menu and select **Properties** option
- Select the **Tools** tab
- Click the **Check Now** button
- The scanning process will then initiate

How to Run Scan Disk in Windows Vista

- Click the **Computer** icon on the desktop
- Right click the drive you want to scan with Scandisk and select **Properties**
- Click on the **Tools** tab. Under the **Error-checking** sub heading, click the **Check Now** button
- A window named **Check Local Disk** will appear. If you want to attempt to correct errors, check the **Scan for and attempt recovery of bad sectors** checkbox
- Click **Start** to initiate the disk scan. In Vista, it is required to schedule the Scandisk to make it run at boot time, as Vista has mechanisms which do not allow it to run while the system is operating.

CHAPTER - III

NETWORKING AND INTERNET

In the world of computers, **networking** is the practice of linking two or more computing devices together for the purpose of sharing data. Networks are built with a mix of computer hardware and computer software.

COMPUTER NETWORK AND ITS NEED

Computer network

A **computer network**, often simply referred to as a **network**, is a collection of computers and devices connected by communications channels that facilitates communications among users and allows users to share resources with other users. Networks may be classified according to a wide variety of characteristics.

A computer network allows sharing of resources and information among devices connected to the network. The Advanced Research Projects Agency (ARPA) founded the design of the Advanced Research Projects Agency Network (ARPANET) for the United States Department of Defense. It was the first operational computer network in the world. Development of the network began in 1969, based on designs developed during the 1960s.

Need

Computer networks can be used for several purposes:

- **Facilitating communications**. Using a network, people can communicate efficiently and easily via e-mail, instant messaging, chat rooms, telephone, video telephone calls, and video conferencing.
- **Sharing hardware**. In a networked environment, each computer on a network can access and use hardware on the network. Suppose several personal computers on a network each require the use of a laser printer. If the personal computers and a laser printer are connected to a network,

each user can then access the laser printer on the network, as they need it.

- **Sharing files, data and information**. In a net-work environment, any authorized user can access data and information stored on other computers on the network. The capability of providing access to data and information on shared storage devices is an important feature of many networks.
- **Sharing software**. Users connected to a network can access application programs on the network.

TYPE OF NETWORKS

The following presents categories used for type of networks.

Connection method

Computer networks can be classified according to the hardware and software technology that is used to interconnect the individual devices in the network, such as optical fiber, Ethernet, Wireless LAN, HomePNA, and Power line communication.

Ethernet uses physical wiring to connect devices. Frequently deployed devices include hubs, switches, bridges and/or routers. Wireless LAN technology is designed to connect devices without wiring. These devices use radio waves or infrared signals as a transmission medium. ITU-T G.hn technology uses existing home wiring (coaxial cable, phone lines and power lines) to create a high-speed (up to 1 Gigabytes) local area network.

Wired technologies

- **Twisted pair wire** is the most widely used medium for telecommunication. Twisted-pair wires are ordinary telephone wires which consist of two insulated copper wires twisted into pairs and are used for both voice and data transmission. The use of two wires twisted together helps to reduce crosstalk and electromagnetic induction. The transmission speed ranges from 2 million bytes per second to 100 million bytes per second.
- **Coaxial cable** is widely used for cable television systems, office buildings, and other worksites for local area networks. The cables consist of copper or aluminum wire wrapped with insulating layer typically of a flexible material with a high dielectric constant, all of which are surrounded by a conductive layer. The layers of insulation help minimize interference and distortion. Transmission speed range from 200 million to more than 500 million bytes per second.

- **Optical fiber cable** consists of one or more filaments of glass fiber wrapped in protective layers. It transmits light which can travel over extended distances without signal loss. Fiber-optic cables are not affected by electromagnetic radiation. Transmission speed may reach trillions of bytes per second. The transmission speed of fiber optics is hundreds of times faster than for coaxial cables and thousands of times faster than for twisted-pair wire.

Wireless technologies

- **Terrestrial Microwave** – Terrestrial microwaves use Earth-based transmitter and receiver. The equipment look similar to satellite dishes. Terrestrial microwaves use low-gigahertz range, which limits all communications to line-of-sight. Path between relay stations is spaced approx. 30 miles apart. Microwave antennas are usually placed on top of buildings, towers, hills, and mountain peaks.
- **Communications Satellites** – The satellites use microwave radio waves as their telecommunications medium which are not deflected by the Earth's atmosphere. The satellites are stationed in space, typically 22,000 miles (for geosynchronous satellites) above the equator. These Earth-orbiting systems are capable of receiving and relaying voice, data, and TV signals.
- **Cellular and PCS Systems** – Use several radio communications technologies. The systems are divided to different geographic area. Each area has low-power transmitter or radio relay antenna device to relay calls from one area to the next area.
- **Wireless LANs** – Wireless local area network use a high-frequency radio technology similar to digital cellular and a low-frequency radio technology. Wire-less LANs use spread spectrum technology to enable communication between multiple devices in a limited area. An example of open-standards wireless radio-wave technology is IEEE 802.11b.
- **Bluetooth** – A short range wireless technology. Operate at approx. 1Mbps with range from 10 to 100 meters. Bluetooth is an open wireless protocol for data exchange over short distances. An example of Bluetooth for data exchange i.e. musical or video clips from mobile phone to another mobile phone or mobile phone to PC.

Scale

Networks are often classified as given below depending on their scale, scope and purpose:

LAN - Local Area Network

WLAN - Wireless Local Area Network

WAN - Wide Area Network

MAN - Metropolitan Area Network

VPN- Virtual Private Network

SAN - Storage Area Network, System Area Network, Server Area Network, or sometimes Small Area Network

CAN - Campus Area Network, Controller Area Network, or sometimes Cluster Area Network

PAN - Personal Area Network

DAN - Desk Area Network

VAN- Value Added Network

LAN and WAN were the original categories of area networks, while the others have gradually emerged over many years of technology evolution. Usage, trust level, and access right often differ between these types of networks. For example, LANs tend to be designed for internal use by an organization's internal systems and employees in individual physical locations (such as a building), while WANs may connect physically separate parts of an organization and may include connections to third parties. These network types are a separate concept from network topologies such as bus, ring and star which are described in details later on.

Personal area network

A personal area network (PAN) is a computer network used for communication among computer and different information technological devices close to one person. Some examples of devices that are used in a PAN are personal computers, printers, fax machines, telephones, PDAs, scanners, and even video game consoles. A PAN may include wired and wireless connections between devices. The reach of a PAN typically extends to 10 meters. A wired PAN is usually constructed with USB and Firewire connections while technologies such as Bluetooth and infrared communication typically form a wireless PAN.

Local area network

A LAN connects network devices over a relatively short distance. A networked office building, school, or home usually contains a single LAN, though sometimes one building will contain a few small LANs (perhaps one per room), and occasionally a LAN will span a group of nearby buildings. In TCP/IP networking, a LAN is often but not always implemented as a single IP subnet.

In addition to operating in a limited space, LANs are also typically owned, controlled, and managed by a single person or organization. They also tend to use certain conne-ctivity technologies, primarily Ethernet and Token Ring.

A local area network (LAN) is a network that connects computers and devices in a limited geographical area such as home, school, computer laboratory, office building, or closely positioned group of buildings. Each computer or device on the network is a node. Current wired LANs are most likely to be based on Ethernet technology, although new standards like ITU-T G.hn also provide a way to create a wired LAN using existing home wires (coaxial cables, phone lines and power lines).

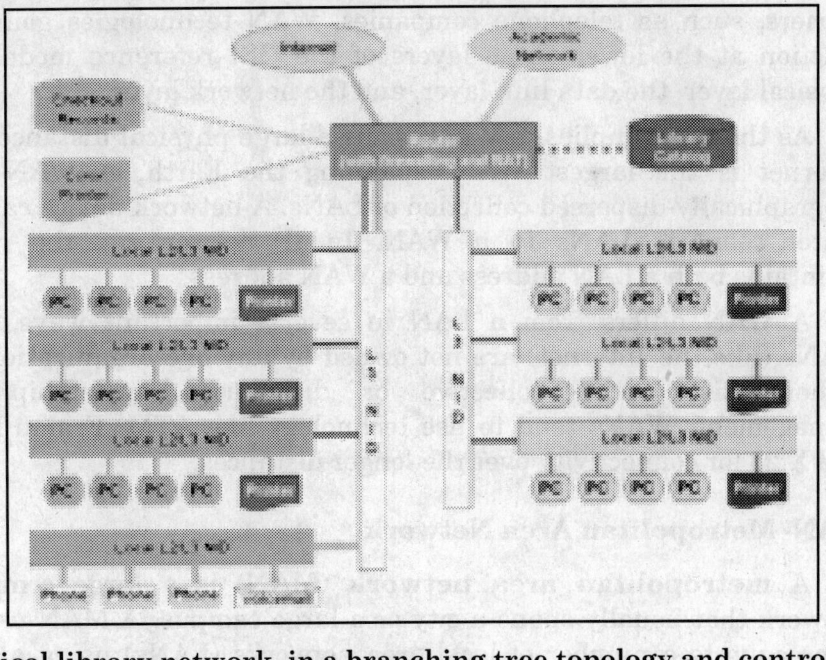

Typical library network, in a branching tree topology and controlled access to resources

All interconnected devices must understand the network layer (layer 3), because they are handling multiple subnets (the different colors). Those inside the library, which have only 10/100 MB Ethernet connections to the user device and a Gigabyte Ethernet connection to the central router, could be called "layer 3 switches" because they only have Ethernet interfaces and must understand IP. It would be more correct to call them access routers, where the router at the top is a distribution router that connects to the Internet and academic networks' customer access routers.

The defining characteristics of LANs, in contrast to WANs (Wide Area Networks), include their higher data transfer rates, smaller geographic range, and no need for leased telecommunication lines. Current Ethernet or other IEEE 802.3 LAN technologies operate at speeds up to 10 GB. This is the data transfer rate. IEEE has projects investigating the standardization of 40 and 100 GB.

WAN - Wide Area Network

A wide area network (WAN) is a computer network that covers a large geographic area such as a city, country, or spans even intercontinental distances, using a communi-cations channel that combines many types of media such as telephone lines, cables, and air waves. A WAN often uses transmission facilities provided by common carriers, such as telephone companies. WAN technologies generally function at the lower three layers of the OSI reference model: the physical layer, the data link layer, and the network layer.

As the term implies, a WAN spans a large physical distance. The Internet is the largest WAN, spanning the Earth. A WAN is a geographically-dispersed collection of LANs. A network device called a router connects LANs to a WAN. In IP networking, the router maintains both a LAN address and a WAN address.

A WAN differs from a LAN in several important ways. Most WANs (like the Internet) are not owned by any one organization but rather exist under collective or distributed ownership and management. WANs tend to use technology like ATM, Frame Relay and X.25 for connectivity over the longer distances.

MAN- Metropolitan Area Network

A **metropolitan area network** (MAN) is a large computer network that usually spans a city or a large campus. A MAN usually interconnects a number of local area networks (LANs) using a high-capacity backbone technology, such as fiber-optical links, and provides up-link services to wide area networks and the Internet.

A MAN is optimized for a larger geographical area than a LAN, ranging from several blocks of buildings to entire cities. MANs can also depend on communications channels of moderate-to-high data rates. A MAN might be owned and operated by a single organization, but it usually will be used by many individuals and organizations. A physical area larger than a LAN but smaller than a WAN, such as a city. A MAN is typically owned an operated by a single entity such as a government body or large corporation.

MANs might also be owned and operated as public utilities. They will often provide means for internetworking of local networks

A Metropolitan Area Network (MAN) is a large com-puter network that spans a metropolitan area or campus. Its geographic scope falls between a WAN and LAN. MANs provide Internet connectivity for LANs in a metropolitan region, and connect them to wider area networks like the Internet. It can also be used in cable television.

VAN- Value Added Network

VAN is also an acronym for virtual area network. A **Value-added Network** (VAN) is a hosted service offering that acts as an intermediary between business partners sharing standards based or proprietary data via shared Business Processes. The offered service is referred to as "Value-added Network Service".

A value-added network (VAN) is a private network provider (sometimes called a turnkey communications line) that is hired by a company to facilitate electronic data interchange (EDI) or provide other network services. Before the arrival of the World Wide Web, some companies hired value-added networks to move data from their company to other companies. With the arrival of the World Wide Web, many companies found it more cost-efficient to move their data over the Internet instead of paying the minimum monthly fees and per-character charges found in typical VAN contracts. In response, contemporary value-added network providers now focus on offering EDI translation, encryption, secure e-mail, management reporting, and other extra services for their customers.

LAN, WAN and Home Networking

Residences typically employ one LAN and connect to the Internet WAN via an Internet Service Provider (ISP) using a broadband modem. The ISP provides a WAN IP address to the modem, and all of the computers on the home network use LAN (so-called private) IP addresses. All computers on the home LAN can communicate directly with each other but must go through a central gateway, typically a broadband router, to reach the ISP.

Home area network

A home area network is a residential LAN which is used for communication between digital devices typically deployed in the home, usually a small number of personal computers and accessories, such as printers and mobile computing devices. An important function is the sharing of Internet access, often a broadband service through a CATV or Digital Subscriber Line (DSL) provider.

Campus network

A network spanning multiple LANs but smaller than a MAN, such as on a university or local business campus. A campus network is a computer network made up of an interconnection of local area networks (LANs) within a limited geographical area. The networking equipments (switches, routers) and transmission media (optical fiber, copper plant, Cat5 cabling etc.) are almost entirely owned (by the campus tenant / owner: an enterprise, university, government etc.).

In the case of a university campus-based campus network, the network is likely to link a variety of campus buildings including; academic departments, the university library and student residence halls.

Global area network

A global area network (GAN) is a network used for supporting mobile communications across an arbitrary number of wireless LANs, satellite coverage areas, etc. The key challenge in mobile communications is handing off the user communications from one local coverage area to the next. In IEEE Project 802, this involves a succession of terrestrial WIRELESS local area networks (WLAN).

Enterprise Private Network

An **Enterprise Private Network** is a network build by an enterprise to interconnect the various company sites (production sites, head offices, remote offices, shops etc.) in order to share computer resources over the network.

Beginning with the digitalization of telecommunication networks started in the 70's in the USA (by AT&T) and propelled by the growth in computer systems availability and demands private networks have been built for decades without the need to append the term **private** to them. The networks were operated over telecommunication networks and as per voice communications a certain amount of security and secrecy was expected and assumed.

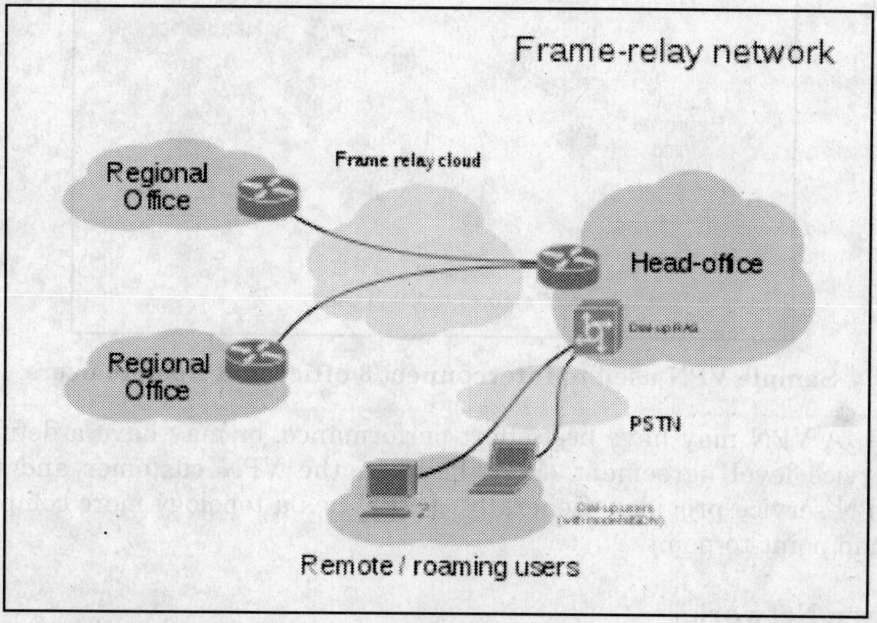

Sample EPN made of Frame relay WAN connections and dialup remote access

But with the Internet in the 90's came a new type of network built over this Public infrastructure, using encryp-tion to protect the data traffic from eaves-dropping (VPN). So the enterprise networks are now commonly referred to Enterprise Private Network in order to clarify that these are private networks (in opposition to public networks).

Virtual private network

A virtual private network (VPN) is a computer network in which some of the links between nodes are carried by open connections or virtual circuits in some larger network (e.g., the Internet) instead of by physical wires. The data link layer protocols of the virtual network are said to be tunneled through the larger network when this is the case. One common application is secure communications through the public Internet, but a VPN need not have explicit security features, such as authentication or content encryption. VPNs, for example, can be used to separate the traffic of different user communities over an underlying network with strong security features.

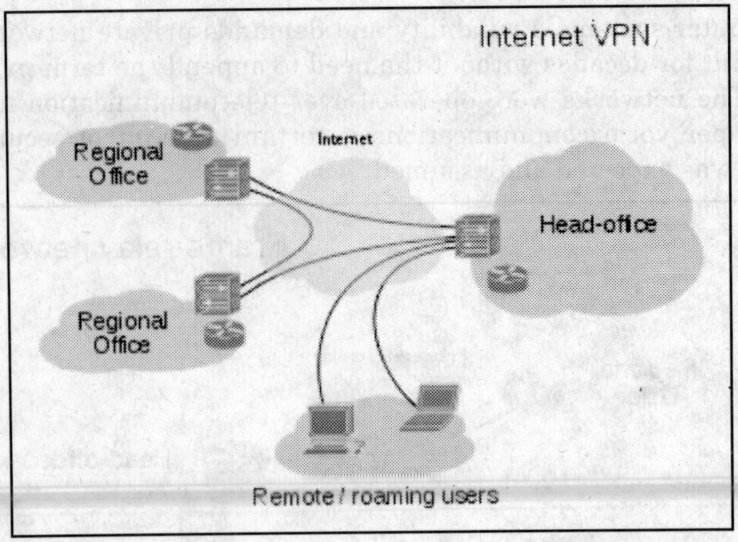

Sample VPN used to interconnect 3 office and Remote users

A VPN may have best-effort performance, or may have a defined service level agreement (SLA) between the VPN customer and the VPN service provider. Generally, a VPN has a topology more complex than point-to-point.

Area Networks

Networks can be categorized in several different ways. One approach defines the type of network according to the geographic area it spans. Local area networks (LANs), for example, typically reach across a single home, whereas wide area networks (WANs), reach across cities, states, or even across the world. The Internet is the world's largest public WAN.

Functional relationship (network architecture)

Computer networks may be classified according to the functional relationships which exist among the elements of the network, e.g., active networking, client–server and peer-to-peer (workgroup) architecture.

Other Types of Area Networks

You may also commonly see references to these others:

Wireless Local Area Network - a LAN based on WiFi wireless network technology

Storage Area Network - connects servers to data storage devices through a technology like Fibre Channel.

System Area Network - links high-performance computers with high-speed connections in a cluster configuration. Also known as Cluster Area Network.

Network Design

Computer networks also differ in their design. The two types of high-level network design are called client-server and peer-to-peer. Client-server networks feature centralized server computers that store email, Web pages, files and or applications. On a peer-to-peer network, conversely, all computers tend to support the same functions. Client-server networks are much more common in business and peer-to-peer networks much more common in homes.

Network Protocols

In networking, the communication language used by computer devices is called the protocol. Yet another way to classify computer networks is by the set of protocols they support. Networks often implement multiple protocols to support specific applications. Popular protocols include TCP/ IP, the most common protocol found on the Internet and in home networks.

Wired vs Wireless Networking

Many of the same network protocols, like TCP/IP, work in both wired and wireless networks. Networks with Ethernet cables predominated in businesses, schools, and homes for several decades. Recently, however, wireless networking alternatives have emerged as the premier technology for building new computer networks.

CONCEPT OF NETWORK TOPOLOGY

A network topology represents its layout or structure from the point of view of data flow. In so-called bus networks, for example, all of the computers share and communicate across one common conduit, whereas in a star network, all data flows through one centralized device. Common types of network topologies include bus, star, ring and mesh.

In computer networking, topology refers to the layout of connected devices. Computer networks may be classified according to the network topology upon which the network is based, such as bus network, star network, ring network, mesh network, star-bus network, tree or hierarchical topology network. Network topology is the coordination by which devices in the network are arranged in their logical relations to one another, independent of physical arrangement. Even if networked computers are physically placed in a linear arrangement and are connected to a hub, the network has a star topology, rather than a bus topology. In this regard the visual and operational characteristics of a network are distinct. Networks may be classified based on the method of data used to convey the data, these include digital and analog networks.

Network topology is defined as the interconnection of the various elements (links, nodes, etc.) of a computer network. Network Topologies can be physical or logical. Physical Topology means the physical design of a network including the devices, location and cable installation. Logical topology refers to the fact that how data actually transfers in a network as opposed to its physical design.

Topology can be considered as a virtual shape or structure of a network. This shape actually does not correspond to the actual physical design of the devices on the computer network. The computers on the home network can be arranged in a circle shape but it does not necessarily mean that it presents a ring topology.

Any particular network topology is determined only by the graphical mapping of the configuration of physical and/or logical connections between nodes. The study of network topology uses graph theory. Distances between nodes, physical interconnections, transmission rates, and/or signal types may differ in two networks and yet their topologies may be identical.

A Local Area Network (LAN) is one example of a network that exhibits both a physical topology and a logical topology. Any given node in the LAN has one or more links to one or more nodes in the network and the mapping of these links and nodes in a graph results in a geometrical shape that may be used to describe the physical topology of the network. Likewise, the mapping of the data flow between the nodes in the network determines the logical topology of the network. The physical and logical topologies may or may not be identical in any particular network.

Basic topology types

The study of network topology recognizes six basic topologies:

- Bus topology
- Star topology

- Ring topology
- Hybrid topology
- Tree topology
- Mesh topology

This classification is based on the interconnection between computers - be it physical or logical.

CLASSIFICATION OF NETWORK TOPOLOGIES

There are also three basic categories of network topologies:

- Physical topologies
- Signal topologies
- Logical topologies

The terms Signal topology and logical topology are often used interchangeably, though there is a subtle difference between the two.

Physical topologies

The mapping of the nodes of a network and the physical connections between them – i.e., the layout of wiring, cables, the locations of nodes, and the interconnections between the nodes and the cabling or wiring system.

Classification of physical topologies

Point-to-point

The simplest topology is a permanent link between two endpoints. Switched point-to-point topologies are the basic model of conventional telephony. The value of a permanent point-to-point network is the value of guaranteed, or nearly so, communications between the two endpoints. The value of an on-demand point-to-point connection is proportional to the number of potential pairs of subscribers, and has been expressed as Metcalfe's Law.

Permanent (dedicated)

Easiest to understand, of the variations of point-to-point topology, is a point-to-point communications channel that appears, to the user, to be permanently associated with the two endpoints. Children's "tin-can telephone" is one example, with a microphone to a single public address speaker is another. These are examples of physical dedicated channels.

Within many switched telecommunications systems, it is possible to establish a permanent circuit. One example might be a telephone in the lobby of a public building, which is programmed to ring only the number of a telephone dispatcher. "Nailing down" a switched connection saves the cost of running a physical circuit between the two points. The resources in such a connection can be released when no longer needed, for example, a television circuit from a parade route back to the studio.

Switched

Using circuit-switching or packet-switching technologies, a point-to-point circuit can be set up dynamically, and dropped when no longer needed. This is the basic mode of conventional telephony.

Bus network topology

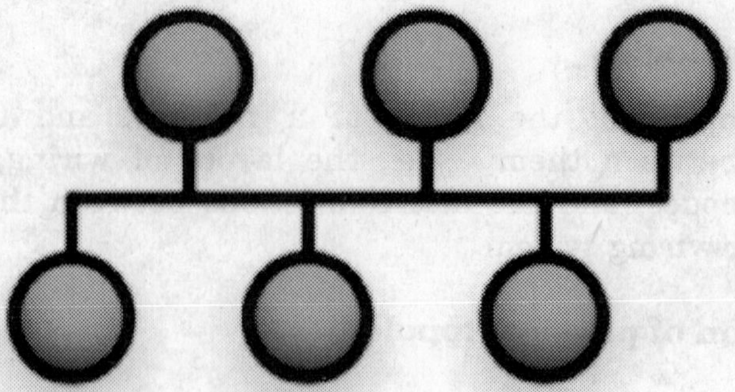

In local area networks where bus topology is used, each machine is connected to a single cable. Each computer or server is connected to the single bus cable through some kind of connector. A terminator is required at each end of the bus cable to prevent the signal from bouncing back and forth on the bus cable. A signal from the source travels in both directions to all machines connected on the bus cable until it finds the MAC address or IP address on the network that is the intended recipient. If the machine address does not match the intended address for the data, the machine ignores the data. Alternatively, if the data does match the machine address, the data is accepted. Since the bus topology consists of only one wire, it is rather inexpensive to implement when compared to other topologies. However, the low cost of implementing the technology is offset by the high cost of managing the network. Additionally, since only one cable is utilized, it can be the single point of failure. If the network cable breaks, the entire network will be down.

Linear bus

The type of network topology in which all of the nodes of the network are connected to a common transmission medium which has exactly two endpoints (this is the 'bus', which is also commonly referred to as the backbone, or trunk) – all data that is transmitted between nodes in the network is transmitted over this common transmission medium and is able to be received by all nodes in the network virtually simultaneously (disregarding propagation delays).

Note

The two endpoints of the common transmission medium are normally terminated with a device called a terminator that exhibits the characteristic impedance of the transmis-sion medium and which dissipates or absorbs the energy that remains in the signal to prevent the signal from being reflected or propagated back onto the transmission medium in the opposite direction, which would cause interference with and degradation of the signals on the transmission medium.

Distributed bus

The type of network topology in which all of the nodes of the network are connected to a common transmission medium which has more than two endpoints that are created by adding branches to the main section of the transmission medium–the physical distributed bus topology functions in exactly the same fashion as the physical linear bus topology (i.e., all nodes share a common transmission medium).

Notes

(1) All of the endpoints of the common transmission medium are normally terminated with a device called a 'terminator' (see the note under linear bus).

(2) The physical linear bus topology is sometimes considered to be a special case of the physical distributed bus topology – i.e., a distributed bus with no branching segments.

(3) The physical distributed bus topology is sometimes incorrectly referred to as a physical tree topology – however, although the physical distributed bus topology resembles the physical tree topology, it differs from the physical tree topology in that there is no central node to which any other nodes are connected, since this hierarchical functionality is replaced by the common bus.

Star network topology

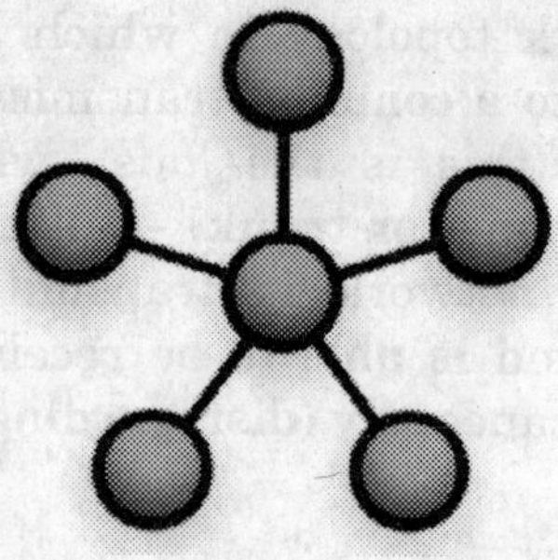

In local area networks with a star topology, each network host is connected to a central hub. In contrast to the bus topology, the star topology connects each node to the hub with a point-to-point connection. All traffic that transverse the network passes through the central hub. The hub acts as a signal booster or repeater. The star topology is considered the easiest topology to design and implement. An advantage of the star topology is the simplicity of adding additional nodes. The primary disadvantage of the star topology is that the hub represents a single point of failure.

Notes

(1) A point-to-point link (described above) is sometimes categorized as a special instance of the physical star topology – therefore, the simplest type of network that is based upon the physical star topology would consist of one node with a single point-to-point link to a second node, the choice of which node is the 'hub' and which node is the 'spoke' being arbitrary.

(2) After the special case of the point-to-point link, as in note 1) above, the next simplest type of network that is based upon the physical star topology would consist of one central node – the 'hub' – with two separate point-to-point links to two peripheral nodes – the 'spokes'.

(3) Although most networks that are based upon the physical star topology are commonly implemented using a special device such as a hub or switch as the central node (i.e., the 'hub' of the star), it is also possible to implement a network that is based upon the physical star topology using a computer or even a simple common connection point as the 'hub' or central node – however, since many illustrations of the physical star network topology depict the central node as one of these special devices, some confusion is possible, since

this practice may lead to the misconception that a physical star network requires the central node to be one of these special devices, which is not true because a simple network consisting of three computers connected as in note 2) above also has the topology of the physical star.

(4) Star networks may also be described as either broadcast multi-access or nonbroadcast multi-access (NBMA), depending on whether the technology of the network either automatically propagates a signal at the hub to all spokes, or only addresses individual spokes with each communication.

Extended star

A type of network topology in which a network that is based upon the physical star topology has one or more repeaters between the central node (the 'hub' of the star) and the peripheral or 'spoke' nodes, the repeaters being used to extend the maximum transmission distance of the point-to-point links between the central node and the peripheral nodes beyond that which is supported by the transmitter power of the central node or beyond that which is supported by the standard upon which the physical layer of the physical star network is based.

If the repeaters in a network that is based upon the physical extended star topology are replaced with hubs or switches, then a hybrid network topology is created that is referred to as a physical hierarchical star topology, although some texts make no distinction between the two topologies.

Distributed Star

A type of network topology that is composed of individual networks that are based upon the physical star topology connected together in a linear fashion – i.e., 'daisy-chained' – with no central or top level connection point (e.g., two or more 'stacked' hubs, along with their associated star connected nodes or 'spokes').

Ring network topology

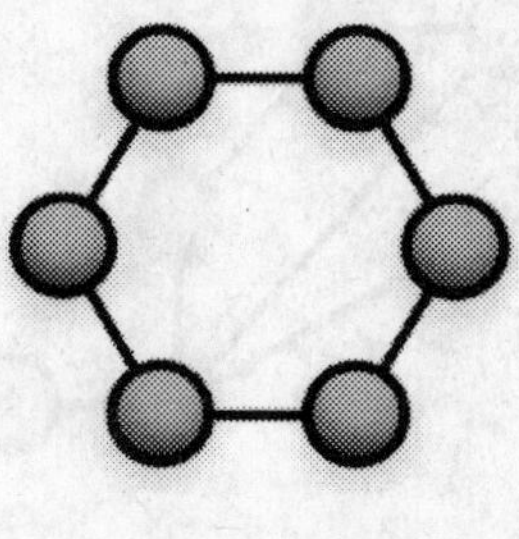

In local area networks where the ring topology is used, each computer is connected to the network in a closed loop or ring. Each machine or computer has a unique address that is used for identification purposes. The signal passes through each machine or computer connected to the ring in one direction. Ring topologies typically utilize a token passing scheme, used to control access to the network. By utilizing this scheme, only one machine can transmit on the network at a time. The machines or computers connected to the ring act as signal boosters or repeaters which strengthen the signals that transverse the network. The primary disadvantage of ring topology is the failure of one machine will cause the entire network to fail.

Mesh topology

Fully connected mesh topology

The value of fully meshed networks is proportional to the exponent of the number of subscribers, assuming that communicating groups of any two endpoints, up to and including all the endpoints, is approximated by Reed's Law.

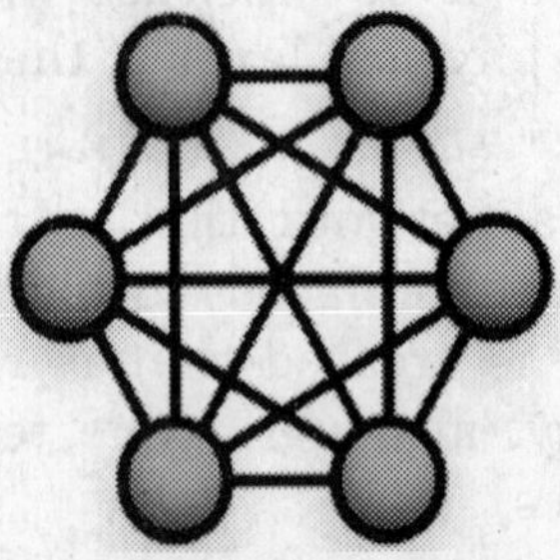

Fully connected mesh topology

Note

The physical fully connected mesh topology is generally too costly and complex for practical networks, although the topology is used when there are only a small number of nodes to be interconnected.

Partially connected mesh topology

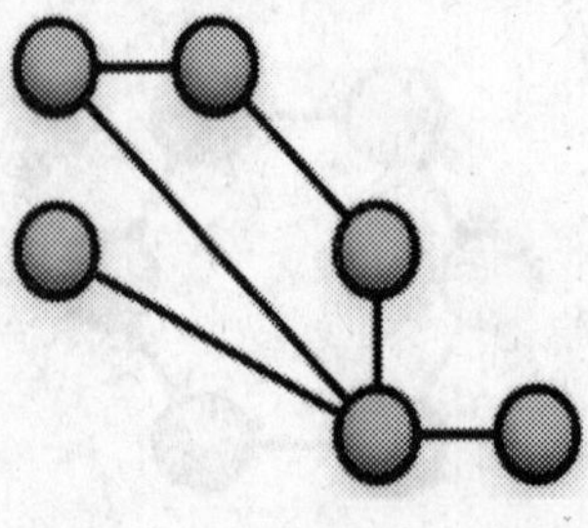

The type of network topology in which some of the nodes of the network are connected to more than one other node in the network with a point-to-point link – this makes it possible to take advantage of some of the redundancy that is provided by a physical fully connected mesh topology without the expense and complexity required for a connection between every node in the network.

Note

In most practical networks that are based upon the physical partially connected mesh topology, all of the data that is transmitted between nodes in the network takes the shortest path (or an approximation of the shortest path) between nodes, except in the case of a failure or break in one of the links, in which case the data takes an alternative path to the destination. This requires that the nodes of the network possess some type of logical 'routing' algorithm to determine the correct path to use at any particular time.

Tree network topology

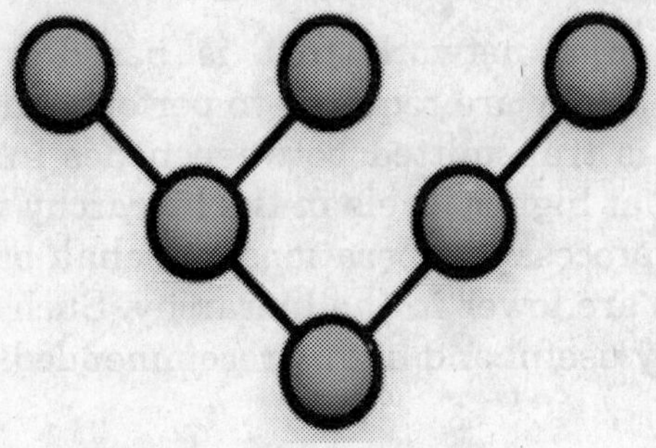

Also known as hierarchical **network**. The type of network topology in which a central 'root' node (the top level of the hierarchy) is connected to one or more other nodes that are one level lower in the hierarchy (i.e., the second level) with a point-to-point link between each of the second level nodes and the top level central 'root' node, while each of the second level nodes that are connected to the top level central 'root' node will also have one or more other nodes that are one level lower in the hierarchy (i.e., the third level) connected to it, also with a point-to-point link, the top level central 'root' node being the only node that has no other node above it in the hierarchy (The hierarchy of the tree is symmetrical.) Each node in the network having a specific fixed number, of nodes connected to it at the next lower level in the hierarchy, the number, being referred to as the 'branching factor' of the hierarchical tree.

Note

(1) A network that is based upon the physical hierarchical topology must have at least three levels in the hierarchy of the tree, since a network with a central 'root' node and only one hierarchical level below it would exhibit the physical topology of a star.

(2) A network that is based upon the physical hierarchical topology and with a branching factor of 1 would be classified as a physical linear topology.

(3) The branching factor, f, is independent of the total number of nodes in the network and, therefore, if the nodes in the network require ports for connection to other nodes the total number of ports per node may be kept low even though the total number of nodes is large – this makes the effect of the cost of adding ports to each node totally dependent upon the branching factor and may therefore be kept as low as required without any effect upon the total number of nodes that are possible.

(4) The total number of point-to-point links in a network that is based upon the physical hierarchical topology will be one less than the total number of nodes in the network.

(5) If the nodes in a network that is based upon the physical hierarchical topology are required to perform any processing upon the data that is transmitted between nodes in the network, the nodes that are at higher levels in the hierarchy will be required to perform more processing operations on behalf of other nodes than the nodes that are lower in the hierarchy. Such a type of network topology is very useful and highly recommended.

Signal topology

The mapping of the actual connections between the nodes of a network, as evidenced by the path that the signals take when propagating between the nodes.

Note

The term 'signal topology' is often used synonymously with the term 'logical topology', however, some confusion may result from this practice in certain situations since, by definition, the term 'logical topology' refers to the apparent path that the data takes between nodes in a network while the term 'signal topology' generally refers to the actual path that the signals (e.g., optical, electrical, electro-magnetic, etc.) take when propagating between nodes.

Logical topology

The logical topology, in contrast to the "physical", is the way that the signals act on the network media, or the way that the data passes through the network from one device to the next without regard to the physical interconnection of the devices. A network's logical topology is not necessarily the same as its physical topology. For example, twisted pair Ethernet is a logical bus topology in a physical star topology layout. While IBM's Token Ring is a logical ring topology, it is physically set up in a star topology.

Classification of logical topologies

The logical classification of network topologies generally follows the same classifications as those in the physical classifications of network topologies, the path that the data takes between nodes being used to determine the topology as opposed to the actual physical connections being used to determine the topology

Notes

(1) Logical topologies are often closely associated with media access control (MAC) methods and protocols.

(2) The logical topologies are generally determined by network protocols as opposed to being determined by the physical layout of cables, wires, and network devices or by the flow of the electrical signals, although in many cases the paths that the electrical signals take between nodes may closely match the logical flow of data, hence the convention of using the terms 'logical topology' and 'signal topology' interchangeably.

(3) Logical topologies are able to be dynamically reconfigured by special types of equipment such as routers and switches.

Daisy chains

Except for star-based networks, the easiest way to add more computers into a network is by daisy-chaining, or connecting each computer in series to the next. If a message is intended for a computer partway down the line, each system bounces it along in sequence until it reaches the destination. A daisy-chained network can take two basic forms: linear and ring.

- A **linear topology** puts a two-way link between one computer and the next. However, this was expensive in the early days of computing, since each computer (except for the ones at each end) required two receivers and two transmitters.

- By connecting the computers at each end, a **ring topology** can be formed. An advantage of the ring is that the number of transmitters and receivers can be cut in half, since a message will eventually loop all of the way around. When a node sends a message, the message is processed by each computer in the ring. If a computer is not the destination node, it will pass the message to the next node, until the message arrives at its destination. If the message is not accepted by any node on the network, it will travel around the entire ring and return to the sender. This potentially results in a doubling of travel time for data.

Centralization

The **star topology** reduces the probability of a network failure by connecting all of the peripheral nodes (computers, etc.) to a central node. When the physical star topology is applied to a logical bus network such as Ethernet, this central node (traditionally a hub) rebroadcasts all transmissions received from any peripheral node to all peripheral nodes on the network, sometimes including the originating node. All peripheral nodes may thus communicate with all others by transmitting to, and receiving from, the central node only. The failure of a transmission line linking any peripheral node to the central node will result in the isolation of that peripheral node from all others, but the remaining peripheral nodes will be unaffected. However, the disadvantage is that the failure of the central node will cause the failure of all of the peripheral nodes also.

If the central node is passive, the originating node must be able to tolerate the reception of an echo of its own transmission, delayed by the two-way round trip transmission time (i.e. to and from the central node) plus any delay generated in the central node. An active star network has an active central node that usually has the means to prevent echo-related problems.

A **tree topology** (**hierarchical topology**) can be viewed as a collection of star networks arranged in a hierarchy. This tree has individual peripheral nodes (e.g. leaves) which are required to transmit to and receive from one other node only and are not required to act as repeaters or regenerators. Unlike the star network, the functionality of the central node may be distributed.

As in the conventional star network, individual nodes may thus still be isolated from the network by a single-point failure of a transmission path to the node. If a link connecting a leaf fails, that leaf is isolated; if a connection to a non-leaf node fails, an entire section of the network becomes isolated from the rest.

In order to alleviate the amount of network traffic that comes from broadcasting all signals to all nodes, more advanced central nodes were developed that are able to keep track of the identities of the nodes that are connected to the network. These network switches will "learn" the layout of the network by "listening" on each port during normal data transmission, examining the data packets and recording the address/identifier of each connected node and which port it's connected to in a lookup table held in memory. This lookup table then allows future transmissions to be forwarded to the intended destination only.

Decentralization

In a **mesh topology** (i.e., a partially connected mesh topology), there are at least two nodes with two or more paths between them to provide redundant paths to be used in case the link providing one of the paths fails. This decentralization is often used to advantage to compensate for the single-point-failure disadvantage that is present when using a single device as a central node (e.g., in star and tree networks). A special kind of mesh, limiting the number of hops between two nodes, is a hypercube. The number of arbitrary forks in mesh networks makes them more difficult to design and implement, but their decentralized nature makes them very useful. This is similar in some ways to a **grid network**, where a linear or ring topology is used to connect systems in multiple directions. A multi-dimensional ring has a toroidal topology, for instance.

A fully connected network, complete topology or **full mesh topology** is a network topology in which there is a direct link between all pairs of nodes. In a fully connected network with n nodes, there are n(n-1)/2 direct links. Networks designed with this topology are usually very expensive to set up, but provide a high degree of reliability due to the multiple paths for data that are provided by the large number of redundant links between nodes. This topology is mostly seen in military applications. However, it can also be seen in the file sharing protocol BitTorrent in which users connect to other users in the "swarm" by allowing each user sharing the file to connect to other users also involved. Often in actual usage of BitTorrent any given individual node is rarely connected to every single other node as in a true fully connected network but the protocol does allow for the possibility for any one node to connect to any other node when sharing files.

Hybrids

Hybrid networks use a combination of any two or more topologies in such a way that the resulting network does not exhibit one of the standard topologies (e.g., bus, star, ring, etc.). For example, a tree network connected to a tree network is still a tree network, but two star networks connected together exhibit a hybrid network topology. A hybrid topology is always produced when two different basic network topologies are connected. Two common examples for Hybrid network are: star ring network and star bus network

- A Star ring network consists of two or more star topologies connected using a multistation access unit (MAU) as a centralized hub.
- A Star Bus network consists of two or more star topologies connected using a bus trunk (the bus trunk serves as the network's backbone).

While grid networks have found popularity in high-performance computing applications, some systems have used genetic algorithms to design custom networks that have the fewest possible hops in between different nodes. Some of the resulting layouts are nearly incomprehensible, although they function quite well.

INTERNET

The Internet is a global system of interconnected governmental, academic, corporate, public, and private computer networks. It is based on the networking techno-logies of the Internet Protocol Suite. It is the successor of the Advanced Research Projects Agency Network (ARPANET) developed by DARPA of the U.S. Department of Defense. The Internet is also the communications backbone under-lying the World Wide Web (WWW). The 'Internet' is most commonly spelled with a capital 'I' as a proper noun, for historical reasons and to distinguish it from other generic internetworks.

Participants in the Internet use a diverse array of methods of several hundred documented, and often standardized, protocols compatible with the Internet Protocol Suite and an addressing system (IP Addresses) administered by the Internet Assigned Numbers Authority and address registries. Service providers and large enterprises exchange information about the reachability of their address spaces through the Border Gateway Protocol (BGP), forming a redundant worldwide mesh of transmission paths.

Internetwork

An Internetwork is the connection of two or more private computer networks via a common switching (OSI Layer 2) or routing technology (OSI Layer 3) and owned by separate entities (public or private). The result is called an internetwork. The Internet is an aggregation of many internetworks, hence its name was shortened to Internet.

Any interconnection between public, private, commercial, industrial, or governmental networks may also be defined as an internetwork or (more often) an extranet.

Intranets and extranets

Intranets and extranets are parts or extensions of a computer network, usually a local area network.

An intranet is a set of networks, using the Internet Protocol and IP-based tools such as web browsers and file transfer applications that are under the control of a single administrative entity. That administrative entity closes the intranet to all but specific, authorized users. Most commonly, an intranet is the internal network of an organization. A large intranet will typically have at least one web server to provide users with organizational information.

An extranet is a network that is limited in scope to a single organization or entity and also has limited connections to the networks of one or more other usually, but not necessarily, trusted organizations or entities (e.g., a company's customers may be given access to some part of its intranet creating in this way an extranet, while at the same time the customers may not be considered 'trusted' from a security standpoint). Technically, an extranet may also be categorized as a CAN, MAN, WAN, or other type of network, although, by definition, an extranet cannot consist of a single LAN; it must have at least one connection with an external network.

Overlay Network

An overlay network is a computer network that is built on top of another network. Nodes in the overlay can be thought of as being connected by virtual or logical links, each of which corresponds to a path, perhaps through many physical links, in the underlying network.

Nodes in the overlay can be thought of as being connected by virtual or logical links, each of which corresponds to a path, perhaps through many physical links, in the underlying network. For example, many peer-to-peer networks are overlay networks because they run on top of the Internet. Internet was built as an overlay on the telephone network.

Overlay networks have been around since the invention of networking when computer systems were connected over telephone lines using modem, before any data network existed.

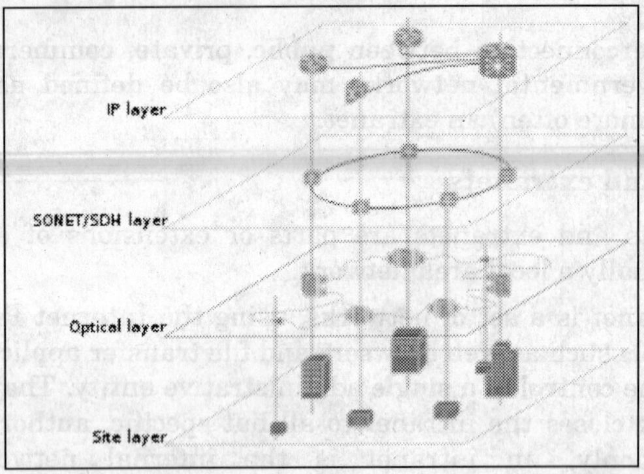

A sample overlay network: IP over SONET over Optical

Nowadays the Internet is the basis for many overlaid networks that can be constructed to permit routing of messages to destinations not specified by an IP address. For example, distributed hash tables can be used to route messages to a node having a specific logical address, whose IP address is not known in advance.

Overlay networks have also been proposed as a way to improve Internet routing, such as through quality of service guarantees to achieve higher-quality streaming media. Previous proposals such as IntServ, DiffServ, and IP Multicast have not seen wide acceptance largely because they require modification of all routers in the network. On the other hand, an overlay network can be incrementally deployed on end-hosts running the overlay protocol software, without cooperation from ISPs. The overlay has no control over how packets are routed in the underlying network between two overlay nodes, but it can control, for example, the sequence of overlay nodes a message traverses before reaching its destination.

For example, Akamai Technologies manages an overlay network that provides reliable, efficient content delivery (a kind of multicast).

Academic research includes End System Multicast and Overcast for multicast; RON (Resilient Overlay Network) for resilient routing; and OverQoS for quality of service guarantees, among others.

Basic hardware components

All networks are made up of basic hardware building blocks to interconnect network nodes, such as Network Interface Cards (NICs), Bridges, Hubs, Switches, and Routers. In addition, some method of connecting these building blocks is required, usually in the form of galvanic cable (most commonly Category 5 cable). Less common are microwave links or optical cable (optical fiber). An Ethernet card may also be required.

Network interface cards

A network card, network adapter, or NIC (network interface card) is a piece of computer hardware designed to allow computers to communicate over a computer network. It provides physical access to a networking medium and often provides a low-level addressing system through the use of MAC (Medium Access Control) addresses.

Repeaters

A repeater is an electronic device that receives a signal, cleans it of unnecessary noise, regenerates it, and retransmits it at a higher power level, or to the other side of an obstruction, so that the signal can cover longer distances without degradation. In most twisted pair Ethernet configurations, repeaters are required for cable that runs longer than 100 meters. Repeaters work on the Physical Layer of the Open System Intervention (OSI) model.

Hubs

A network hub contains multiple ports. When a packet arrives at one port, it is copied unmodified to all ports of the hub for transmission. The destination address in the frame is not changed to a broadcast address. It works on the Physical Layer of the OSI model.

Bridges

A network bridge connects multiple network segments at the data link layer (layer 2) of the OSI model. Bridges do send broadcasts to all ports except the one on which the broadcast was received. However, bridges do not promiscuously copy traffic to all ports, as hubs do, but learn which MAC addresses are reachable through specific ports. Once the bridge associates a port and an address, it will send traffic for that address to that port only.

Bridges learn the association of ports and addresses by examining the source address of frames that it sees on various ports. Once a frame arrives through a port, its source address is stored and the bridge assumes that MAC address is associated with that port. The first time that a previously unknown destination address is seen, the bridge will forward the frame to all ports other than the one on which the frame arrived.

Bridges come in three basic types

- Local bridges: Directly connect local area networks (LANs)
- Remote bridges: Can be used to create a wide area network (WAN) link between LANs. Remote bridges, where the connecting link is slower than the end networks, largely have been replaced with routers.
- Wireless bridges: Can be used to join LANs or connect remote stations to LANs.

Switches

A network switch is a device that forwards and filters OSI layer 2 datagrams (chunk of data communication) between ports (connected cables) based on the MAC addresses in the packets. This is distinct from a hub in that it only forwards the frames to the ports involved in the communication rather than all ports connected. A switch breaks the collision domain but represents itself as a broadcast domain. Switches make forwarding decisions of frames on the basis of MAC addresses. A switch normally has numerous ports, facilitating a star topology for devices, and cascading additional switches. Some switches are capable of routing based on Layer 3 addressing or additional logical levels; these are called multi-layer switches. The term switch is used loosely in marketing to encompass devices including routers and bridges, as well as devices that may distribute traffic on load or by application content (e.g., a Web URL identifier).

Routers

A router is an internetworking device that forwards packets between networks by processing information found in the datagram or packet (Internet protocol information from Layer 3 of the OSI Model). In many situations, this information is processed in conjunction with the routing table (also known as forwarding table). Routers use routing tables to determine what interface to forward packets (this can include the "null" also known as the "black hole" interface because data can go into it, however, no further processing is done for said data).

The **Internet** is a global system of interconnected computer networks that use the standard Internet Protocol Suite (TCP/IP) to serve billions of users worldwide. It is a network of networks that consists of millions of private, public, academic, business, and government networks of local to global scope that are linked by a broad array of electronic and optical networking technologies. The Internet carries a vast array of information resources and services, most notably the inter-linked hypertext documents of the World Wide Web (WWW) and the infrastructure to support electronic mail.

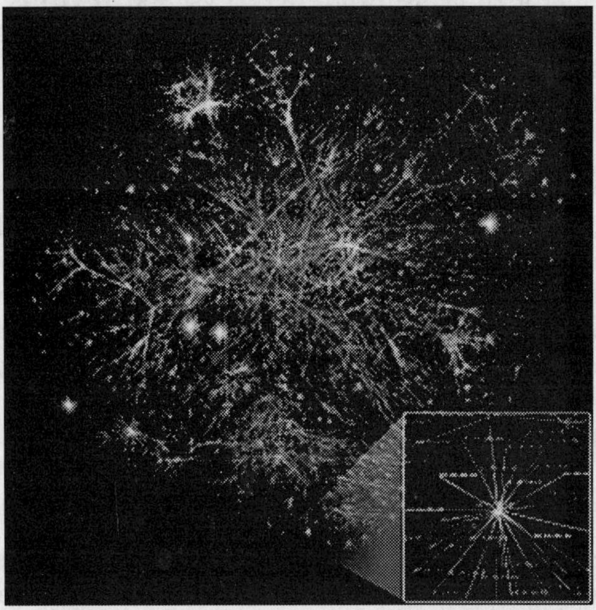

Visualization of the various routes through a portion of the Internet.

Most traditional communications media, such as telephone and television services, are reshaped or redefined using the technologies of the Internet, giving rise to services such as Voice over Internet Protocol (VoIP) and IPTV. Newspaper publishing has been reshaped into Web sites, blogging, and web feeds. The Internet has enabled or accelerated the creation of new forms of human interactions through instant messaging, Internet forums, and social networking sites.

The origins of the Internet reach back to the 1960s when the United States funded research projects of its military agencies to build robust, fault-tolerant and distributed computer networks. This research and a period of civilian funding of a new U.S. backbone by the National Science Foundation spawned worldwide participation in the development of new networking technologies and led to the commercialization of an international network in the mid 1990s, and resulted in the following popularization of countless applications in virtually every aspect of modern human life.

The Internet has no centralized governance in either technological implementation or policies for access and usage; each constituent network sets its own standards. Only the overreaching definitions of the two principal name spaces in the Internet, the Internet Protocol address space and the Domain Name System, are directed by a maintainer organization, the Internet Corporation for Assigned Names and Numbers (ICANN). The technical underpinning and standardization of the core protocols (IPv4 and IPv6) is an activity of the Internet Engineering Task Force (IETF), a non-profit organization of loosely affiliated international participants that anyone may associate with by contributing technical expertise.

Terminology

The term the Internet, when referring to the Internet, has traditionally been treated as a proper noun and written with an initial capital letter. There is a trend to regard it as a generic term or common noun and thus write it as "the internet", without the capital. The word Internet can be shortened to Net. The term cloud is also for the Internet, especially in the contexts of cloud computing and software as a service.

Internet vs. Web

The terms Internet and World Wide Web are often used in everyday speech without much distinction. However, the Internet and the World Wide Web are not one and the same. The Internet is a global data communications system. It is a hardware and software infrastructure that provides connectivity between computers. In contrast, the Web is one of the services communicated via the Internet. It is a collection of interconnected documents and other resources, linked by hyperlinks and URLs.

HISTORY OF INTERNET

The USSR's launch of Sputnik spurred the United States to create the Advanced Research Projects Agency (ARPA or DARPA) in

February 1958 to regain a techn-ological lead. ARPA created the Information Processing Technology Office (IPTO) to further the research of the Semi Automatic Ground Environment (SAGE) program, which had networked country-wide radar systems together for the first time. The IPTO's purpose was to find ways to address the US Military's concern about survivability of their communications networks, and as a first step interconnect their computers at the Pentagon, Cheyenne Mountain, and SAC HQ. J.C.R. Licklider, a promoter of universal networking, was selected to head the IPTO. Licklider moved from the Psycho-Acoustic Laboratory at Harvard University to MIT in 1950, after becoming interested in information technology. At MIT, he served on a committee that established Lincoln Laboratory and worked on the SAGE project. In 1957 he became a Vice President at BBN, where he bought the first production PDP-1 computer and conducted the first public demonstration of time-sharing.

At the IPTO, Licklider's successor Ivan Sutherland in 1965 got Lawrence Roberts to start a project to make a network, and Roberts based the technology on the work of Paul Baran, who had written an exhaustive study for the United States Air Force that recommended packet switching (opposed to circuit switching) to achieve better network robustness and disaster survivability. Roberts had worked at the MIT Lincoln Laboratory originally established to work on the design of the SAGE system. UCLA professor Leonard Kleinrock had provided the theoretical foundations for packet networks in 1962, and later, in the 1970s, for hierarchical routing, concepts which have been the underpinning of the development towards today's Internet.

Sutherland's successor Robert Taylor convinced Roberts to build on his early packet switching successes and come and be the IPTO Chief Scientist. Once there, Roberts prepared a report called Resource Sharing Computer Networks which was approved by Taylor in June 1968 and laid the foundation for the launch of the working ARPANET the following year.

After much work, the first two nodes of what would become the ARPANET were interconnected between Kleinrock's Network Measurement Center at the UCLA's School of Engineering and Applied Science and Douglas Engelbart's NLS system at SRI International (SRI) in Menlo Park, California, on October 29, 1969. The third site on the ARPANET was the Culler-Fried Interactive Mathematics centre at the University of California at Santa Barbara, and the fourth was the University of Utah Graphics Department. In an early sign of future growth, there were already fifteen sites connected to the young ARPANET by the end of 1971.

The ARPANET was one of the "eve" networks of today's Internet. In an independent development, Donald Davies at the UK National Physical Laboratory also discovered the concept of packet switching in the early 1960s, first giving a talk on the subject in 1965, after which the teams in the new field from two sides of the Atlantic ocean first became acquainted. It was actually Davies' coinage of the wording "packet" and "packet switching" that was adopted as the standard terminology. Davies also built a packet switched network in the UK called the Mark I in 1970.

Following the demonstration that packet switching worked on the ARPANET, the British Post Office, Telenet, DATAPAC and TRANSPAC collaborated to create the first international packet-switched network service. In the UK, this was referred to as the International Packet Switched Service (IPSS), in 1978. The collection of X.25-based networks grew from Europe and the US to cover Canada, Hong Kong and Australia by 1981. The X.25 packet switching standard was developed in the CCITT (now called ITU-T) around 1976. X.25 was independent of the TCP/IP protocols that arose from the experimental work of DARPA on the ARPANET, Packet Radio Net and Packet Satellite Net during the same time period.

The early ARPANET ran on the Network Control Program (NCP), a standard designed and first implemented in December 1970 by a team called the Network Working Group (NWG) led by Steve Crocker. To respond to the network's rapid growth as more and more locations connected, Vinton Cerf and Robert Kahn developed the first description of the now widely used TCP protocols during 1973 and published a paper on the subject in May 1974. Use of the term "Internet" to describe a single global TCP/IP network originated in December 1974 with the publication of RFC 675, the first full specification of TCP that was written by Vinton Cerf, Yogen Dalal and Carl Sunshine, then at Stanford University. During the next nine years, work proceeded to refine the protocols and to implement them on a wide range of operating systems. The first TCP/IP-based wide-area network was operational by January 1, 1983 when all hosts on the ARPANET were switched over from the older NCP protocols. In 1985, the United States' National Science Foundation (NSF) commissioned the construction of the NSFNET, a university 56 kilobit/second network backbone using computers called "fuzzballs" by their inventor, David L. Mills. The following year, NSF sponsored the conversion to a higher-speed 1.5 MB/second network. A key decision to use the DARPA TCP/IP protocols was made by Dennis Jennings, then in charge of the Supercomputer program at NSF.

The opening of the network to commercial interests began in 1988. The US Federal Networking Council approved the interconnection of the NSFNET to the commercial MCI Mail system in that year and the link was made in the summer of 1989. Other commercial electronic e-mail services were soon connected, including OnTyme, Telemail and Compuserve. In that same year, three commercial Internet service providers (ISPs) were created: UUNET, PSINet and CERFNET. Important, separate networks that offered gateways into, then later merged with, the Internet include Usenet and BITNET. Various other commercial and educational networks, such as Telenet, Tymnet, Compuserve and JANET were interconnected with the growing Internet. Telenet (later called Sprintnet) was a large privately funded national computer network with free dial-up access in cities throughout the U.S. that had been in operation since the 1970s. This network was eventually interconnected with the others in the 1980s as the TCP/IP protocol became increasingly popular. The ability of TCP/IP to work over virtually any pre-existing communication networks allowed for a great ease of growth, although the rapid growth of the Internet was due primarily to the availability of an array of standardized commercial routers from many companies, the availability of commercial Ethernet equipment for local-area networking, and the widespread implementation and rigorous standardization of TCP/IP on UNIX and virtually every other common operating system.

NeXT Computer the world's first Web server used by Tim Berners-Lee at CERN

Although the basic applications and guidelines that make the Internet possible had existed for almost two decades, the network did not gain a public face until the 1990s. On 6 August 1991, CERN, a pan European organization for particle research, publicized the new World

Wide Web project. The Web was invented by British scientist Tim Berners-Lee in 1989. An early popular web browser was Viola WWW, patterned after HyperCard and built using the X Window System. It was eventually replaced in popularity by the Mosaic web browser. In 1993, the National Center for Supercomputing Applications at the University of Illinois released version 1.0 of Mosaic, and by late 1994 there was growing public interest in the previously academic, technical Internet. By 1996 usage of the word Internet had become commonplace, and consequently, so had its use as a synecdoche in reference to the World Wide Web.

Meanwhile, over the course of the decade, the Internet successfully accommodated the majority of previously existing public computer networks (although some networks, such as FidoNet, have remained separate). During the 1990s, it was estimated that the Internet grew by 100 percent per year, with a brief period of explosive growth in 1996 and 1997. This growth is often attributed to the lack of central administration, which allows organic growth of the network, as well as the non-proprietary open nature of the Internet protocols, which encourages vendor interoperability and prevents any one company from exerting too much control over the network. The estimated population of Internet users is 2 billion as of June 30, 2010.

Technology

Protocols

The complex communications infrastructure of the Internet consists of its hardware components and a system of software layers that control various aspects of the architecture. While the hardware can often be used to support other software systems, it is the design and the rigorous standardization process of the software architecture that characterizes the Internet and provides the foundation for its scalability and success. The responsibility for the architectural design of the Internet software systems has been delegated to the Internet Engineering Task Force (IETF). The IETF conducts standard-setting work groups, open to any individual, about the various aspects of Internet architecture. Resulting discussions and final standards are published in a series of publications, each called a Request for Comments (RFC), freely available on the IETF web site. The principal methods of networking that enable the Internet are contained in specially designated RFCs that constitute the Internet Standards. Other less rigorous documents are simply informative, experimental, or historical, or document the best current practices (BCP) when implementing Internet technologies.

The Internet Standards describe a framework known as the Internet Protocol Suite. This is a model architecture that divides methods into a layered system of protocols (RFC 1122, RFC 1123). The layers correspond to the environment or scope in which their services operate. At the top is the Application Layer, the space for the application-specific networking methods used in software applications, e.g., a web browser program. Below this top layer, the Transport Layer connects applications on different hosts via the network (e.g., client–server model) with appropriate data exchange methods. Underlying these layers are the core networking technologies, consisting of two layers. The Internet Layer enables computers to identify and locate each other via Internet Protocol (IP) addresses, and allows them to connect to one-another via intermediate (transit) networks. Lastly, at the bottom of the architecture, is a software layer, the Link Layer, that provides connectivity between hosts on the same local network link, such as a local area network (LAN) or a dial-up connection. The model, also known as TCP/IP, is designed to be independent of the underlying hardware which the model therefore does not concern itself with in any detail. Other models have been developed, such as the Open Systems Interconnection (OSI) model, but they are not compatible in the details of description, nor implementation, but many similarities exist and the TCP/IP protocols are usually included in the discussion of OSI networking.

The most prominent component of the Internet model is the Internet Protocol (IP) which provides addressing systems (IP addresses) for computers on the Internet. IP enables internetworking and essentially establishes the Internet itself. IP Version 4 (IPv4) is the initial version used on the first generation of the today's Internet and is still in dominant use. It was designed to address up to ~4.3 billion (10^9) Internet hosts. However, the explosive growth of the Internet has led to IPv4 address exhaustion which is estimated to enter its final stage in approximately 2011. A new protocol version, IPv6, was developed in the mid 1990s which provides vastly larger addressing capabilities and more efficient routing of Internet traffic. IPv6 is currently in commercial deployment phase around the world and Internet address registries (RIRs) have begun to urge all resource managers to plan rapid adoption and conversion.

IPv6 is not interoperable with IPv4. It essentially establishes a "parallel" version of the Internet not directly accessible with IPv4 software. This means software upgrades or translator facilities are necessary for every networking device that needs to communicate on the IPv6 Internet. Most modern computer operating systems are already converted to operate with both versions of the Internet Protocol. Network infrastructures, however, are still lagging in this development. Aside from the complex physical connections that make up its infrastructure, the Internet is facilitated by bi- or multi-lateral commercial contracts (e.g., peering agreements), and by technical specifications or protocols that describe how to exchange data over the network. Indeed, the Internet is defined by its interconnections and routing policies.

Structure

The Internet structure and its usage characteristics have been studied extensively. It has been determined that both the Internet IP routing structure and hypertext links of the World Wide Web are examples of scale-free networks. Similar to the way the commercial Internet providers connect via Internet exchange points, research networks tend to interconnect into large subnetworks such as GEANT, GLORIAD, Internet2 (successor of the Abilene Network), and the UK's national research and education network JANET. These in turn are built around smaller networks.

Many computer scientists describe the Internet as a "prime example of a large-scale, highly engineered, yet highly complex system". The Internet is extremely heterogeneous; for instance, data transfer rates and physical characteristics of connections vary widely. The Internet exhibits "emergent phenomena" that depend on its large-scale organization. For example, data transfer rates exhibit temporal self-similarity. The principles of the routing and addressing methods for traffic in the Internet reach back to their origins the 1960s when the eventual scale and popul-arity of the network could not be anticipated. Thus, the poss-ibility of developing alternative structures is investigated.

Internet Governance

The Internet is a globally distributed network comprising many voluntarily interconnected autonomous networks. It operates without a central governing body. However, to maintain interoperability, all technical and policy aspects of the underlying core infrastructure and the principal name spaces are administered by the Internet Corporation for Assigned Names and Numbers (ICANN), headqua-rtered in Marina del Rey, California. ICANN is the authority that coordinates the assignment of unique identifiers for use on the Internet, including domain names, Internet Protocol (IP) addresses, application port numbers in the transport protocols, and many other parameters. Globally unified name spaces, in which names and numbers are uniquely assigned, are essential for the global reach of the Internet. ICANN is governed by an international board of directors drawn from across the Internet technical, business, academic, and other non-commercial communities. The US government continues to have the primary role in approving changes to the DNS root zone that lies at the heart of the domain name system. ICANN's role in coordinating the assignment of unique identifiers distinguishes it as perhaps the only central coordinating body on the global Internet. On November 16, 2005, the World Summit on the Information Society, held in Tunis, established the Internet Governance Forum (IGF) to discuss Internet-related issues.

ICANN headquarters in Marina Del Rey, California, United States

Modern uses

The Internet is allowing greater flexibility in working hours and location, especially with the spread of unmetered high-speed connections and web applications.

The Internet can now be accessed almost anywhere by numerous means, especially through mobile Internet devices. Mobile phones, datacards, handheld game consoles and cellular routers allow users to connect to the Internet from anywhere there is a wireless network supporting that device's technology. Within the limitations imposed by small screens and other limited facilities of such pocket-sized devices, services of the Internet, including email and the web, may be available. Service providers may restrict the services offered and wireless data transmission charges may be significantly higher than other access methods.

The Internet has also become a large market for companies; some of the biggest companies today have grown by taking advantage of the efficient nature of low-cost advertising and commerce through the Internet, also known as e-commerce. It is the fastest way to spread information to a vast number of people simultaneously. The Internet has also subsequently revolutionized shopping—for example; a person can order a CD online and receive it in the mail within a couple of days, or download it directly in some cases. The Internet has also greatly facilitated personalized marketing which allows a company to market a product to a specific person or a specific group of people more so than any other advertising medium. Examples of personalized marketing include online communities such as MySpace, Friendster, Facebook, Twitter, Orkut and others which thousands of Internet users join to advertise themselves and make friends online. Many of these users are young teens and adolescents ranging from 13 to 25 years old. In turn, when they advertise themselves they advertise interests and hobbies, which online marketing companies can use as information as to what those users will purchase online, and advertise their own companies' products to those users.

The low cost and nearly instantaneous sharing of ideas, knowledge, and skills has made collaborative work dramatically easier, with the help of collaborative software. Not only can a group cheaply communicate and share ideas, but the wide reach of the Internet allows such groups to easily form in the first place. An example of this is the free software movement, which has produced, among other programs, Linux, Mozilla Firefox, and OpenOffice.org. Internet "chat", whether in the form of IRC chat rooms or channels, or via instant messaging systems, allow colleagues to stay in touch in a very convenient way when working at their computers during the day. Messages can be exchanged even more quickly and conveniently than via e-mail. Extensions to these systems may allow files to be exchanged, "whiteboard" drawings to be shared or voice and video contact between team members.

Version control systems allow collaborating teams to work on shared sets of documents without either accid-entally overwriting each other's work or having members wait until they get "sent" documents to be able to make their contributions. Business and project teams can share calendars as well as documents and other information. Such collaboration occurs in a wide variety of areas including scientific research, software development, conference planning, political activism and creative writing. Social and political collaboration is also becoming more widespread as both Internet access and computer literacy grow.

The Internet allows computer users to remotely access other computers and information stores easily, wherever they may be across the world. They may do this with or without the use of security, authentication and encryption technologies, depending on the requirements. This is encouraging new ways of working from home, collaboration and information sharing in many industries. An accountant sitting at home can audit the books of a company based in another country, on a server situated in a third country that is remotely maintained by IT specialists in a fourth. These accounts could have been created by home-working bookkeepers, in other remote locations, based on information e-mailed to them from offices all over the world. Some of these things were possible before the widespread use of the Internet, but the cost of private leased lines would have made many of them infeasible in practice. An office worker away from their desk, perhaps on the other side of the world on a business trip or a holiday, can open a remote desktop session into his normal office PC using a secure Virtual Private Network (VPN) connection via the Internet. This gives the worker complete access to all of his or her normal files and data, including e-mail and other applications, while away from the office. This concept is also referred to by some network security people as the Virtual Private Nightmare, because it extends the secure perimeter of a corporate network into its employees' homes.

Services

Information

Many people use the terms Internet and World Wide Web, or just the Web, interchangeably, but the two terms are not synonymous. The World Wide Web is a global set of documents, images and other resources, logically interrelated by hyperlinks and referenced with Uniform Resource Identifiers (URIs). URIs allow providers to symbolically identify services and clients to locate and address web servers, file servers, and other databases that store documents and provide resources and access them using the Hypertext Transfer Protocol (HTTP), the primary carrier protocol of the Web. HTTP is only one of the hundreds of communication protocols used on the Internet. Web services may also use HTTP to allow software systems to communicate in order to share and exchange business logic and data.

World Wide Web browser software, such as Microsoft's Internet Explorer, Mozilla Firefox, Opera, Apple's Safari, and Google Chrome, let users navigate from one web page to another via hyperlinks embedded in the documents. These documents may also contain any combination of computer data, including graphics, sounds, text, video, multimedia and interactive content including games, office applications and scientific demonstrations. Through keyword-driven Internet research using search engines like Yahoo! and Google, users worldwide have easy, instant access to a vast and diverse amount of online information. Compared to printed encyclopedias and traditional libraries, the World Wide Web has enabled the decentralization of information.

The Web has also enabled individuals and organizations to publish ideas and information to a potentially large audience online at greatly reduced expense and time delay. Publishing a web page, a blog, or building a website involves little initial cost and many cost-free services are available. Publishing and maintaining large, professional web sites with attractive, diverse and up-to-date information is still a difficult and expensive proposition, however many individuals and some companies and groups use web logs or blogs, which are largely used as easily updatable online diaries. Some commercial organizations encourage staff to communicate advice in their areas of specialization in the hope that visitors will be impressed by the expert knowledge and free information, and be attracted to the corporation as a result. One example of this practice is Microsoft, whose product developers publish their personal blogs in order to create the public's interest in their work. Collections of personal web pages published by large service providers remain popular, and have become increasingly sophisticated. Whereas operations such as Angelfire and GeoCities have existed since the early days of the Web, newer offerings from, for example, Facebook and MySpace currently have large followings. These operations often brand themselves as social network services rather than simply as web page hosts.

Advertising on popular web pages can be lucrative, and e-commerce or the sale of products and services directly via the Web continues to grow. In the early days, web pages were usually created as sets of complete and isolated HTML text files stored on a web server. More recently, websites are more often created using content management or wiki software with, initially, very little content. Contributors to these systems, who may be paid staff, members of a club or other organization or members of the public, fill underlying databases with content using editing pages designed for that purpose, while casual visitors view and read this content in its final HTML form. There may or may not be editorial, approval and security systems built into the process of taking newly entered content and making it available to the target visitors.

Communication

E-mail is an important communications service available on the Internet. The concept of sending electronic text messages between parties in a way analogous to mailing letters or memos predates the creation of the Internet. Today it can be important to distinguish between internet and internal e-mail systems. Internet e-mail may travel and be stored unencrypted on many other networks and machines out of both the sender's and the recipient's control. During this time it is quite possible for the content to be read and even tampered with by third parties, if anyone considers it important enough. Purely internal or intranet mail systems, where the information never leaves the corporate or organization's network, are much more secure, although in any organization there will be IT and other personnel whose job may involve monitoring, and occasionally accessing, the e-mail of other employees not addressed to them. Pictures, documents and other files can be sent as e-mail attachments. E-mails can be sent to multiple e-mail addresses.

Internet telephony is another common communications service made possible by the creation of the Internet. VoIP stands for Voice-over-Internet Protocol, referring to the protocol that underlies all Internet communication. The idea began in the early 1990s with walkie-talkie-like voice applications for personal computers. In recent years many VoIP systems have become as easy to use and as convenient as a normal telephone. The benefit is that, as the Internet carries the voice traffic, VoIP can be free or cost much less than a traditional telephone call, especially over long distances and especially for those with always-on Internet connections such as cable or ADSL. VoIP is maturing into a competitive alternative to traditional telephone service. Interoperability between different providers has improved and the ability to call or receive a call from a traditional telephone is available. Simple, inexpensive VoIP network adapters are available that eliminate the need for a personal computer.

Voice quality can still vary from call to call but is often equal to and can even exceed that of traditional calls. Remaining problems for VoIP include emergency telephone number dialling and reliability. Currently, a few VoIP providers provide an emergency service, but it is not universally available. Traditional phones are line-powered and operate during a power failure; VoIP does not do so without a back-up power source for the phone equipment and the Internet access devices. VoIP has also become increasingly popular for gaming applications, as a form of communication between players. Popular VoIP clients for gaming include Ventrilo and Teamspeak. PlayStation 3, and Xbox 360 also offer VoIP chat features.

Data transfer

File sharing is an example of transferring large amounts of data across the Internet. A computer file can be e-mailed to customers, colleagues and friends as an attachment. It can be uploaded to a website or FTP server for easy download by others. It can be put into a "shared location" or onto a file server for instant use by colleagues. The load of bulk downloads to many users can be eased by the use of "mirror" servers or peer-to-peer networks. In any of these cases, access to the file may be controlled by user authentication, the transit of the file over the Internet may be obscured by encryption, and money may change hands for access to the file. The price can be paid by the remote charging of funds from, for example, a credit card whose details are also passed—usually fully encrypted—across the Internet. The origin and authenticity of the file received may be checked by digital signatures or by MD5 or other message digests. These simple features of the Internet, over a worldwide basis, are changing the production, sale, and distribution of anything that can be reduced to a computer file for transmission. This includes all manner of print publications, software products, news, music, film, video, photography, graphics and the other arts. This in turn has caused seismic shifts in each of the existing industries that previously controlled the production and distribution of these products.

Streaming media refers to the act that many existing radio and television broadcasters promote Internet "feeds" of their live audio and video streams (for example, the BBC). They may also allow time-shift viewing or listening such as Preview, Classic Clips and Listen Again features. These providers have been joined by a range of pure Internet "broadcasters" who never had on-air licenses. This means that an Internet-connected device, such as a computer or something more specific, can be used to access on-line media in much the same way as was previously possible only with a television or radio receiver. The range of available types of content is much wider, from specialized technical webcasts to on-demand popular multimedia services. Podcasting is a variation on this theme, where—usually audio—material is downloaded and played back on a computer or shifted to a portable media player to be listened to on the move. These techniques using simple equipment allow anybody, with little censorship or licensing control, to broadcast audio-visual material worldwide.

Webcams can be seen as an even lower-budget extension of this phenomenon. While some webcams can give full-frame-rate video, the picture is usually either small or updates slowly. Internet users can watch animals around an African waterhole, ships in the Panama Canal, traffic at a local roundabout or monitor their own premises, live and in real time. Video chat rooms and video conferencing are also popular with many uses being found for personal webcams, with and without two-way sound. YouTube was founded on 15 February 2005 and is now the leading website for free streaming video with a vast number of users. It uses a flash-based web player to stream and show video files. Registered users may upload an unlimited amount of video and build their own personal profile. YouTube claims that its users watch hundreds of millions, and upload hundreds of thousands of videos daily.

The prevalent language for communication on the Internet is English. This may be a result of the origin of the Internet, as well as English's role as a lingua franca. It may also be related to the poor capability of early computers, largely originating in the United States, to handle characters other than those in the English variant of the Latin alphabet. After English (29% of Web visitors) the most requested languages on the World Wide Web are Chinese (22%), Spanish (8%), Japanese (6%), French (5%), Portuguese and German (4% each), Arabic (3%) and Russian and Korean (2% each). By region, 42% of the world's Internet users are based in Asia, 24% in Europe, 15% in North America, 11% in Latin America and the Caribbean taken together, 4% in Africa, 3% in the Middle East and 1% in Australia/Oceania. The Internet's technologies have developed enough in recent years, especially in the use of Unicode that good facilities are available for development and communication in most widely used languages. However, some glitches such as mojibake (incorrect display of foreign language characters, also known as kryakozyabry) still remain.

Common methods of Internet access in homes include dial-up, landline broadband (over coaxial cable, fiber optic or copper wires), Wi-Fi, satellite and 3G technology cell phones. Public places to use the Internet include libraries, offices and Internet cafes, where computers with Internet connections are available. There are also Internet access points in many public places such as airport halls and coffee shops, in some cases just for brief use while standing. Various terms are used, such as "public Internet kiosk", "public access terminal", and "Web payphone". Many hotels now also have public terminals, though these are usually fee-based. These terminals are widely accessed for various usages like ticket booking, bank deposit, online payment etc. Wi-Fi provides wireless access to computer networks, and therefore can do so to the Internet itself. Hotspots providing such access include Wi-Fi cafes, where would-be users need to bring their own wireless-enabled devices such as a laptop or PDA. These services may be free to all, free to customers only, or fee-based. A hotspot need not be limited to a confined location. A whole campus or park, or even an entire city can be enabled. Grassroots efforts have led to wireless community networks. Commercial Wi-Fi services covering large city areas are in place in London, Vienna, Toronto, San Francisco, Philadelphia, Chicago, Sanghai Airport and Pittsburgh. The Internet can then be accessed from such places as a park bench. Apart from Wi-Fi, there have been experiments with proprietary mobile wireless networks like Ricochet, various high-speed data services over cellular phone networks, and fixed wireless services. High-end mobile phones such as smartphones generally come with Internet access through the phone network. Web browsers such as Opera are available on these advanced handsets, which can also run a wide variety of other Internet software. More mobile phones have Internet access than PCs, though this is not as widely used. An Internet access provider and protocol matrix differentiates the methods used to get online.

Social impact

The Internet has enabled entirely new forms of social interaction, activities, and organizing, thanks to its basic features such as widespread usability and access. Social networking websites such as Orkut, Facebook, Twitter and MySpace have created new ways to socialize and interact. Users of these sites are able to add a wide variety of information to pages, to pursue common interests, and to connect with others. It is also possible to find existing acquaintances, to allow communication among existing groups of people. Sites like LinkedIn foster commercial and business connections. YouTube and Flickr specialize in users' videos and photographs.

In the first decade of the 21st century the first generation is raised with widespread availability of Internet connectivity, bringing consequences and concerns in areas such as personal privacy and identity, and distribution of copyrighted materials. These "digital natives" face a variety of challenges that were not present for prior generations.

The Internet has achieved new relevance as a political tool, leading to Internet censorship by some states. The presidential campaign of Howard Dean in 2004 in the United States was notable for its success in soliciting donation via the Internet. Many political groups use the Internet to achieve a new method of organizing in order to carry out their mission, having given rise to Internet activism. Some governments, such as those of Iran, North Korea, Myanmar, the People's Republic of China, and Saudi Arabia, restrict what people in their countries can access on the Internet, especially political and religious content. This is accomplished through software that filters domains and content so that they may not be easily accessed or obtained without elaborate circumvention.

In Norway, Denmark, Finland and Sweden, major Internet service providers have voluntarily, possibly to avoid such an arrangement being turned into law, agreed to restrict access to sites listed by authorities. While this list of forbidden URLs is only supposed to contain addresses of known child pornography sites, the content of the list is secret. Many countries, including the United States, have enacted laws against the possession or distribution of certain material, such as child pornography, via the Internet, but do not mandate filtering software. There are many free and commercially available software programs, called content-control software, with which a user can choose to block offensive websites on individual computers or networks, in order to limit a child's access to pornographic materials or depiction of violence.

The Internet has been a major outlet for leisure activity since its inception, with entertaining social experiments such as MUDs and MOOs being conducted on university servers, and humor-related Usenet groups receiving much traffic. Today, many Internet forums have sections devoted to games and funny videos; short cartoons in the form of Flash movies are also popular. Over 6 million people use blogs or message boards as a means of communication and for the sharing of ideas. The pornography and gambling industries have taken advantage of the World Wide Web, and often provide a significant source of advertising revenue for other websites. Although many governments have attempted to restrict both industries' use of the Internet, this has generally failed to stop their widespread popularity.

One main area of leisure activity on the Internet is multiplayer gaming. This form of recreation creates communities, where people of all ages and origins enjoy the fast-paced world of multiplayer games. These range from MMORPG to first-person shooters, from role-playing games to online gambling. This has revolutionized the way many people interact while spending their free time on the Internet. While online gaming has been around since the 1970s modern modes of online gaming began with subscription services such as GameSpy and MPlayer. Non-subscribers were limited to certain types of game play or certain games. Many people use the Internet to access and download music, movies and other works for their enjoyment and relaxation. Free and fee-based services exist for all of these activities, using centralized servers and distributed peer-to-peer technologies. Some of these sources exercise more care with respect to the original artists' copyrights than others.

Many people use the World Wide Web to access news, weather and sports reports, to plan and book vacations and to find out more about their interests. People use chat, messaging and e-mail to make and stay in touch with friends worldwide, sometimes in the same way as some previously had pen pals. The Internet has seen a growing number of Web desktops, where users can access their files and settings via the Internet. Cyber slacking can become a serious drain on corporate resources; the average UK employee spent 57 minutes a day surfing the Web while at work, according to a 2003 study by Peninsula Business Services.

The Internet has been criticized for its Identity Performativity. Users define and label themselves on social networking sites through artistic tastes, personal experiences and relationships, and visuals (photographs, blogs, etc.). Some argue that the ability to construct a user's identity is limited by other's work and criticize the internet's lack of physical interaction.

Mental effects

The effect of the internet on the human brain has been studied a great deal. Nicholas Carr asserts that the internet reduces the deep thinking that leads to true creativity. He also says that hyperlinks and overstimulation means that the brain must give most of its attention to short-term decisions. Carr also states that the internet overwhelms the brain and hurts long-term memory. He points out that the great deal of stimuluses on the internet leads to a very large cognitive load, which makes it difficult to remember anything.

Psychologist Steven Pinker, however, argues otherwise. He points out that people have control over what they do, and that research and reasoning never came naturally to people. He says that, "Experience does not revamp the basic information-processing capacities of the brain" and asserts that the internet is actually making people smarter.

WORLD WIDE WEB (WWW)

The World Wide Web, abbreviated as WWW and commonly known as the Web, is a system of interlinked hypertext documents accessed via the Internet. With a web browser, one can view web pages that may contain text, images, videos, and other multimedia and navigate between them by using hyperlinks. Using concepts from earlier hypertext systems, British engineer and computer scientist Sir Tim Berners-Lee, now the Director of the World Wide Web Consortium, wrote a proposal in March 1989 for what would eventually become the World Wide Web. He was later joined by Belgian computer scientist Robert Cailliau while both were working at CERN in Geneva, Switzerland. In 1990, they proposed using "HyperText to link and access information of various kinds as a web of nodes in which the user can browse at will", and released that web in December.

The World-Wide Web (W3) was developed to be a pool of human knowledge, which would allow collaborators in remote sites to share their ideas and all aspects of a common project. If two projects are independently created, rather than have a central figure make the changes, the two bodies of information could form into one cohesive piece of work.

The World Wide Web is a collection of documents written and encoded with the Hypertext Markup Language (HTML). With the aid of a relatively small piece of software (called a "browser"), a user can ask for these documents and display them on the user's local computer, although the document can be on a computer on a totally different network elsewhere in the world. HTML documents (or "pages," as they are called) can contain many different kinds of information such as text, pictures, video, sound, and pointers, which take users immediately to other web pages. Because Web pages are continually available through the Internet, these pointers may call up pages from anywhere in the world. It is this ability to jump from site to site that gave rise to the term "World Wide Web." Browsing the Web (or "surfing the Net") can be a fascinating activity, especially to people new to the Internet. The World Wide Web is by far the most heavily used application on the Internet.

WEB BROWSER

A **web browser** is a software application for retrieving, presenting, and traversing information resources on the World Wide Web. An information resource is identified by a Uniform Resource Identifier (URI) and may be a web page, image, video, or other piece of content. Hyperlinks present in resources enable users to easily navigate their browsers to related resources.

Although browsers are primarily intended to access the World Wide Web, they can also be used to access information provided by Web servers in private networks or files in file systems. Some browsers can be also used to save information resources to file systems.

The history of the Web browser dates back in to the late 1980s, when a variety of technologies laid the foundation for the first Web browser, WorldWideWeb, by Tim Berners-Lee in 1991. That browser brought together a variety of existing and new software and hardware technologies.

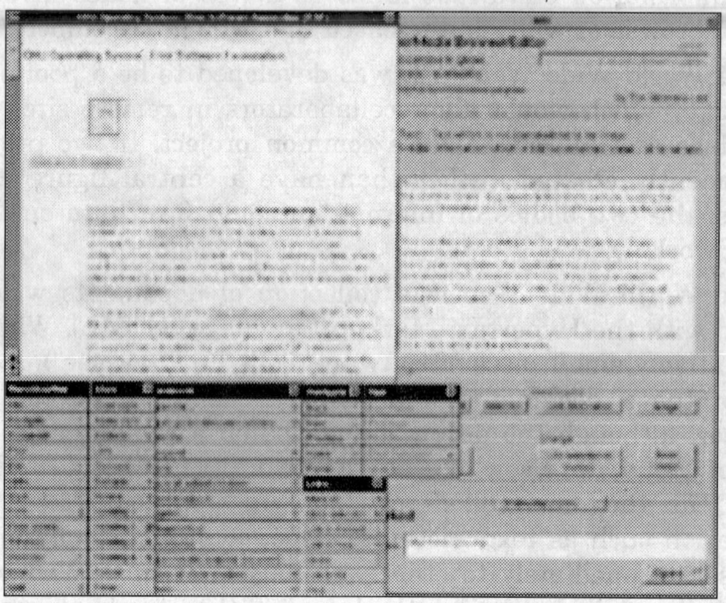

WorldWideWeb, the first Web browser for NeXT, released in 1991

Ted Nelson and Douglas Engelbart developed the concept of hypertext long before Berners-Lee and CERN. It became the core of the World Wide Web. Berners-Lee does acknowledge Engelbart's contribution.

The introduction of the NCSA Mosaic Web browser in 1993 – one of the first graphical Web browsers – led to an explosion in Web use. Marc Andreessen, the leader of the Mosaic team at NCSA, soon started his own company, named Netscape, and released the Mosaic-influenced Netscape Navigator in 1994, which quickly became the world's most popular browser, accounting for 90% of all Web use at its peak.

Microsoft responded with its browser Internet Explorer in 1995 (also heavily influenced by Mosaic), initiating the industry's first browser war. By bundling Internet Explorer with Windows, Microsoft was able to leverage its dominance in the operating system market to take over the Web browser market; Internet Explorer usage share peaked at over 95% by 2002. Internet Explorer has 60% browser usage share as of April 2010 according to Net Applications.

Opera first appeared in 1996; although it has never achieved widespread use, having 2% browser usage share as of April 2010, it has a substantial share of the fast-growing mobile phone Web browser market, being preinstalled on over 40 million phones. It is also available on several other embedded systems, including Nintendo's Wii video game console.

In 1998, Netscape launched what was to become the Mozilla Foundation in an attempt to produce a competitive browser using the open source software model. That browser would eventually evolve into Firefox, which developed a respectable following while still in the beta stage of development; shortly after the release of Firefox 1.0 in late 2004, Firefox (all versions) accounted for 7.4% of browser use. As of April 2010, Firefox has a 25% usage share.

Apple's Safari had its first beta release in January 2003; as of October 2009, it has a dominant share of Apple-based Web browsing, accounting for just under 5% of the entire browser market as of April 2010. Its rendering engine, called WebKit, is also running in the standard browsers of several mobile phone platforms, including the iPhone OS, Google Android, Nokia S60 and Palm WebOS. The most recent major entrant to the browser market is Google's WebKit-based Chrome, first released in September 2008. As of April 2010, it has a 7% usage share.

Function

The primary purpose of a web browser is to bring information resources to the user. This process begins when the user inputs a Uniform Resource Identifier (URI), for example http://en.wikipedia.org/, into the browser. The prefix of the URI determines how the URI will be interpreted. The most commonly used kind of URI starts with http: and identifies a resource to be retrieved over the Hypertext Transfer Protocol (HTTP). Many browsers also support a variety of other prefixes, such as https: for HTTPS, ftp: for the File Transfer Protocol, and file: for local files. Prefixes that the web browser cannot directly handle are often handed off to another application entirely. For example, mailto: URIs are usually passed to the user's default e-mail application, and news: URIs are passed to the user's default newsgroup reader.

In the case of http, https, file, and others, once the resource has been retrieved the web browser will display it. HTML is passed to the browser's layout engine to be transformed from markup to an interactive document. Aside from HTML, web browsers can generally display any kind of content that can be part of a web page. Most browsers can display images, audio, video, and XML files, and often have plug-ins to support Flash applications and Java applets. Upon encountering a file of an unsupported type or a file that is set up to be downloaded rather than displayed, the browser prompts the user to save the file to disk.

Interactivity in a web page can also be supplied by Javascript, which usually does not require a plugin. Javascript can be used along with other technologies to allow "live" interaction with the web page's server via AJAX.

Information resources may contain hyperlinks to other information resources. Each link contains the URI of a resource to go to. When a link is clicked, the browser navigates to the resource indicated by the link's target URI, and the process of bringing content to the user begins again.

Features

Available web browsers range in features from minimal, text-based user interfaces with bare-bones support for HTML to rich user interfaces supporting a wide variety of file formats and protocols. Browsers which include additional components to support e-mail, Usenet news, and Internet Relay Chat (IRC), are sometimes referred to as "Internet suites" rather than merely "web browsers".

All major web browsers allow the user to open multiple information resources at the same time, either in different browser windows or in different tabs of the same window. Major browsers also include pop-up blockers to prevent unwanted windows from "popping up" without the user's consent.

Most web browsers can display a list of web pages that the user has bookmarked so that the user can quickly return to them. Bookmarks are also called "Favorites" in Internet Explorer. In addition, all major web browsers have some form of built-in web feed aggregator. In Mozilla Firefox, web feeds are formatted as "live bookmarks" and behave like a folder of bookmarks corresponding to recent entries in the feed. In Opera, a more traditional feed reader is included which stores and displays the contents of the feed. Furthermore, most browsers can be extended via plug-ins, downloadable components that provide additional features.

User interface

Most major web browsers have these user interface elements in common:

- Back and forward buttons to go back to the previous resource and forward again.
- A refresh or reload button to reload the current resource.
- A stop button to cancel loading the resource. In some browsers, the stop button is merged with the reload button.
- A home button to return to the user's home page.
- An address bar to input the Uniform Resource Identifier (URI) of the desired resource and display it.
- A search bar to input terms into a search engine.
- A status bar to display progress in loading the resource and also the URI of links when the cursor hovers over them, and page zooming capability.

Major browsers also possess incremental find features to search within a web page.

Privacy and security

Most browsers support HTTP Secure and offer quick and easy ways to delete the web cache, cookies, and browsing history.

Standards support

Early web browsers supported only a very simple version of HTML. The rapid development of proprietary web browsers led to the development of non-standard dialects of HTML, leading to problems with interoperability. Modern web browsers support a combination of standards-based and de facto HTML and XHTML, which should be rendered in the same way by all browsers

Internet Explorer

Windows Internet Explorer (formerly **Microsoft Internet Explorer**; abbreviated to **MSIE** or, more comm-only, **IE**), is a series of graphical web browsers developed by Microsoft and included as part of the Microsoft Windows line of operating systems starting in 1995. It has been the most widely used web browser since 1999, attaining a peak of about 95% usage share during 2002 and 2003 with IE5 and IE6.

That percentage share has since declined in the face of renewed competition from other web browsers. Its usage share now sits at approximately 50% to 60% and is slowly trending downward. Microsoft spent over $100 million a year on IE in the late 1990s, with over 1,000 people working on it by 1999.

The latest release is Internet Explorer 8, which is available as a free update for Windows XP with Service Pack 2 or later, Windows Server 2003 with Service Pack 1 or later, Windows Vista, and Windows Server 2008, and is included with Windows 7 and Windows Server 2008 R2. Internet Explorer was originally planned to be omitted from Windows 7 and Windows Server 2008 R2 in Europe but Microsoft later dropped the plans, and instead included a browser ballot screen with the products, allowing users to select a different web browser if they wish. Versions of Internet Explorer for other operating systems have also been produced, including Internet Explorer Mobile (Windows CE and Windows Mobile), Internet Explorer for Mac (discontinued), and Internet Explorer for UNIX (Solaris and HP-UX).

Mozila

Mozilla is a global community dedicated to building free, open source products like the award winning Firefox web browser and Thunderbird email software.

Firefox

The Firefox Web Browser is the faster, more secure, and fully customizable way to surf the web. The award-winning Firefox browser is now faster, more secure, and fully customizable for online life.

Mozilla Firefox is a free and open source web browser descended from the Mozilla Application Suite and managed by Mozilla Corporation. As of June 2010, Firefox was the second most widely used browser, with 23.81% of worldwide usage share of web browsers, according to Net Applications. To display web pages, Firefox uses the Gecko layout engine, which implements most current web standards in addition to several features which are intended to anticipate likely additions to the standards.

Latest Firefox features include tabbed browsing, spell checking, incremental find, live bookmarking, a download manager, private browsing, location-aware browsing (also known as "geolocation") based exclusively on a Google service and an integrated search system that uses Google by default in most localizations. Functions can be added through add-ons, created by third-party developers, of which there is a wide selection, a feature that has attracted many of Firefox's users.

Firefox runs on various versions of GNU/Linux, Mac OS X, Microsoft Windows and many other Unix-like operating systems. Its current stable release is version 3.6.6, released on June 26, 2010. Firefox's source code is free software, released under a tri-license GNU GPL/GNU LGPL/MPL.

Netscape Navigator

Netscape Navigator and **Netscape** are the names for the proprietary web browser popular in the 1990s. It was the flagship product of the Netscape Communications Corporation and the dominant web browser in terms of usage share, although by 2002 its usage had almost disappeared. This was partly due to the increased usage of Microsoft's Internet Explorer web browser software and other web browsers, and partly because the Netscape Corporation (later purchased by AOL) did not sustain Netscape Navigator's technical innovation after the late 1990s.

The business demise of Netscape was a central premise of Microsoft's antitrust trial, wherein the Court ruled that Microsoft Corporation's bundling of Internet Explorer with the Windows operating system was a monopolistic and illegal business practice.

The **Netscape Navigator** web browser was succeeded by the Netscape Communicator Internet suite, in turn succeeded by Netscape 6, Netscape 7, Netscape Browser 8, and Netscape Navigator 9.

AOL formally stopped development of Netscape Navigator on December 28, 2007, but continued supporting the web browser with security updates until March 1, 2008, when AOL canceled technical support. AOL allows downloading of archived versions of the Netscape Navigator web browser family. Moreover, AOL maintains the Netscape website as an Internet portal. Netscape source code was the base for Mozilla Firefox.

MacWeb

MacWeb was an early Mac OS-only web browser for 68k and PowerPC Apple Macintosh computers, developed by TradeWave (formerly EINet) between 1994 and 1996. MacWeb's major attraction was its ability to run well on low-end hardware, with small memory (1

MB or less) and disk (680 kB, small enough to fit on a floppy disk) footprints as well as fast (but simple) page display. This compactness led to MacWeb's inclusion on many "Internet starter kit" floppy disks that were popular at the time. TradeWave also developed a similar Microsoft Windows browser named WinWeb. However, they were eclipsed by more full-featured competitors such as Netscape Navigator, and development was eventually abandoned.

The first public release was 0.98-alpha on May 31, 1994, and the final official release was version 2.0 in 1996. An unofficial "2.0c" patch was released by Antoine Hébert in 1998 to correct a problem on old machines not supporting color QuickDraw.

Although Morgan (1995) states that MacWeb was the second web browser released for the Macintosh, this is not quite true. The MacWWW browser became available in 1992 and the Mosaic web browser was released for the Mac in 1993.

WinWeb

WinWeb Small Business Software and Support Services offers the best possible software solutions for small business. WinWeb.com have launched a new website, along with some changes to the software and services. WinWeb have divided their software in to Small Business Applications, all designed to make small business life easier. The Applications that WinWeb now offer are:

- Online Accounting Software
- Bookkeeping Software
- Invoicing Software
- Business Email
- Email Marketing
- Business Website
- Business Planning
- Online Shop
- Online Disk
- Website Hosting

By offering all this software as individual applications, WinWeb allows small business owners to pick and choose the business software that is most relevant for their small business.

WinWeb are still offering a range of Business Services, but have revised the selection of services on offer from the WinWeb Business

Support Services team. Please visit the WinWeb website for more details.

WinWeb will also collated application and services bundles, specifically designed with your business in mind. These bundles allow you to purchase a selection WinWeb applications and services at a significantly lower price. OnlineOffice is still available, and will include all of WinWeb's Applications, for one great low price.

Google Chrome

Google Chrome is a browser that combines a minimal design with sophisticated technology to make the web faster, safer, and easier. It is a web browser developed by Google that uses the WebKit layout engine and application framework. It was first released as a beta version for Microsoft Windows on 2 September, 2008, and the public stable release was on 11 December, 2008. The name is derived from the graphical user interface frame, or "chrome", of web browsers. As of June 2010, Chrome was the third most widely used browser, with 7.24% of worldwide usage share of web browsers, according to Net Applications.

In September, 2008, Google released a large portion of Chrome's source code, including its V8 JavaScript engine, as an open source project entitled Chromium. This move enabled third-party developers to study the underlying source code and help port the browser to Mac OS X and Linux. The Google also expressed hope that other browsers would adopt V8 to improve web application performance. The Google-authored portion of Chromium is released under the permissive BSD license, which allows portions to be incorporated into both open source and closed-source soft-ware programs. Other portions of the source code are subject to a variety of open-source licenses. Chromium implements the same feature set as Chrome, but lacks built in automatic updates and Google branding, and most notably has a blue-colored logo in place of the multicolored Google logo.

Cello

Cello was an early shareware 16-bit multipurpose web browser for Windows 3.1 developed by Thomas R. Bruce of the Legal Information Institute at Cornell Law School. It was the first web browser for Microsoft Windows, and thus was among the first free winsock browsers. It was reported that it worked without any problems on Windows NT 3.5 and with small modifications on OS/2.

Cello was created because, at the time, lawyers used Microsoft Windows on their computers, but the web browsers available at the time were mostly for Unix operating systems. This meant many legal experts were unable to access legal information made available in hypertext on the World Wide Web. Cello was popular during 1993/1994, but fell out of favor following the release of Mosaic and Netscape, during which development was abandoned.

Cello was first publicly released on June 8, 1993. Although a version 2.0 had been announced, development was abandoned prior to a public release leaving version 1.01a, released on April 16, 1994, to be the last version. Since then, the Legal Information Institute at Cornell Law School has licensed out the Cello 2.0 source code which has been used to develop commercial software. The browser is no longer available from its original homepage. However, it can still be downloaded from mirror sites.

INTERNET SERVERS

Internet server (web server) - this is a special computer, which is constantly switched on and connected to the Internet so that each Internet user around the world can access your website at all times. This computer is built up with selected high quality components, which can endure incessant work and high load. Depending on the expected load and the type of services, which this computer will provide, different configurations can be set up. As far as database hosting is concerned, for example, a multiprocessor solution combined with small-sized but very fast and stable hard disks would do just great, whereas a single processor configuration with many large size hard disks would be apt with file/image hosting. To ensure better Internet connectivity, the given server is stored in a data center, where it is mounted into a special rack, which offers good ventilation and easy maintenance.

Putting the machine itself in a data center and connecting it to the Internet do not automatically make it an "Internet server". For this purpose, specific web server software has to be installed on it and configured according to the given platform. Among the most popular web server packages are: Apache Server, Microsoft ISS, Google GWS, lighttpd, nginx. After the installation and configuration of the web server software, FTP, E-mail, DNS, database, etc. software packages can be added as well. Depending on the manner the given sever is organized and the services it's offering, it can be a separate independent system or a part of a hosting platform.

SERVER TYPES

A computer on a network or other network device that stores all necessary information and is dedicated to provide a particular service. For example, a database server would store all data and software related to a certain database and allows other network devices to access and process database queries. A file server is a computer and storage device dedicated to storing files for any user on the network to store files on the server. A print server is a device that manages one or more printers, and a network server is a computer that manages network traffic.

On multiprocessing operating systems, however, a single computer can execute several programs at once. A server in this case could refer to the program that is managing resources rather than the entire computer. The latest virtual server technology allows one computer to provide multiple server processing simultaneously and independently. The major server types are listed as follows:

Application Servers: Application servers connect between database servers and the end user.

Audio/Video Servers: Provide multimedia capabilities to Web sites by enabling them to broadcast streaming multimedia content.

Chat Servers: Provide service to a large number of users to exchange real time information and discussion.

Database Server: Store all data and software related to a certain database and allows other network devices to access and process database queries.

File Servers: dedicated to storing files for any user on the network to store files on the server.

FTP Servers: File Transfer Protocol makes it possible to move one or more files securely between computers while providing file security and organization as well as transfer control.

Groupware Servers: Enable users to collaborate, regardless of location, via the Internet or a corporate intranet and to work together in a virtual atmosphere.

IRC Servers: Internet Relay Chat consists of various separate networks (or "nets") of servers that allow users to connect to each other via an IRC network.

List Servers: Manage mailing lists (interactive discussions and announcements), newsletters, or advertising.

Mail Servers: Move and store emails over corporate networks and across the Internet.

News Servers: Distribute and deliver public news groups currently accessible over the USENET news network.

Printer Server: Manages one or more printers

Proxy Servers: It sits between a client program (such as a Web browser) and an external server (typically another server on the Web) to filter requests, improve performance, and share connections.

Telnet Servers: Enables users to log on to a host computer and perform tasks as if they're working on the remote computer itself.

Web Servers: Provide content to a Web browser by loading a file from a disk and deliver it across the network to a user's Web browser.

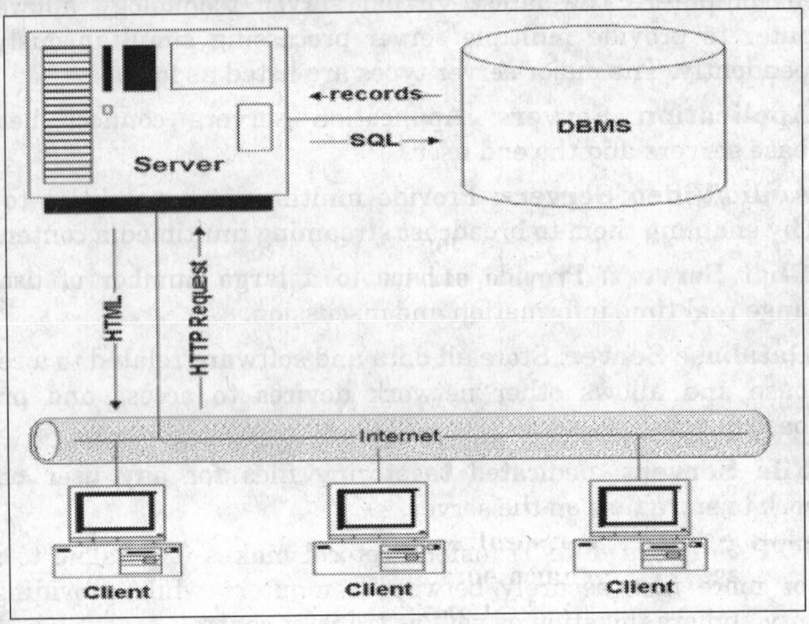

Server

UNIFORM RESOURCE LOCATOR (URL)

In computing, a **Uniform Resource Locator (URL)** is a Uniform Resource Identifier (URI) that specifies where an identified resource is available and the mechanism for retrieving it. In popular usage and in many technical documents and verbal discussions it is often incorrectly used as a synonym for URI,. The best-known example of a URL is the "address" of a web page on the World Wide Web, e.g. http://www.example.com.

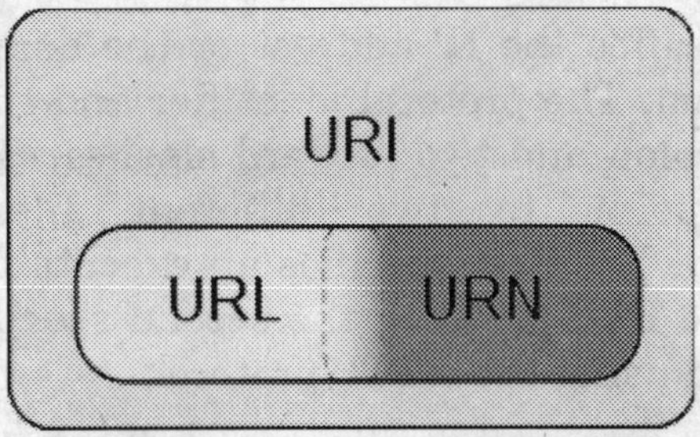

The relationship of URL to URI and URN

A URL (Uniform Resource Locator, previously Universal Resource Locator) - usually pronounced by sounding out each letter but, in some quarters, pronounced "Earl" - is the unique address for a file that is accessible on the Internet. A common way to get to a Web site is to enter the URL of its home page file in your Web browser's address line. However, any file within that Web site can also be specified with a URL. Such a file might be any Web (HTML) page other than the home page, an image file, or a program such as a common gateway interface application or Java applet. The URL contains the name of the protocol to be used to access the file resource, a domain name that identifies a specific computer on the Internet, and a pathname, a hierarchical description that specifies the location of a file in that computer. On the Web (which uses the Hypertext Transfer Protocol, or HTTP), an example of a URL is:

http://www.ietf.org/rfc/rfc2396.txt

which specifies the use of a HTTP (Web browser) application, a unique computer named www.ietf.org, and the location of a text file or page to be accessed on that computer whose pathname is /rfc/rfc2396.txt. A URL for a particular image on a Web site might look like this:

http://searchnetworking.techtarget.com/WhatIs/images/coaxla.gif

A URL for a file meant to be downloaded using the File Transfer Protocol (FTP) would require that the "ftp" protocol be specified like this hypothetical URL:

ftp://www.somecompany.com/whitepapers/widgets.ps

A URL is a type of URI (Uniform Resource Identifier, formerly called Universal Resource Identifier). Abbreviation of Uniform Resource Locator, the global address of documents and other resources on the World Wide Web.

The first part of the address is called a protocol identifier and it indicates what protocol to use, and the second part is called a resource name and it specifies the IP address of the domain name where the resource is located. The protocol identifier and the resource name are separated by a colon and two forward slashes. For example, the two URLs below point to two different files at the domain pcwebopedia.com. The first specifies an executable file that should be fetched using the FTP protocol; the second specifies a Web page that should be fetched using the HTTP protocol:

- ftp://www.pcwebopedia.com/stuff.exe
- http://www.pcwebopedia.com/index.html

INTERNET ARCHITECTURE

It is by definition a meta-network, a constantly changing collection of thousands of individual networks intercommunicating with a common protocol.

The Internet's architecture is described in its name, a short from of the compound word "inter-networking". This architecture is based in the very specification of the standard TCP/IP protocol, designed to connect any two networks which may be very different in internal hardware, software, and technical design. Once two networks are interconnected, communication with TCP/IP is enabled end-to-end, so that any node on the Internet has the near magical ability to communicate with any other no matter where they are. This openness of design has enabled the Internet architecture to grow to a global scale.

In practice, the Internet technical architecture looks a bit like a multi-dimensional river system, with small tributaries feeding medium-sized streams feeding large rivers. For example, an individual's access to the Internet is often from home over a modem to a local Internet service provider who connects to a regional network connected to a national network. At the office, a desktop computer might be connected to a local area network with a company connection to a corporate Intranet connected to several national Internet service providers. In general, small local Internet service providers connect to medium-sized regional networks which connect to large national networks, which then connect to very large bandwidth networks on the Internet backbone. Most Internet service providers have several redundant network cross-connections to other providers in order to ensure continuous availability.

The companies running the Internet backbone operate very high bandwidth networks relied on by governments, corporations, large organizations, and other Internet service providers. Their technical infrastructure often includes global connections through underwater cables and satellite links to enable communication between countries and continents. As always, a larger scale introduces new phenomena: the number of packets flowing through the switches on the backbone is so large that it exhibits the kind of complex non-linear patterns usually found in natural, analog systems like the flow of water or development of the rings of Saturn.

Each communication packet goes up the hierarchy of Internet networks as far as necessary to get to its destination network where local routing takes over to deliver it to the addressee. In the same way, each level in the hierarchy pays the next level for the bandwidth they use, and then the large backbone companies settle up with each other. Bandwidth is priced by large Internet service providers by several methods, such as at a fixed rate for constant availability of a certain number of megabits per second, or by a variety of use methods that amount to a cost per gigabyte. Due to economies of scale and efficiencies in management, bandwidth cost drops dramatically at the higher levels of the architecture.

CYBER SPACE

Cyber space is the electronic medium of computer networks, in which online communication takes place. It is readily identified with the interconnected information technology required to achieve the wide range of system capabilities associated with the transport of communication and control products and services. Current technology integrates a number of capabilities (sensors, signals, connections, transmissions, processors, and controllers) sufficient to generate a virtual interactive experience accessible regardless of a geographic location.

Cyber space is the dynamic realization of electromagnetic energy through the application of communication and control technology. In pragmatic terms, operations within this global domain allow an interdependent network of information technology infrastructures (ITI), telecommunications networks, computer processing systems, integrated sensors, system control networks, embedded processors and controllers common to global control and communications across the electro-magnetic environment. As a social experience, individuals can interact, exchange ideas, share information, provide social support, conduct business, direct actions, create artistic media, play games, engage in political discussion, and so on. The term is rooted in the science of cybernetics from the Greek κυβερνήτης (kybernētēs, steersman, governor, pilot, or rudder) and Norbert Wiener's pioneering work in electronic communication and control science, a forerunner to current information theory and computer science.

The term "cyberspace" was first used by the cyberpunk science fiction author William Gibson in his sci-fi novel Neuromancer (1984). which he would later describe as an "evocative and essentially meaningless" buzzword that could serve as a cipher for all of his cybernetic musings. Now ubiquitous, the term has become a conventional means to describe anything associated with computers, information technology, the internet and the diverse internet culture. The United States government recognizes the interconnected information technology and the interdependent network of information technology infrastructures operating across this medium as part of the US National Critical Infrastructure.

According to Chip Morningstar and F. Randall Farmer, cyberspace is defined more by the social interactions involved rather than it's technical implementation. The core characteristic is that must be an environment which consists of many participants with the ability to affect and influence each other. They derive this concept from the observation that people seek richness, complexity, and depth within a virtual world. Hence in cyberspace, the computational medium is an augmentation of the communication channel between real people.

A metaphor for describing the non-physical terrain created by computer systems. Online system, for example, create a cyberspace within which people can communicate with one another (via e-mail), do research, or simply window shop. Like physical space, cyberspace contains objects (files, mail messages, graphics, etc.) and different modes of transportation and delivery. Unlike real space, though, exploring cyberspace does not require any physical movement other than pressing keys on a keyboard or moving a mouse.

Some programs, particularly computer games, are designed to create a special cyberspace, one that resembles physical reality in some ways but defies it in others. In its extreme form, called virtual reality, users are presented with visual, auditory, and even tactile feedback that makes cyberspace feel real.

TCP/IP INTERNET SERVICE PROVIDER

The **Transmission Control Protocol** (**TCP**) is one of the core protocols of the Internet Protocol Suite. TCP is one of the two original components of the suite (the other being Internet Protocol, or IP), so the entire suite is commonly referred to as TCP/IP. Whereas IP handles lower-level transmissions from computer to computer as a message makes its way across the Internet, TCP operates at a higher level, concerned only with the two end systems, for example a Web browser and a Web server. In particular, TCP provides reliable, ordered delivery of a stream of bytes from a program on one computer to another program on another computer. Besides the Web, other common applications of TCP include e-mail and file transfer. Among other management tasks, TCP controls segment size, flow control, and data exchange rate.

TCP/IP (pronounced as separate letters) Short for Transmission Control Protocol/Internet Protocol, the suite of communications protocols used to connect hosts on the Internet. TCP/IP uses several protocols, the two main ones being TCP and IP. TCP/IP is built into the UNIX operating system and is used by the Internet, making it the de facto standard for transmitting data over networks. Even network operating systems that have their own protocols, such as Netware, also support TCP/IP.

TCP/IP (Transmission Control Protocol/Internet Protocol) is the basic communication language or protocol of the Internet. It can also be used as a communications protocol in a private network (either an intranet or an extranet). When you are set up with direct access to the Internet, your computer is provided with a copy of the TCP/IP program just as every other computer that you may send messages to or get information from also has a copy of TCP/IP.

TCP/IP is a two-layer program. The higher layer, Transmission Control Protocol, manages the assembling of a message or file into smaller packets that are transmitted over the Internet and received by a TCP layer that reassembles the packets into the original message. The lower layer, Internet Protocol, handles the address part of each packet so that it gets to the right destination. Each gateway computer on the network checks this address to see where to forward the message. Even though some packets from the same message are routed differently than others, they'll be reassembled at the destination.

TCP/IP uses the client/server model of communication in which a computer user (a client) requests and is provided a service (such as sending a Web page) by another computer (a server) in the network. TCP/IP communication is primarily point-to-point, meaning each communication is from one point (or host computer) in the network to another point or host computer. TCP/IP and the higher-level applications that use it are collectively said to be "stateless" because each client request is considered a new request unrelated to any previous one (unlike ordinary phone conversations that require a dedicated connection for the call duration). Being stateless frees network paths so that everyone can use them continuously. (Note that the TCP layer itself is not stateless as far as any one message is concerned. Its connection remains in place until all packets in a message have been received).

Many Internet users are familiar with the even higher layer application protocols that use TCP/IP to get to the Internet. These include the World Wide Web's Hypertext Transfer Protocol (HTTP), the File Transfer Protocol (FTP), Telnet (Telnet) which lets you logon to remote computers, and the Simple Mail Transfer Protocol (SMTP). These and other protocols are often packaged together with TCP/IP as a "suite."

Personal computer users with an analog phone modem connection to the Internet usually get to the Internet through the Serial Line Internet Protocol (SLIP) or the Point-to-Point Protocol (PPP). These protocols encapsulate the IP packets so that they can be sent over the dial-up phone connection to an access provider's modem.

Protocols related to TCP/IP include the User Datagram Protocol (UDP), which is used instead of TCP for special purposes. Other protocols are used by network host computers for exchanging router information. These include the Internet Control Message Protocol (ICMP), the Interior Gateway Protocol (IGP), the Exterior Gateway Protocol (EGP), and the Border Gateway Protocol (BGP).

DOMAIN NAME

A **domain name** is an identification label that defines a realm of administrative autonomy, authority, or control on the Internet, based on the Domain Name System (DNS).

Domain names are used in various networking contexts and application-specific naming and addressing purposes. They are organized in subordinate levels (subdomains) of the DNS root domain, which is nameless. The first-level set of domain names are the top-level domains (TLDs), including the generic top-level domains (gTLDs), such as the prominent domains com, net and org, and the country code top-level domains (ccTLDs). Below these top-level domains in the DNS hierarchy are the second-level and third-level domain names that are typically open for reservation by end-users that wish to connect local area networks to the Internet, run web sites, or create other publicly accessible Internet resources. The registration of these domain names is usually administered by domain name registrars who sell their services to the public.

Individual Internet host computers use domain names as host identifiers, or hostnames. Hostnames are the leaf labels in the domain name system usually without further subordinate domain name space. Hostnames appear as a component in Uniform Resource Locators (URLs) for Internet resources such as web sites (e.g., en.wikipedia.org).

Domain names are also used as simple identification labels to indicate ownership or control of a resource. Such examples are the realm identifiers used in the Session Initiation Protocol (SIP), the DomainKeys used to verify DNS domains in e-mail systems, and in many other Uniform Resource Identifiers (URIs).

An important purpose of domain names is to provide easily recognizable and memorizable names to numerically addressed Internet resources. This abstraction allows any resource (e.g., website) to be moved to a different physical location in the address topology of the network, globally or locally in an intranet. Such a move usually requires changing the IP address of a resource and the corresponding translation of this IP address to and from its domain name.

Domain names are often referred to simply as domains and domain name registrants are frequently referred to as domain owners, although domain name registration with a registrar does not confer any legal ownership of the domain name, only an exclusive right of use.

This article primarily discusses the group of domain names that are offered by domain name registrars for registration by the public. The Domain Name System article discusses the technical facilities and infrastructure of the domain name space and the hostname article deals with specific information about the use of domain names as identifiers of network hosts.

A name that identifies one or more IP addresses. For example, the domain name microsoft.com represents about a dozen IP addresses. Domain names are used in URLs to identify particular Web pages. For example, in the URL http://www.pcwebopedia.com/index.html, the domain name is pcwebopedia.com.

Every domain name has a suffix that indicates which top level domain (TLD) it belongs to. There are only a limited number of such domains. For example:

- **gov** - Government agencies

- **edu** - Educational institutions
- **org** - Organizations (nonprofit)
- **mil** – Military
- **com** - commercial business
- **net** - Network organizations
- **ca** – Canada
- **th** - Thailand
- **int**- International organisation
- **in**- India

Because the Internet is based on IP addresses, not domain names, every Web server requires a Domain Name System (DNS) server to translate domain names into IP addresses.

ELECTRONIC MAIL (e mail)

Electronic mail, most commonly abbreviated **email** or **e-mail**, is a method of exchanging digital messages across the Internet or other computer networks. E-mail systems are based on a store-and-forward model in which e-mail server computer systems accept, forward, deliver and store messages on behalf of users, who only need to connect to the e-mail infrastructure, typically an e-mail server, with a network-enabled device for the duration of message submission or retrieval. Originally, e-mail was always transmitted directly from one user's device to another's, but because that required both computers to be online at the same time, this is rarely the case nowadays.

An electronic mail message consists of two components, the message header, and the message body, which is the email's content. The message header contains control information, including, minimally, an originator's email address or sender‘s e mail address and one or more recipient addresses. An e-mail address serve a similar purpose to an address on an envelope –the electronic postman needs to know where to deliver the letter and to whom it's intended. Usually additional information is added, such as a subject header field. In pkjain3661@gmail.com for example, everything to the right of the @ symbol relates to the actual computer where your account is held, while anything to the left of the @ symbol relates to user at that address.

Originally a text-only communications medium, email was extended to carry multi-media content attachments. The foundation for today's global Internet e-mail service was created in the early ARPANET and standards for encoding of messages were proposed as early as 1973. An e-mail sent in the early 1970s looked very similar to one sent on the Internet today. Conversion from the ARPANET to the Internet in the early 1980s produced the core of the current service.

Network-based e-mail was initially exchanged on the ARPANET in extensions to the File Transfer Protocol (FTP), but is today carried by the Simple Mail Transfer Protocol (SMTP), first published as Internet standard 10 in 1982. In the process of transporting e-mail messages between systems, SMTP communicates delivery parameters using a message envelope separately from the message (header and body) itself.

A sample E mail Message

From : pkjain3661@gmail.com

To: info@scientificpub.com

Subject: Publishing a book on computer for Law students

As discussed please find attached files to do needful for publishing a book on computer for the benefit of Law students of RTM Nagpur University.

Regards

Yours faithfully

Dr. P.K. Jain

COMMUNICATION USING EMAIL

Email has revolutionized the way that we communicate with others. It has given us the ability to process work and information faster and cheaper. Sending documents across multiple sites is instantaneous. We are able to stay in communication via a laptop, phone or PDA anywhere; giving us the ability to be far more productive. It's almost hard to believe how businesses functioned without email. Although sending an email rather than personally meeting with someone is more efficient, it tends to be less personal and can hinder social interaction and relationship building. The use of e-mail to avoid conflict or sending bad or negative feedback should be avoided. Messages can also easily be misconstrued. "Because it is so difficult to convey via email that something was meant ironically, misunderstandings are common and can lead to major fights. Usually, that's neither wonderful nor funny."

Electronic mail has strongly in the value in both corporate and personal domains. Email is cheaper and faster than a letter, less intrusive than a phone call, less hassle than a FAX. Using email, differences in location and time zone are less of an obstacle to communication. There is also evidence that email leads to a more egalitarian information structure.

Because of these advantages, email use is exploding. By 1998, 30% of adults in the United States and Canada had come on-line. A 2007 Pew Internet and American Life Project survey found that 73% of U.S. adults connect to the Internet regularly. Almost all of those use electronic mail.

This is not a document on the mechanics of sending email - which buttons to push or how to attach a photograph. Those details are different for every different email software package, and are better handled by manuals for the program.

What Makes Email Different?

Electronic communication, because of its speed and broadcasting ability, is fundamentally different from paper-based communication. Because the turnaround time can be so fast, email is more conversational than traditional paper-based media.

In a paper document, it is absolutely essential to make everything completely clear and unambiguous because your audience may not have a chance to ask for clarification. With email documents, your recipient can ask questions immediately. Email thus tends, like conversational speech, to be sloppier than communications on paper.

This is not always bad. It makes little sense to slave over a message for hours, making sure that your spelling is faultless, your words eloquent, and your grammar beyond reproach, if the point of the message is to tell your co-worker that you are ready to go to lunch.

However, your correspondent also won't have normal status cues such as dress, diction, or dialect, so may make assumptions based on your name, address, and - above all - facility with language. You need to be aware of when you can be sloppy and when you have to be meticulous.

Email also does not convey emotions nearly as well as face-to-face or even telephone conversations. It lacks vocal inflection, gestures, and a shared environment. Your correspondent may have difficulty telling if you are serious or kidding, happy or sad, frustrated or euphoric. Sarcasm is particularly dangerous to use in email.

Another difference between email and older media is that what the sender sees when composing a message might not look like what the reader sees. Vocal cords make sound waves that are perceived basically the same by both your ears as your audience's. The paper that you write your love note on is the same paper that the object of your affection sees. But with email, the software and hardware that you use for composing, sending, storing, downloading, and reading may be completely different from what your correspondent uses. Consequently visual qualities of Your message's may be quite different by the time it reaches to receivers screen. Thus email compositions should be different from both paper compositions and speech.

CHAPTER - IV

E-COMMERCE

Electronic commerce or e-commerce, has completely revolutionized the traditional concept of doing business by enabling its presence in the global market. Commerce is original Latin word Commercium means the activity of buying and selling, especially on a large scale. Electronic commerce or in short e-commerce, refers to business activities like selling and purchasing of products and services and exchanging of goods and services carried out over electronic systems like the Internet and computer networks through which transactions or terms of sale are performed electronically. Contrary to popular belief, e-commerce is not just on the Web. The history of e-commerce dates back to 1970, when for the first time, electronic data interchange (EDI) and electronic fund transfer were introduced. Since then, a rapid growth of e-commerce has pervaded almost every other aspects of business such as supply chain management, transaction processing, Internet marketing and inventory management.

INTRODUCTION

Electronic commerce, commonly known as **e-commerce** or **e-Commerce**, or e-business consists of the buying and selling of products or services over electronic systems such as the Internet and other computer networks. The amount of trade conducted electronically has grown extraordinarily with widespread Internet usage. The use of commerce is conducted in this way, spurring and drawing on innovations in electronic funds transfer, supply chain management, Internet marketing, online transaction processing, electronic data interchange (EDI), inventory management systems, and automated data collection systems. Modern electronic commerce typically uses the World Wide Web at least at some point in the transaction's lifecycle, although it can encompass a wider range of technologies such as e-mail as well.

A large percentage of electronic commerce is conducted entirely electronically for virtual items such as access to premium content on a website, but most electronic commerce involves the transportation of physical items in some way. Online retailers are sometimes known as e-tailers and online retail is sometimes known as **e-tail**. Almost all big retailers have electronic commerce presence on the World Wide Web.

Electronic commerce that is conducted between businesses is referred to as business-to-business or B2B. B2B can be open to all interested parties (e.g. commodity exchange) or limited to specific, pre-qualified participants (private electronic market). Electronic commerce that is conducted between businesses and consumers, on the other hand, is referred to as business-to-consumer or B2C. This is the type of electronic commerce conducted by companies such as Amazon.com. Online shopping is a form of electronic commerce where the buyer is directly online to the seller's computer usually via the internet. There is no intermediary service. The sale and purchase transaction is completed electronically and interactively in real-time such as Amazon.com for new books. If an intermediary is present, then the sale and purchase transaction is called electronic commerce such as eBay.com.

Electronic commerce is generally considered to be the sales aspect of e-business. It also consists of the exchange of data to facilitate the financing and payment aspects of the business transactions.

HISTORY

Early development

The meaning of electronic commerce has changed over the last 30 years. Originally, electronic commerce meant the facilitation of commercial transactions electronically, using technology such as Electronic Data Interchange (EDI) and Electronic Funds Transfer (EFT). These were both introduced in the late 1970s, allowing businesses to send commercial documents like purchase orders or invoices electronically. The growth and acceptance of credit cards, automated teller machines (ATM) and telephone banking in the 1980s were also forms of electronic commerce. Another form of e-commerce was the airline and railway reservation system in USA and UK.

From the 1990s onwards, electronic commerce would additionally include enterprise resource planning systems (ERP), data mining and data warehousing.

An early example of many-to-many electronic commerce in physical goods was the Boston Computer Exchange, a marketplace for used computers launched in 1982. An early online information marketplace, including online consulting, was the American

Information Exchange, another pre -Internet online system introduced in 1991.

In 1990, Tim Berners-Lee invented the World Wide Web web browser and transformed an academic telecommunication network into a worldwide everyman everyday communication system called internet/www. Commercial enterprise on the Internet was strictly prohibited until 1991. Although the Internet became popular worldwide around 1994 when the first internet online shopping started, it took about five years to introduce security protocols and DSL allowing continual connection to the Internet. By the end of 2000, many European and American business companies offered their services through the World Wide Web. Since then people began to associate a word "ecommerce" with the ability of purchasing various goods through the Internet using secure protocols and electronic payment services. Today E-commerce is a byword in Indian society and it has become an integral part of our daily life. There are websites providing any number of goods and services. Then there are those, which provide a specific product along with its allied services.

Chronology

- 1979: Michael Aldrich invented online shopping
- 1981: Thomson Holidays, UK is first B2B online shopping
- 1982: Minitel was introduced nationwide in France by France Telecom and used for online ordering.
- 1984: Gateshead SIS/Tesco is first B2C online shopping and Mrs Snowball, 72, is the first online home shopper
- 1985: Nissan UK sells cars and finance with credit checking to customers online from dealers' lots.
- 1987: Swreg begins to provide software and share-ware authors means to sell their products online through an electronic Merchant account.
- 1990: Tim Berners-Lee writes the first web browser, WorldWideWeb, using a NeXT computer.
- 1992: J.H. Snider and Terra Ziporyn publish Future Shop: How New Technologies Will Change the Way We Shop and What We Buy. St. Martin's Press. ISBN 0-312-06359-8.
- 1994: Netscape releases the Navigator browser in October under the code name Mozilla. Pizza Hut offers online ordering on its Web page. The first online bank opens. Attempts to offer flower delivery and magazine subscriptions online. Adult

materials also become commercially available, as do cars and bikes. Netscape 1.0 is introduced in late 1994 SSL encryption that made transactions secure.

- 1995: Jeff Bezos launches Amazon.com and the first commercial-free 24 hour, internet-only radio stations, Radio HK and NetRadio start broadcasting. Dell and Cisco begin to aggressively use Internet for comme-rcial transactions. eBay is founded by computer programmer Pierre Omidyar as AuctionWeb.
- 1998: Electronic postal stamps can be purchased and downloaded for printing from the Web.
- 1999: Business.com sold for US $7.5 million to eCompanies, which was purchased in 1997 for US $149,000. The peer-to-peer filesharing software Napster launches. ATG Stores launches to sell decorative items for the home online.
- 2000: The dot-com bust.
- 2002: eBay acquires PayPal for $1.5 billion. Niche retail companies CSN Stores and NetShops are founded with the concept of selling products through several targeted domains, rather than a central portal.
- 2003: Amazon.com posts first yearly profit.
- 2007: Business.com acquired by R.H. Donnelley for $345 million.
- 2009: Zappos.com acquired by Amazon.com for $928 million. Retail Convergence, operator of private sale website RueLaLa.com, acquired by GSI Commerce for $180 million, plus up to $170 million in earn-out payments based on performance through 2012.
- 2010: US e Commerce and Online Retail sales projec-ted to reach $173 billion, an increase of 7 percent over 2009.

SCOPE

The scope of e-commerce is as wide as an ocean and there by the implementation hurdles.

When one thinks of the electronic commerce even through final goal remains the same as that of the traditional commerce, but the way in which they function in order to improve the performance is different. As information sharing is the major part of the commerce industries networking has given boost to e-commerce. This change in view-point has opened door for new opportunities.

Business applications

Some common applications related to electronic commerce are the following:

- Email
- Enterprise content management
- Instant messaging
- Newsgroups
- Online shopping and order tracking
- Online banking
- Online office suites
- Domestic and international payment systems
- Shopping cart software
- Teleconferencing
- Electronic tickets

Forms

Contemporary electronic commerce involves everything from ordering "digital" content for immediate online consu-mption, to ordering conventional goods and services, to "meta" services to facilitate other types of electronic commerce.

On the consumer level, electronic commerce is mostly conducted on the World Wide Web. An individual can go online to purchase anything from books or groceries, to expensive items like real estate. Another example would be online banking, i.e. online bill payments, buying stocks, transferring funds from one account to another, and initiating wire payment to another country. All of these activities can be done with a few strokes of the keyboard.

On the institutional level, big corporations and financial institutions use the internet to exchange financial data to facilitate domestic and international business. Data integrity and security are very hot and pressing issues for electronic commerce today.

DEFINATION

Electronic commerce, commonly known as (electronic marketing) e-commerce or eCommerce, consists of the buying and selling of products or services over electronic systems such as the Internet and other computer networks. There is no kind of physical contact between buyer and seller. Amazon and eBay are prime examples, but many major businesses have an e-commerce component.

TRADITIONAL COMMERCE VS E-COMMERCE

Principle

Multiple media vs a single one

The company's **positioning** towards traditional commerce or e-commerce affects directly its processes and strategy. The main difference between exercising traditional commerce and e-commerce is that in the former **multiple media** (like magazines, letters, mail, fax, etc) are used while in the latter **everything is digital.**

Definition

Traditional commerce

Traditional commerce means **communicating** (ordering, paying) with customer and supplier using different applications in **many time-consuming different steps.**

E-commerce

E-commerce means processing of information using **one digital application** (EDI or Internet) and only **a few quick steps** .

Positioning

Positioning is a plan showing the **situation** and setting **priorities** of the company towards other actors of the market.

Interactivity

Interactivity characterises a system when it is in a steady dynamic process of data interchange between many equal and free access system users at the same time.

ADVANTAGES AND DISADVANTAGES OF E-COMMERCE

Here is some of the important advantages and disadvantages of electronic commerce.

Advantages

The greatest and the most important advantage of e-commerce, is that it enables a business concern or individual to reach the global market. It caters to the demands of both the national and the international market, as your business activities are no longer restricted by geographical boundaries. With the help of electronic commerce, even small enterprises can access the global market for selling and purchasing products and services. Even time restrictions are nonexistent while conducting businesses, as e-commerce empowers one to execute business transactions 24 hours a day and even on holidays and weekends. This in turn significantly increases sales and profit.

Electronic commerce gives the customers the opportunity to look for cheaper and quality products. With the help of e-commerce, consumers can easily research on a specific product and sometimes even find out the original manufacturer to purchase a product at a much cheaper price than that charged by the wholesaler. Shopping online is usually more convenient and time saving than conventional shopping. Besides these, people also come across reviews posted by other customers, about the products purchased from a particular e-commerce site, which can help make purchasing decisions.

For business concerns, e-commerce significantly cuts down the cost associated with marketing, customer care, processing, information storage and inventory management. It reduces the time period involved with business process re-engineering, customization of products to meet the demand of particular customers, increasing productivity and customer care services. Electronic commerce reduces the burden of infrastructure to conduct businesses and thereby raises the amount of funds available for profitable investment. It also enables efficient customer care services. On the other hand, it collects and manages information related to customer behavior, which in turn helps develop and adopt an efficient marketing and promotional strategy.

- Companies have a bigger increase in their profits if they use Ecommerce
- Ecommerce increases sales for companies and decrease costs
- Advertising on the Web can promote small businesses
- Companies can ship their products to different people in the world

Disadvantages

Electronic commerce is also characterized by some technological and inherent limitations which has restricted the number of people using this revolutionary system. One important disadvantage of e-commerce is that the Internet has still not touched the lives of a great number of people, either due to the lack of knowledge or trust. A large number of people do not use the Internet for any kind of financial transaction. Some people simply refuse to trust the authenticity of completely impersonal business transactions, as in the case of e-commerce. Many people have reservations regarding the requirement to disclose personal and private information for security concerns. Many times, the legitimacy and authenticity of different e-commerce sites have also been questioned.

Another limitation of e-commerce is that it is not suitable for perishable commodities like food items. People prefer to shop in the conventional way than to use e-commerce for purchasing food products. So e-commerce is not suitable for such business sectors. The time period required for delivering physical products can also be quite significant in case of e-commerce. A lot of phone calls and e-mails may be required till you get your desired products. However, returning the product and getting a refund can be even more troublesome and time consuming than purchasing, in case if you are not satisfied with a particular product. Some more limitations are as follows:

- Expensive things such as jewelry may be impossible to inspect
- The rapid development of new technology on the Internet
- Some of the companies only ship their products to certain cities or countries

These are only some of the problems that face Ecommerce today. But computer programmers say that in the future they will develop a new technology for people who would like to perform Ecommerce so that it is easier for them. Thus, on evaluating the various pros and cons of electronic commerce, we can say that the advantages of e-commerce have the potential to outweigh the disadvantages. A proper strategy to address the technical issues and to build up customers trust in the system, can change the present scenario and help e-commerce adapt to the changing needs of the world.

E-COMMERCE AND TRADE CYCLE

The Trade Cycle

A trade cycle is the series of exchanges, between a customer and supplier, that take place when a commercial exchange is executed. A general trade cycle consists of:

Pre-Sales

Execution

Settlement

After-Sales

Finding a supplier and agreeing the terms

Selecting goods and taking delivery

Invoice (if any) and payment

Following up complaints or providing maintenance.

For business-to-business transactions the trade cycle typically involves the provision of credit with execution preceding settlement whereas in consumer-to-business these two steps are typically co-incident. The nature of the trade cycle can indicate the e-Commerce technology most suited to the exchange.

Commercial transactions that are repeated on a regular basis, such as supermarkets replenishing their shelves, is one category of trade cycle. EDI is the e-Commerce technology appropriate to these exchanges.

FUNCTIONS OF E-COMMERCE

The four function of e commerce are:

Communication

Aimed at the delivery of information and/ or documents to facilitate business transaction. Example E-mail

Process Management

Covers the automation and improvement of business processes. Example Networking two computers together so that they can share and transfer data rather than have a person to take data from one computer to another.

Service Management

Application of technology to improve the quality of service. Example Citibank website. It permit customers to track credit and debit details, offers, online payments, air ticketing, etc. without having to take service representative. Customer services is greatly enhanced due to the site's capabilities.

Transaction capabilities

Provides the ability to buy/sell on the Internet or some other online service. Example IRCTCs railway e-ticketing services

TYPES OF E-COMMERCE

The major different types of e-commerce are: business-to-business (B2B); business-to-consumer (B2C); consumer-to-business (C2B), consumer-to-consumer (C2C); business-to-government (B2G); and mobile commerce (m-commerce).

Business-to-business (B2B) describes commerce transactions between businesses, such as between a manufacturer and a wholesaler, or between a wholesaler and a retailer. Pricing is based on quantity of order and is often negotiable. Contrasting terms are **business-to-consumer** (B2C) and **business-to-government** (B2G). B2B e-comm-erce is simply defined as e-commerce between companies. This is the type of e-commerce that deals with relationships between and among businesses. About 80% of e-commerce is of this type, and most experts predict that B2B ecommerce will continue to grow faster than the B2C segment. The B2B market has two primary components: **e-frastructure** and **e-markets**. E-frastructure is the architecture of B2B, primarily consisting of the following:

- logistics - transportation, warehousing and distrib-ution (e.g., Procter and Gamble);
- application service providers - deployment, hosting and management of packaged software from a central facility (e.g., Oracle and IBM);
- outsourcing of functions in the process of e-commerce, such as Web-hosting, security and customer care solutions (e.g., outsourcing providers such as eShare, NetSales, iXL Enterprises and Universal Access);
- auction solutions software for the operation and maintenance of real-time auctions in the Internet (e.g., Moai Technologies and OpenSite Technologies);
- content management software for the facilitation of Web site content management and delivery (e.g., Interwoven and ProcureNet); and
- Web-based commerce enablers (e.g., Commerce One, a browser-based, XMLenabled purchasing automation software).

E-markets are simply defined as Web sites where buyers and sellers interact with each other and conduct transactions. The more common B2B examples and best practice models are IBM, Hewlett Packard (HP), Cisco and Dell. Cisco, for instance, receives over 90% of its product orders over the Internet. Most B2B applications are in the areas of supplier management (especially purchase order processing), inventory management (i.e., managing order-ship-bill cycles), distribution management (especially in the transmission of shipping documents), channel management (i.e., information dissemination on changes in operational conditions), and payment management (e.g., electronic payment systems or EPS).

The volume of B2B transactions is much higher than the volume of B2C transactions. The primary reason for this is that in a typical supply chain there will be many B2B transactions involving subcomponent or raw materials, and only one B2C transaction, specifically sale of the finished product to the end customer. For example, an automobile manufacturer makes several B2B transactions such as buying tires, glass for windscreens, and rubber hoses for its vehicles. The final transaction, a finished vehicle sold to the consumer, is a single (B2C).

B2C (Business-to-Consumer)

Businesses selling to the general public typically through catalogs utilizing shopping cart software which allowing customers to choose products to buy, review terms on their orders, add to or delete items from their order and make online purchases.

Business-to-consumer (**B2C**, sometimes also called **Business-to-Customer**) describes activities of businesses serving end consumers with products and/or services. An example of a B2C transaction would be a person buying a pair of shoes from a retailer. The transactions that led to the shoes being available for purchase, that is the purchase of the leather, laces, rubber, etc. as well as the sale of the shoe from the shoemaker to the retailer would be considered (B2B) transactions. B 2C is also called Retailing on the World Wide Web.

C2B (Consumer-to-Business)

A consumer posts his project with a set budget online and within hours companies review the consumer's requirements and bid on the project. The consumer reviews the bids and selects the company that will complete the project. Magic bricks empowers consumers in India by providing the meeting ground and platform for real estate buy and sell, rental accommodation etc..

C2C (Consumer-to-Consumer)

There are many sites offering free classifieds, auctions, and forums where individuals can buy and sell by online payment systems like transferring money from one bank account to other and where people can send and receive money online with ease. eBay's auction service is a great example of where person-to-person transactions take place every day.

Companies using internal networks to offer their employees products and services online--not necessarily online on the Web--are engaging in B2E (Business-to-Employee) ecommerce.

G2G (Government-to-Government), G2E (Government-to-Employee), G2B (Government-to-Business), B2G (Business-to-Government), G2C (Government-to-Citizen), C2G (Citizen-to-Government) are other forms of ecommerce that involve transactions with the government--from procurement to filing taxes to business registrations to renewing licenses. There are other categories of ecommerce out there, but they tend to be superfluous.

E-COMMERCE APPLICATIONS

Various applications of e-commerce are continually affecting trends and prospects for business over the Internet, including e-banking, e-tailing and online publis-hing/online retailing.

A more developed and mature e-banking environment plays an important role in e-commerce by encouraging a shift from traditional modes of payment (i.e., cash, checks or any form of paper-based legal tender) to electronic alternatives (such as e-payment systems), thereby closing the e-commerce loop.

(a) Benefits of e-Commerce • Expanded Geographical Reach • Expanded Customer Base • Increase Visibility thro-ugh Search Engine Marketing • Provide Customers valuable information about your business • Available 24/7/365 - Never Close • Build Customer Loyalty • Reduction of Mar-keting and Advertising Costs • Collection of Customer Data

(b) Basic Benefits of e Business/ e-Commerce are:

- increase sales - this is the first thing that people consider when dealing with e-commerce
- decreasing costs
- increase profits
- understanding that profits is not the same as sales
- Expands the size of the market from regional to national or national to international
- Contract the market

- reach a narrow market
- target market segmentation allows you to focus on a more select group of customers
- and therefore have a competitive advantages in satisfying them

INTERNET PAYMENT SYSTEMS

Internet payment systems refer to the various methods by which individuals and companies doing business online collect money from their customers in exchange for the goods and services they provide. A number of different forms of payment exist for online purchases, and more are being developed all the time. After all, it is in the best interest of both consumers and merchants to make electronic commerce as safe and easy as possible. "The low cost of entry has attracted hundreds of companies, large and small, to the level playing field of cyberspace," Paul J. Dowling, Jr. noted in his book Web Advertising and Marketing. "On the Internet, a small, one-man operation can look as good as or better than a large, multinational corporation. But whether it's an individual working out of a virtual office, or a CEO sitting in an expensive downtown office building, they're going online for one purpose—to sell. And they're leaving no stone unturned in their efforts to make it safe and easy for their customers to buy."

Customers who physically visit retail establishments can choose among a variety of payment methods, including cash, checks, credit cards, and debit cards. Customers who shop on the Internet are beginning to expect online merchants to offer the same variety and convenience in payment terms. Credit cards remain the most common form of payment for online purchases, although the options have expanded to include digital cash, smart cards, electronic checks, and other technologies. In addition, some customers continue to make online purchases using traditional payment methods, such as placing orders by telephone or fax, or sending a check via snail mail. Dowling recommends that companies conducting sales online make as many payment methods available as possible and advertise their acceptance of those methods on their Web sites. He claims that small businesses can add value to their product or service offerings by making payment easy, comfortable, and secure for their customers. "Getting paid on the Web ultimately testifies to your marketing plan's effectiveness," Dowling wrote. "And when everything goes as it should, customers will place the order."

Perhaps the biggest issue affecting online payment systems—from both the sellers' and the buyers' perspectives—is maintaining the security of financial information sent over the Internet. A survey conducted by Visa showed that 91 percent of consumers were concerned about privacy and security on the Internet. Another study, conducted by the Boston Consulting Group and quoted in Computerworld, indicated that 28 percent of consumers' online purchase efforts failed—meaning that they intended to buy online but did not complete the transaction. Concerns about security and the perception that online credit card transactions are extremely unsafe seem to be among the biggest issues keeping many retailers and consumers from closing sales electronically.

Online Payment Options

Credit card: Credit cards are the most common means of online payment. They are also among the easiest payment methods, for consumers as well as for merchants. From the consumer's standpoint, ordering merchandise from the Internet required only entering a credit card number and expiration date in the appropriate fields on a merchant's Web site. Many consumers felt greater confidence in online transactions when they used a credit card, knowing that a third party (the credit card company or issuing bank) was involved and could help protect them against fraud. In most cases, the consumer's liability for fraudulent credit card charges is limited depending upon issuing authorities' terms and conditions.

For merchants who already accept credit cards offline, taking credit card payments over the Internet is relatively simple. It basically involves setting up two Web pages, one to promote the company and its products or services, and the other to process order information. As Dowling explained, however, it can be difficult for online retailers to establish the merchant accounts needed to begin accepting credit cards. Many banks are reluctant to set up accounts for online merchants because they deal with "card-not-present transactions," or transactions in which the physical credit card and holder's signature are not used. The approval process for these accounts is usually quite rigorous, and the fees on sales tend to be higher than those charged to regular merchants. These high fees can pose a particular problem for online merchants who sell small-ticket items.

Once a small business has established a merchant account with a bank, the next step in accepting credit cards is to select a payment processing firm or service bureau. It is also necessary to obtain card authorization software—which can be run on a computer network—or a point-of-sale (POS) terminal to transmit sale data to the payment processing firm via a modem and telephone line. The processing firm checks the validity of the credit card number, expiration date, and purchase amount, and then provides the merchant with an authorization number. The preferred method for handling online sales is to pass the transaction information along to the payment processing firm for authorization while the customer is still online. An e-mail confirmation completes the transaction.

Smart card: Smart cards are similar to credit cards, except they store information on an imbedded chip instead of on a magnetic strip on the back. Consumers can load money into an account on the card by using an automatic teller machine (ATM) or by placing the card in a slot in a specially equipped computer. The imbedded chip keeps track of how much money is added to and withdrawn from the account. Smart cards are already quite popular for online sales in some international markets. It is eventually expected to combine the features of credit, debit, phone, and other cards in one piece of plastic.

Digital cash: Digital cash is a form of electronic currency that functions similarly to a debit card. Customers can transfer money from savings and checking accounts into an online cash account, from which they withdraw to make purchases over the Internet. This form of payment is particularly well suited to purchases of small, low-cost items. In addition, it offers consumers the benefit of anonymity in their purchases, similar to using real cash. The basic technology involved in digital cash transactions is public-key encryption. Digital signatures are used to authenticate the bank issuing the note and the individual computer user who is spending the money.

Some people expect digital cash to become the preferred method of online payment in the near future. Eventually, people using the Net probably will have digital cash on their computer much the same as they have bills and coins in their wallet or purse. In fact, digital cash accounts could be integrated into consumers' Web browsers, and companies that provide content on their Web sites (like online newspapers and magazines) could charge a nominal fee for surfers to view their sites. But methods still need to be established to standardize the use of digital cash. As it stands, consumers sometimes have to install several different payment software programs to do business with various companies over the Internet.

Electronic checks: Small businesses can also allow customers to pay for online purchases by accepting personal or business checks online. Although not as popular as credit cards, electronic checks are also accepted by hundreds of merchants on the Net. While most electronic check schemes require the merchant to use special software, electronic checks might appeal to you if you do not currently have a credit card merchant account. Online merchants who accept electronic checks generally set up a form on a Web page and have their customers enter all the information from their regular checks. The merchant can submit this information to a bank like a regular check. A digital signature is used in place of a handwritten one to verify the identity of the customer. One advantage of electronic checks is that it provides customers with a familiar method of payment. In addition, a number of services are available to simplify the process for both consumers and merchants.

Secure third parties and online banks: Banks have traditionally been reluctant to do business online because of the perceived security risks. But banks have begun offering an increasing number of services online in response to customer demands. Secure third parties may be banks or other institutions that act as middlemen in financial transactions between merchants and customers. For small businesses, conducting transactions through a secure third party eliminates the need and expense of setting up a secure Web site. Secure third parties also provide consumers with added protection from fraud, since the merchants never handle their credit card numbers. Secure third parties will become more popular as smaller merchants with fewer resources continue migrating on-line. While a small company may want to keep Web operations in-house, it may not want to purchase or maintain a secure Web server. Third-party solutions offer an affordable alternative to expensive, secure servers and local Internet providers that don't offer secure transaction capability.

Old-fashioned payment methods: A final alternative for companies that conduct sales over the Internet is to accept payment via traditional, offline methods—by taking orders through an address or phone number listed on their Web site, for example. However, experts warn that limiting payment methods in this manner may cost a company some potential sales. As soon as you add that extra step—writing down your address or phone number, sending out a check or dialing the phone—you give them another chance to reevaluate their decision to buy. When prospective clients click on your order-now button, they'd better be able to do just that.

One avenue in which using traditional payment methods may not hurt sales is business-to-business transactions. Even when sales are made over the Internet, many businesses choose to use existing methods to bill their customers' accounts. In order to protect both parties in an online transaction from fraud, businesses may find it helpful to require all new accounts to be opened in writing via fax or mail. In this way, the seller has a printed document on hand listing the names of authorized buyers, along with approved e-mail addresses, shipping addresses, and purchase amount limits. Any changes to this account information should also be made in writing. Finally, the seller should verify orders by telephone and send an e-mail confirmation upon shipment.

Security Efforts

Security remains the main concern about online payment systems, particularly the use of credit cards for purchases made over the Internet. Although media reports tend to concentrate on the effect of security breaches on consumers, credit card fraud affects merchants as well. For example, when hackers infiltrate a company's computers, steal thousands of customer credit card numbers, and use them to charge fraudulent purchases, the online retailer's reputation suffers severe damage. In addition, companies are sometimes left without recourse when they accept a credit card order and ship the merchandise, only to have the customer claim that they never ordered or received it.

But many e-commerce analysts claim that transmitting credit card numbers online does not have to be any less secure than handing a card to a salesperson at retail store. Credit card numbers sent over the Internet can be protected by sophisticated encryption technology which is often invisible to parties involved in the sale. In fact, encryption capability is built into many popular Web browsers used by consumers, and the software needed to decrypt messages is widely available to online merchants at a reasonable price.

Encryption reassures the merchant that the customer's order has not been altered and that the customer's personal and financial data has not been intercepted and copied. Further-more, if a digital signature is attached, the merchant can verify that the order was actually sent by the person who claimed to have sent it. Encryption also assures the customer that their personal and financial data remains confidential. Of course, it is vital that the online retailer never decrypt or store credit card numbers on any computer that is connected to the Internet.

For small businesses that operate their Web sites on a server belonging to an Internet Service Provider (ISP) or other host, it is still possible to accept credit card payments online. Many hosts will collect customer financial data and pass it along to their clients in encrypted form. Small businesses that do not have access to a secure Web server can also go through a company like Versanet, which allows companies to call their own secure order page on the Versanet server to process credit card transactions. Experts recommend that companies unable to use encryption (for example, companies that are located in countries where encryption is illegal) either not accept credit card orders online or use a two-stage order process that separates credit card numbers and expiration dates into chunks or data that would be difficult for hackers to identify.

A number of organizations were working to address the problem of security in e-commerce, including Visa, American Express, major software vendors, Better Business Bureaus, and the national organization of Certified Public Accoun-tants. Many of these groups provided recommendations and security certification programs for online merchants. Still, some experts claimed that the future of Internet payment systems might lie in an entirely new technology. One possibility is biometrics, which uses physical identifying features such as fingerprints and voice scans to authenticate customers. User authentication is the weakest link in e-commerce, and biometrics could not only solve that problem, it could eliminate online fraud. Currently used in the financial and health care industries for the authentication of transactions and drug purchases, biometrics might be the wave of the future. But it needs to overcome people's reluctance to provide something as personal as a fingerprint, which is often viewed as an invasion of privacy.

CONSUMER ORIENTED E-COMMERCE

The wide range of applications for the consumer marketplace can be broadly classified into

- **Entertainment**: Movies on demand, Video catalo-ging, interactive ads, multi-user games, on-line discussions
- **Financial services and information**: Home banking, financial services, financial news
- **Essential services**: Home shopping, electronic catalogs, telemedicine, remote diagnostics
- **Educational and training**: Interactive education, video conferencing, on-line databases

BUSINESS ORIENTED E-COMMERCE

A company that uses a network or the Internet for ordering from its suppliers, receiving invoices and making payments. This application of e commerce has been well established for several years, though its true potential is now being utilized. These companies never interact with the customer or end user. E commerce presents a vast spectrum of possibilities to every businessman worldwide.

The most apparent and equally valuable benefit would be of global presence. Any business concern will be able to address not only but also a global one at same time and market its products globally without cost or capital restraints. All this without even stepping out of one's office. Moreover, the businessman will able to identify and satisfy his customer's needs better as well as be able to provide customers with pre-as well as post-sale support, more product information, prompter response to customer enquiries and better chance on how to use its products. Since transactions are done electronically, unnecessary and redundant intermediaries in the chain of business may be eliminated which will drive down inventory, lead times, ordering costs and response time.

E-SERVICE

The concept of **E-service** (short for electronic service), represents one prominent application of utilizing the use of Information and communication technologies (ICTs) in different areas. However, providing an exact definition of e-service is hard to come by as researchers have been using different definitions to describe e-service. Despite these different definitions, it can be argued that they all agree about the role of technology in facilitating the delivery of services which make them more of electronic services. An e-service defines as "...an interactive, content-centered and Internet-based customer service, driven by the customer and integrated with related organizational customer support processes and technologies with the goal of strengthening the customer-service provider relationship"

As the aforementioned definition makes e-service limited to Internet domain; it seems more wise and compelling to adopt other approach defines e-services as: "...deeds, efforts or performances whose delivery is mediated by information technology. Such e-service includes the service element of e-tailing, customer support, and service delivery". This definition reflects three main components-service provider, service receiver and the channels of service delivery (i.e., technology). For example, as concerned to public e-service, public agencies are the service provider and citizens as well as businesses are the service receiver. The channel of service delivery is the third requirement of e-service. Internet is the main channel of e-service delivery while other classic channels (e.g. telephone, call center, public kiosk, mobile phone, television) are also considered.

E-Banking

Online banking (or **Internet banking**) allows customers to conduct financial transactions on a secure website operated by their retail or virtual bank, credit union or building society.

Features

Online banking solutions have many features and capabilities in common, but traditionally also have some that are application specific. The common features fall broadly into several categories such as

- Transactional (e.g., performing a financial transaction such as an account to transfer, paying a bill, wire transfer... and applications... apply for a loan, new account, etc.)
    - Electronic bill presentment and payment - EBPP
    - Funds transfer between a customer's own checking and savings accounts, or to another customer's account
    - Investment purchase or sale
    - Loan applications and transactions, such as repayments of enrollments
- Non-transactional (e.g., online statements, check links, cobrowsing, chat)
    - Bank statements
- Financial Institution Administration -
- Support of multiple users having varying levels of authority
- Transaction approval process
- Wire transfer

Features commonly unique to Internet banking include

- Personal financial management support, such as importing data into personal accounting software. Some online banking platforms support account aggregation to allow the customers to monitor all of their accounts in one place whether they are with their main bank or with other institutions.

History

The precursor for the modern home online banking services were the distance banking services over electronic media from the early 1980s. The term online became popular in the late '80s and referred to the use of a terminal, keyboard and TV (or monitor) to access the banking system using a phone line. 'Home banking' can also refer to the use of a numeric keypad to send tones down a phone line with instructions to the bank. Online services started in New York in 1981 when four of the city's major banks (Citibank, Chase Manhattan, Chemical and Manufacturers Hanover) offered home banking services[1] using the videotex system. Because of the commercial failure of videotex these banking services never became popular except in France where the use of videotex (Minitel) was subsidised by the telecom provider and the UK, where the Prestel system was used.

The UK's first home online banking services was set up by Bank of Scotland for customers of the Nottingham Building Society (NBS) in 1983. The system used was based on the UK's Prestel system and used a computer, such as the BBC Micro, or keyboard (Tandata Td1400) connected to the telephone system and television set. The system (known as 'Homelink') allowed on-line viewing of statements, bank transfers and bill payments. In order to make bank transfers and bill payments, a written instruction giving details of the intended recipient had to be sent to the NBS who set the details up on the Homelink system. Typical recipients were gas, electricity and telephone companies and accounts with other banks. Details of payments to be made were input into the NBS system by the account holder via Prestel. A cheque was then sent by NBS to the payee and an advice giving details of the payment was sent to the account holder. BACS was later used to transfer the payment directly.

Stanford Federal Credit Union was the first financial institution to offer online internet banking services to all of its members in October 1994. Today, many banks are internet only banks. Unlike their predecessors, these internet only banks do not maintain brick and mortar bank branc-hes. Instead, they typically differentiate themselves by offering better interest rates and online banking features.

Security

Security token devices

Protection through single password authentication, as is the case in most secure Internet shopping sites, is not considered secure enough for personal online banking applications in some countries. Basically there exist two different security methods for online banking.

- The PIN/TAN system where the PIN represents a password, used for the login and TANs representing one-time passwords to authenticate transactions. TANs can be distributed in different ways, the most popular one is to send a list of TANs to the online banking user by postal letter. The most secure way of using TANs is to generate them by need using a security token. These token generated TANs depend on the time and a unique secret, stored in the security token (this is called two-factor authent-ication or 2FA). Usually online banking with PIN/ TAN is done via a web browser using SSL secured connections, so that there is no additional encryption needed.
- Signature based online banking where all transa-ctions are signed and encrypted digitally. The Keys for the signature generation and encryption can be stored on smartcards or any memory medium, depending on the concrete implementation.

Attacks

Most of the attacks on online banking used today are based on deceiving the user to steal login data and valid TANs. Two well known examples for those attacks are phishing and pharming. Cross-site scripting and keylogger/ Trojan horses can also be used to steal login information.

A method to attack signature based online banking methods is to manipulate the used software in a way, that correct transactions are shown on the screen and faked transactions are signed in the background.

The most recent kind of attack is the so-called Man in the Browser attack, where a Trojan horses permits a remote attacker to modify the destination account number and also the amount.

Countermeasures

There exist several countermeasures which try to avoid attacks. Digital certificates are used against phishing and pharming, the use of class-3 card readers is a measure to avoid manipulation of transactions by the software in signature based online banking variants. To protect their systems against Trojan horses, users should use virus scanners and be careful with downloaded software or e-mail attachments.

Internet banking (or E-banking) means any user with a personal computer and a browser can get connected to his bank -s website to perform any of the virtual banking functions. In internet banking system the bank has a centralized database that is web-enabled. All the services that the bank has permitted on the internet are displayed in menu. Any service can be selected and further interaction is dictated by the nature of service. The traditional branch model of bank is now giving place to an alternative delivery channels with ATM network. Once the branch offices of bank are interconnected through terrestrial or satellite links, there would be no physical identity for any branch. It would a borderless entity permitting anytime, anywhere and anyhow banking.

Internet banking in India

The Reserve Bank of India constituted a working group on Internet Banking. The group divided the internet banking products in India into 3 types based on the levels of access granted. They are:

(i) Information Only System: General purpose information like interest rates, branch location, bank products and their features, loan and deposit calculations are provided in the banks website. There exist facilities for downloading various types of application forms. The communication is normally done through e-mail. There is no interaction between the customer and bank's application system. No identification of the customer is done. In this system, there is no possibility of any unauthorized person getting into production systems of the bank through internet.

(ii) Electronic Information Transfer System: The system provides customer-specific information in the form of account balances, transaction details, and statement of accounts. The information is still largely of the 'read only' format. Identification and authentication of the customer is through password. The information is fetched from the bank's application system either in batch mode or off-line. The application systems cannot directly access through the internet.

(iii) Fully Electronic Transactional System: This system allows bi-directional capabilities. Transactions can be submitted by the customer for online update. This system requires high degree of security and control. In this environment, web server and application systems are linked over secure infrastructure. It comprises technology covering computerization, networking and security, inter-bank payment gateway and legal infrastructure.

Automated Teller Machine (ATM)

ATM is designed to perform the most important function of bank. It is operated by plastic card with its special features. The plastic card is replacing cheque, personal attendance of the customer, banking hours restrictions and paper based verification. There are debit cards. ATMs used as spring board for Electronic Fund Transfer. ATM itself can provide information about customers account and also receive instructions from customers - ATM cardholders. An ATM is an Electronic Fund Transfer terminal capable of handling cash deposits, transfer between accounts, balance enquiries, cash withdrawals and pay bills. It may be on-line or 0ff-line. The on-line ATN enables the customer to avail banking facilities from anywhere. In off-line the facilities are confined to that particular ATM assigned. Any customer possessing ATM card issued by the Shared Payment Network System can go to any ATM linked to Shared Payment Networks and perform his transactions.

Credit Cards/Debit Cards

The Credit Card holder is empowered to spend wherever and whenever he wants with his Credit Card within the limits fixed by his bank. Credit Card is a **postpaid** card. Debit Card, on the other hand, is a **prepaid** card with some stored value. Every time a person uses this card, the Internet Banking house gets money transferred to its account from the bank of the buyer. The buyers account is debited with the exact amount of purchases. An individual has to open an account with the issuing bank which gives debit card with a Personal Identification Number (PIN). When he makes a purchase, he enters his PIN on shops PIN pad. When the card is slurped through the electronic terminal, it dials the acquiring bank system - either Master Card or VISA that validates the PIN and finds out from the issuing bank whether to accept or decline the transactions. The customer can never overspend because the system rejects any transaction which exceeds the balance in his account. The bank never faces a default because the amount spent is debited immediately from the customer's account.

Smart Card

Banks are adding chips to their current magnetic stripe cards to enhance security and offer new service, called Smart Cards. Smart

Cards allow thousands of times of information storable on magnetic stripe cards. In addition, these cards are highly secure, more reliable and perform multiple functions. They hold a large amount of personal information, from medical and health history to personal banking and personal preferences. You can avail the following services through E-Banking.

Bill payment service: You can facilitate payment of electricity and telephone bills, mobile phone, credit card and insurance premium bills as each bank has tie-ups with various utility companies, service providers and insurance companies, across the country. To pay your bills, all you need to do is complete a simple one-time registration for each biller. You can also set up standing instructions online to pay your recurring bills, automatically. Generally, the bank does not charge customers for online bill payment.

Fund transfer: You can transfer any amount from one account to another of the same or any another bank. Customers can send money anywhere in India. Once you login to your account, you need to mention the payees's account number, his bank and the branch. The transfer will take place in a day or so, whereas in a traditional method, it takes about three working days. ICICI Bank says that online bill payment service and fund transfer facility have been their most popular online services.

Credit card customers: With Internet banking, customers can not only pay their credit card bills online but also get a loan on their cards. If you lose your credit card, you can report lost card online.

Railway pass: This is something that would interest all the aam janta. Indian Railways has tied up with ICICI bank and you can now make your railway pass for local trains online. The pass will be delivered to you at your doorstep. But the facility is limited to Mumbai, Thane, Nashik, Surat and Pune.

Investing through Internet banking: You can now open an FD online through funds transfer.Now investors with interlinked demat account and bank account can easily trade in the stock market and the amount will be automatically debited from their respective bank accounts and the shares will be credited in their demat account. Moreover, some banks even give you the facility to purchase mutual funds directly from the online banking system.

Now-a-days, most leading banks offer both online banking and demat account. However if you have your demat account with independent share brokers, then you need to sign a special form, which will link your two accounts.

Recharging your prepaid phone: Now just top-up your prepaid mobile cards by logging in to Internet banking. By just selecting your operator's name, entering your mobile number and the amount for recharge, your phone is again back in action within few minutes.

Shopping: With a range of all kind of products, you can shop online and the payment is also made conveniently through your account. You can also buy railway and air tickets through Internet banking.

Advantage of Internet banking

As per the Internet and Mobile Association of India's report on online banking 2006, "There are many advantages of online banking. It is convenient, it isn't bound by operational timings, there are no geographical barriers and the services can be offered at a miniscule cost."

Through Internet banking, you can check your transactions at any time of the day, and as many times as you want to. Where in a traditional method, you get quarterly statements from the bank. If the fund transfer has to be made outstation, where the bank does not have a branch, the bank would demand outstation charges. Whereas with the help of online banking, it will be absolutely free for you.

Security Precautions

Customers should never share personal information like PIN numbers, passwords etc with anyone, including employees of the bank. It is important that documents that contain confidential information are safeguarded. PIN or password mailers should not be stored, the PIN and/or passwords should be changed immediately and memorised before destroying the mailers.

Customers are advised not to provide sensitive account-related information over unsecured e-mails or over the phone. Take simple precautions like changing the ATM PIN and online login and transaction passwords on a regular basis. Also ensure that the logged in session is properly signed out.

E- stock Trading

On line stock trading and investing A **stock market** or **equity market** is a public market (a loose network of economic transactions, not a physical facility or discrete entity) for the trading of company stock and derivatives at an agreed price; these are securities listed on a stock exchange as well as those only traded privately.

The value of the derivatives market, because it is stated in terms of notional values, cannot be directly compared to a stock or a fixed income security, which traditionally refers to an actual value. Moreover, the vast majority of derivatives 'cancel' each other out (i.e., a derivative 'bet' on an event occurring is offset by a comparable derivative 'bet' on the event not occurring). Many such relatively illiquid securities are valued as marked to model, rather than an actual market price.

The stocks are listed and traded on stock exchanges which are entities of a corporation or mutual organization specialized in the business of bringing buyers and sellers of the organizations to a listing of stocks and securities together. The largest stock market in the United States, by market cap is the New York Stock Exchange, NYSE, while in Canada, it is the Toronto Stock Exchange. Major European examples of stock exchanges include the London Stock Exchange, Paris Bourse, and the Deutsche Börse. Asian examples include the Tokyo Stock Exchange, the Hong Kong Stock Exchange, the Shanghai Stock Exchange, and the Bombay Stock Exchange. In Latin America, there are such exchanges as the BM&F Bovespa and the BMV.

Online Stock Trading

When you visit many financial sites on the Internet, they have a vested interest to win you over as a client so they can make money on commissions. Online stock trading is an extremely competitive field, and can be confusing for beginner investors. SBI provides online stock trading to demit account holder. A number of private financial companies also do online stock trading on behalf of their customer on commission basis.

E-Investing

Through a financial institution that provides a variety of services for clients e investment can be made. An investment bank is a financial institution that helps companies take new bond or stock issues to market, usually acting as the intermediary between the issuer and investors.

Investment banks may underwrite the securities by buying all the available shares at a set price and then reselling them to the public. Or the banks may act as agents for the issuer and take a commission on the securities they sell.

Investment banks are also responsible for preparing the company prospectus, which presents important data about the company to potential investors. In addition, investment banks handle the sales of large blocks of previously issued securities, including sales to institutional investors, such as mutual fund companies.

Unlike a commercial bank or a savings and loan company, an investment bank doesn't usually provide retail banking services to individuals. Example Angle Broking is providing on line share trading to investors for stocks.

E-Auction

Auctions are common in markets where the goods sold are valuable (like art) or when their prices can't be easily determined. The process of an auction aims to find a fair price for the goods by identifying buyers who need them the most. Such auctions are called forward auctions. In forward auctions buyers compete with each other by placing bids for the goods to be sold.

MMTC pioneered the concept of e-Auctions for steel by moving the entire process of auctions to the Internet. With state-of-art technology and unique services to support buyers and sellers in the decision making, financing and logistics stages MMTC make sure that auction tools help enterprises realize their sales and procurement goals with considerable cost savings.

MMTC auction a diverse range of products ranging from Secondary Steel, Iron, and Chemicals to Automobiles and Idle Assets. We have also auctioned specialty metals like Platinum and other products in the past.

Example

MMTC

(A GOVERNMENT OF INDIA ENTERPRISE)

e-AUCTION

At present MSTC sells scrap/obsolete stores/spares/ capital equipments worth around Rs. 1,000 crore per year. Besides it sells coal from various coal subsidiaries of Coal India Ltd. to the tune of roughly 1 million tonne per year. It also sells diamonds on behalf of NMDC as also confiscated diamonds of Customs dept. Mumbai

- The modus operandi followed by MSTC for this purpose is to put only a select number of items on auction, which can be offered on a regular and sustained basis.
- Initiate drive to register actual buyers of the item for permanent registration.

- Advance notice of selling events is sent by e-mail to the registered customers.
- Auctions are thereafter held on pre-announced date and time.

Some of the unique features of e-Auction system are

- Permanent registration of coal buyers - thereby ensuring that information about forthcoming sale events is made known. Customers get information only about items of their choice.
- Before the auction starts, either floor price or reserve price is fed into the system by the stock-holder (Principal).
- If the highest price exceeds floor price or the reserve price as the case may be, then automatic sale intim-ation letter is issued by the system without any manual intervention making the system transparent.
- The auction continues even beyond the stipulated closing hours until no bid is received for a specified period of time (5 to 8 minutes depending upon the item)

If you are a buyer of -Scrap/obsolete/surplus stores/ spares and capital equipments or coal or diamonds then please register yourself with us as buyer. We are also condu-cting auction of Manganese Ore and Iron Ore. To facilitate depositing your EMD etc. you can avail our e-banking services. For more details, click radio button of e-banking in the home page **www.mstcecommerce.com** or mail to **sanjibpoddar@mstcindia.co.in**. For details of the registration procedure, the customers may please go to the home page of our website **http://www.mstcecommerce. com** If you are a seller of any of these items and wish to use our services, then please e-mail to sschaudhuri@mstc-india.co.in. If you propose to sell any other items through our portal, kindly send your query by e-mail to **asinha@mstcindia.co.in**

E-Employments

E employments means search relevant employment as per your qualification with the various employment specific portal within local or global domain. Application for job can be filled on line even written examination has been conduc-ted on line including interview by video conferencing. Exam-ple website naukari.com provide **employment** screening

e-Governance

e-Government (short for electronic government, also known as **e-gov**, **digital government**, **online government**, **connected government** or **transformational government**) is creating a comfortable, transparent, and cheap interaction between government and citizens (G2C – government to citizens), government and business enterprises (G2B–government to business enterprises) and relationship between governments (G2G – inter-agency relationship). There are four domains of **e-government** namely, governance, information and communication technology(ICT), business process re-engineering(BPR)and e-citizen.

Defining e-Government and e-Governance

Definitions of e-Government and e-Governance abound in literature. Definitions for e-Government and e-Governance range from the working definitions like "the ability for anyone visiting the city website to communicate and/or interact with the city via the Internet in any way more sophisticated than a simple email letter to the generic city (or webmaster) email address provided at the site" to "the use of technology to enhance the access to and delivery of government services to benefit citizens, business partners and employees". Focus of these definitions range from those focusing on Information and communication technologies (ICTs) to those focusing on ICT-enabled government and governance transformation. Some examples of such definitions include:

- The use of ICTs, and particularly the Internet, as a tool to achieve better government.
- The use of information and communication technologies in all facets of the operations of a government organization.
- The continuous optimization of service delivery, constituency participation and governance by transforming internal and external relationships through technology, the Internet and new media.

Whilst e-Government has traditionally been understood as being centered around the operations of government, e-Governance is understood to extend the scope by including citizen engagement and participation in governance. As such, following in line with the OECD definition of e-Government, e-Governance can be defined as the use of ICTs as a tool to achieve better governance.

Delivery models and activities of e-Government

The primary delivery models of e-Government can be divided into:

- Government-to-Citizen or Government-to-Consumer (G2C)
- Government-to-Business (G2B)
- Government-to-Government (G2G)
- Government-to-Employees (G2E)

Within each of these interaction domains, four kinds of activities take place:

- pushing information over the Internet, e.g: regulatory services, general holidays, public hearing schedules, issue briefs, notifications, etc.
- two-way communications between the agency and the citizen, a business, or another government agency. In this model, users can engage in dialogue with agencies and post problems, comments, or requests to the agency.
- conducting transactions, e.g: lodging tax returns, applying for services and grants.
- governance, e.g: online polling, voting, and campaigning.

Non-internet e-Government

While e-government is often thought of as "online government" or "Internet-based government," many non-Internet "electronic government" technologies can be used in this context. Some non-Internet forms include telephone, fax, PDA, SMS text messaging, MMS, wireless networks and services, Bluetooth, CCTV, tracking systems, RFID, biometric identification, road traffic management and regulatory enforcement, identity cards, smart cards and other Near Field Communication applications; polling station technology (where non-online e-voting is being considered), TV and radio-based delivery of government services, email, online community facilities, newsgroups and electronic mailing lists, online chat, and instant messaging technologies.

Potential benefits and risks of e-Government

Risks

There are many considerations and potential implications of implementing and designing e-government, including disintermediation of the government and its citizens, impacts on economic, social, and political factors, vulnerability to cyber attacks, and disturbances to the status quo in these areas.

Hyper-surveillance

Increased contact between government and its citizens goes both ways. Once e-government begins to develop and become more sophisticated, citizens will be forced to interact electronically with the government on a larger scale. This could potentially lead to a lack of privacy for civilians as their government obtains more and more information on them. In a worse case scenario, with so much information being passed electronically between government and civilians, a totalitarian-like system could develop. When the government has easy access to countless information on its citizens, personal privacy is lost.

With the speed that technology continues to increase, it has become economically feasible for government agencies (from the local level to the federal level), to implement all measures of surveillance. From simple video surveillance systems found in the red light traffic cameras that will automatically take a video of your vehicle running a red light, which then generates an automated ticket to be mailed to you home, to the complex internet surveillance systems used by homeland security.

Hyper-Surveillance has become a part of our everyday lives. There isn't a day that goes by where we aren't monitored with some form of technology. Security cameras in our local supermarket are recording our presence; the firewall at our work is monitoring the web sites we visit, and in some cases, emails are monitored for key words that could be considered offensive.

Some may feel that certain aspects of E-Government's use of hyper-surveillance are encroaching on their civil liberties. While others feel that with the tragic events of 9/11, it's a necessary evil that we must all live with in order to keep our loved ones from harm. Whether the government has gone too far, or if enough safeguards are in place to protect citizens from abuse, is subjective and up to open for debate.

In Local government, Hyper-Surveillance is commonly found in the form of traffic or red light cameras in the more busy intersections. One example of where hyper-surveillance has worked is in the foiled attempt of a terrorist plot to bomb the Holland tunnel. The plot was discovered through the monitoring of Internet chat rooms.

Electronic ease dropping devices such as the Carnivore Surveillance tool are used to perform a digital wire tap of a user's internet activity and record information specific to that user. "Once installed it uses a packet-sniffing software program to trace emails sent and received by the targeted user. The program sifts through all the emails and conversations and records the data on a removable hard drive. In some cases the program can be setup to look for certain words or phrases."

Surveillance means continual observation of a person or group, especially one suspected of doing something illegal.

Cost

Although "a prodigious amount of money has been spent" on the development and implementation of e-government, some say it has yielded only a mediocre product. The outcomes and effects of trial Internet-based governments are often difficult to gauge or unsatisfactory.

Inaccessibility

An e-government site that provides web access and support often does not offer the "potential to reach many users including those who live in remote areas, are homebound, have low literacy levels, exist on poverty line incomes, suffer from chronic illness, are single parents or older adults.

False sense of transparency and accountability

Opponents of e-government argue that online governmental transparency is dubious because it is maintained by the governments themselves. Information can be added or removed from the public eye (i.e. the Internet) with or without public notice. For example, after the World Trade Center in New York City was attacked on September 11, 2001, United States federal officials removed a large amount of government information from its websites in the name of national security. This act went relatively unnoticed by United States citizens. To this day, very few organizations monitor and provide accountability for these modifications. Those that do so, like the United States' OMBWatch and Government Accountability Project, are often nonprofit volunteers. Even the governments themselves do not always keep track of the information they insert and delete. The information of government portals have not been updated since long.

Benefits

It is convenient and cost-effective for businesses, and the public benefits by getting easy access to the most current information available without having to spend time, energy and money to get it.

E-government helps simplify processes and makes access to government information more easily accessible for public sector agencies and citizens. For example, the Indiana Bureau of Motor Vehicles simplified the process of certifying driver records to be admitted in county court proceedings. Indiana became the first state to allow government records to be digitally signed, legally certified and delivered electro-nically by using Electronic Postmark technology. In addition to its simplicity, e-democracy services can reduce costs. Alabama Department of Conservation & Natural Resources, Wal-Mart and NIC developed an online hunting and fishing license service utilizing an existing computer to automate the licensing process. More than 140,000 licenses were pur-chased at Wal-Mart stores during the first hunting season and the agency estimates it will save $200,000 annually from service.

The anticipated benefits of e-government include efficiency, improved services, better accessibility of public services, and more transparency and accountability.

Democratization

One goal of e-government will be greater citizen participation. Through the internet, people from all over the country can interact with politicians or public servants and make their voices heard. Blogging and interactive surveys will allow politicians or public servants to see the views of the people they represent on any given issue. Chat rooms can place citizens in real-time contact with elected officials, their offices or provide them with the means to replace them by interacting directly with public servants, allowing voters to have a direct impact and influence in their government. These technologies can create a more transparent government, allowing voters to immediately see how and why their representation in the capital is voting the way they are. This helps voters better decide who to vote for in the future or how to help the public servants become more productive. A government could theoretically move more towards a true democracy with the proper application of e-government. Government transparency will give insight to the public on how decisions are made and hold elected officials or public servants accountable for their actions. The public could become a direct and prominent influence in government legislature to some degree.

Proponents of e-government argue that online government services would lessen the need for hard copy forms. Due to recent pressures from environmentalist groups, the media, and the public, some governments and organizations have turned to the Internet to reduce this paper use. The United States government utilizes the website http://www.forms.gov to provide "internal government forms for federal employees" and thus "produce significant savings in paper. In India Passport application forms, filing of Income Tax Return etc can be done online.

Speed, efficiency, and convenience

E-government allows citizens to interact with computers to achieve objectives at any time and any location, and eliminates the necessity for physical travel to government agents sitting behind desks and windows. Improved accou-nting and record keeping can be noted through compute-rization, and information and forms can be easily accessed, equaling quicker processing time. On the administrative side, access to help find or retrieve files and linked information can now be stored in databases versus hardcopies stored in various locations. Individuals with disabilities or conditions no longer have to be mobile to be active in government and can be in the comfort of their own homes.

Public approval

Recent trials of e-government have been met with acceptance and eagerness from the public. Citizens participate in online discussions of political issues with increasing frequency, and young people, who traditionally display minimal interest in government affairs, are drawn to e-voting procedures.

Although internet-based governmental programs have been criticized for lack of reliable privacy policies, studies have shown that people value prosecution of offenders over personal confidentiality. Ninety percent of United States adults approve of Internet tracking systems of criminals, and fifty-seven percent are willing to forgo some of their personal internet privacy if it leads to the prosecution of criminals or terrorists.

Technology-specific e-Government

There are also some technology-specific sub-categories of e-government, such as m-government (mobile government), u-government (ubiquitous government), and g-government (GIS/GPS applications for e-government.

E-government portals and platforms The primary delivery models of e-Government are classified depending on who benefits. In the development of public sector or private sector portals and platforms, a system is created that benefits all constituents. Citizens needing to renew their vehicle registration have a convenient way to accomplish it while already engaged in meeting the regulatory inspection requirement. On behalf of a government partner, business provides what has traditionally, and solely, managed by government and can use this service to generate profit or attract new customers. Government agencies are relieved of the cost and complexity of having to process the transactions.

To develop these public sector portals or platforms, governments have the choice to internally develop and manage, outsource, or sign a self-funding contract. The self-funding model creates portals that pay for themselves through convenience fees for certain e-government transactions, known as self-funding portals. Early players in this space include govONE Solutions, First Data Government Solutions and NIC, a company built on the self-funded model.

Social networking is an emerging area for e-democracy. The social networking entry point is within the citizens' environment and the engagement is on the citizens' terms. Proponents of e-government perceive government use of social networks as a medium to help government act more like the public it serves. Examples of state usage can be found at The Official Commonwealth of Virginia Homepage, where citizens can find Google tools and open social forums.

Government and its agents also have the opportunity to follow citizens to monitor satisfaction with services they receive. Through ListServs, RSS feeds, mobile messaging, micro-blogging services and blogs, government and its agencies can share information to citizens who share common interests and concerns. Government is also beginning to Twitter. Interested people can sign up at here. For a full list of state agencies with Twitter feeds, visit Real Life. Live document.

E – Jobs

Employment News is popular weekly publication of government for searching government as well private jobs. Same is now can be browse on line. Job alert facility is available on mobile or email for e-Jobs. Company can search desired profile of suitable candidate who have posted their resume/ bio-data, through internet. This can save time as well money in advertisement. Powerful **employment** classified ads software for **employment** and career sites help in this task.

Examples of e commerce

(A) Multi-Product E-commerce

Some Internet portals provide almost all categories of goods and services in a single site; hence, they are targeting buyers of every possible product/service. The most popular examples are www.indiaplaza.com, www.thebestofindia.com, www.khoj.com, www.sify.com, www.rediff.com, www. india-times.com and so on.

These Indian E-commerce portals provide goods and services in a variety of categories. To name a few:

1. Apparel and accessories for men and women
2. Health and beauty products
3. Books and magazines
4. Computers and peripherals
5. Vehicles
6. Collectibles
7. Software
8. Consumer electronics
9. Household appliances
10. Jewelry
11. Audio/video entertainment goods
12. Gift articles
13. Real estate and services
14. Business opportunities
15. Employment
16. Travel tickets
17. Matrimony
18. Pets...and more.

(B) Single-Product E-commerce

Some Indian portals/websites deal in a specialized field, for example:

(1) Automobiles:

Examples are: http://www.indiacar.com/ and http://www.automartindia.com/.

On these sites we can buy and sell four-wheelers and two-wheelers, new as well as used vehicles, online. Some of the services they provide are:

- Car research and reviews
- Online evaluation
- Technical specifications
- Vehicle Insurance
- Vehicle Finance
- Dealer Locator
- Regional Transport Office regulations
- Expertspeak
- Message board...and more.

(2) Stocks and Shares and E-commerce

In India today, we can even deal in stocks and shares through e-commerce. Some of the sites are: http://www. equitymaster.com/ and www.5paisa.com/.

Some of the services offered to registered members are:

- Online buying/delling of stocks and shares;
- Market analysis and research
- Company information
- Comparison of companies
- Research on Equity and Mutual Funds
- Tracking Market Trends
- Hotline for advice on Risk Management
- 24-Hour helpdesk....and more.

(3) Real Estate and E-commerce

Portals like http://www.indiaproperties.com/ facilitate online dealing in real estate. They offer either outright purchase or lease of a property through their portal. They provide information on new properties as well as properties for resale. One can deal directly with developers/builders or through consultant/brokers.

Allied services:

- Housing Finance

- Insurance companies
- Architects & Interior Designers
- NRI services
- Property Management Consultants
- Packers & Movers
- Security & Maintenance Services
- Vaastu or Feng Shui Consultants...and more.

(4) Travel & Tourism and E-commerce

India has a rich history and heritage and e-commerce is instrumental, to a large extent, in selling India as a product, encouraging Indians as well as foreigners to see its multifaceted culture and beauty. A major Government of India portal, http://www.tourisminindia.com/, has a vast variety of information for a potential tourist.

The tourist destination sites are categorized according to themes like:

- Adventure - trekking, mountain climbing etc
- Eco-Themes pertains to jungles, flora and fauna
- Beaches of India
- Architectural attractions
- Forts and Palaces
- Buddhist attractions
- Hill resorts
- Desert treks
- Pilgrimage sites

Allied services offered are:

1. Passport & visa
2. Travel & accommodation information
3. Weather information
4. Festival & fair dates
5. Shopping
6. Tour Operators
7. Information on Cuisine & Restaurants
8. Car rental services...and more.

There are also sites that highlight the tourist destinations of a specific region in India, like http://www. incredibleindia.org/, which covers North East India.

(5) Gifts and E-commerce

In the bygone days, one had to plan what to gift a loved one, trudge across to your favorite shop, and browse for hours before purchasing a gift. Today there are specific Indian websites making the act of gifting quick and easy to suit ones lifestyle. One such site is http://www. indiangiftsportal.com/.

The gifts are categorized as:

1. Collectibles like paintings and sculptures
2. Luxury items like leather goods, perfumes, jewelry boxes, etc
3. Household curios and carpets, etc
4. Toys & games
5. Chocolates
6. Flowers
7. Wood-craft & metal-craft
8. Idols for worship...and more.

Also the items can be searched by different regions of India, as every region has a special style in making handicrafts.

(6) Hobbies and E-commerce

The most popular hobbies from time immemorial are reading, music and films. On the Indian website http://www.firstandsecond. com/ one can buy more than 300,000 titles of books, cassettes, VCDs and DVDs.

The books cover a wide range of topics like Business, Art, Cookery, Engineering, Children's Stories, Health, Medicine, Biographies, Horror, Home & Garden, etc.

As for music and videos, they are available in English as well as in Indian languages to cater to the varied tastes and the topics range from devotional songs, old-time favorites and retro and jazz to the latest pop, rap, etc.

(7) Matrimony and E-commerce

It is said that marriages are made in heaven, but in the world of E-commerce they are made on marriage portals like http://www.jeevansathi.com/ (meaning life-partner.com in Hindi) and http://www.shaadi.com/ (meaning marriage.com in Hindi).

One can search for a suitable match on their websites by region of residence (India or abroad), religion or caste. Once registered with them, they have email facility and chat rooms too, so that the couple gets to know more about each other before making the biggest decision of their lives.

Allied services for registered members:

1. Astrological services
2. Information on Customs and Rituals
3. Legal issues
4. Health & Beauty
5. Fashion & Style
6. Wedding Planners
7. Honeymoon Destinations...and more.

(8) Employment and E-commerce

Two major portals like www.Monsterindia.com and www.naukri.com (meaning job.com in Hindi) are instrumental in providing job seekers with suitable employment at the click of a mouse. They have directories categorized under the headings Employers and Job Seekers. The service for job seekers is free and for Employers they charge a nominal fee. Jobs are available online in fields ranging from secretarial to software development, and from real estate to education. The opportunities offered are unlimited.

FACILITATORS OF E-COMMERCE IN INDIA

1. Information Directories

Portals like http://www.trade-india.com/ and http://trade.indiamart.com/ maintain directories giving trade details on almost any topic, whether it is from apparel to toys, from gems to heavy machinery, or from food to employment. The products and services are listed with appropriate sub-headings to make it easy for a serious information-seeker to find what he wants. Some other similar sites are http://www.indiagrid.com/, http://indiainfo. com/, and http://in.indiatimes.com/.

Allied services provided by them: Message boards, chat rooms, forums, etc.

2. Banks

a. Netbanking/phone banking

This is an online banking facility available for savings account holders as well as current account holders. Some of the special Netbanking services are:

- Demat accounts for sale/purchase of stocks and shares
- Foreign Exchange services
- Direct/Instant payment of bills on the account-holder's behalf
- Financial Planning & advice
- Electronics Funds Transfer
- Loans to account-holders
- NRI services…and more.

b. Credit/Debit Cards:

Banks facilitate E-commerce by providing the most vital trade instrument, namely the Credit or Debit Card, without which E-commerce would be impossible. Some of the major Indian players in this field are: http://www.hdfcbank.com/, http://www.icicibank.com/ and http://www.statebankofindia. com/.

POTENTIAL OF E-COMMERCE IN INDIA

Microsoft Research India was inaugurated in January 2005 in Bangalore, as the sixth MSR laboratory in the world. The arrival of a giant like Microsoft itself speaks of India's potential as a world-player in the field of Information Technology and e-commerce; and others will soon follow. Indian researchers and technicians can further the fast emerging world of E-commerce in India and take it to greater heights.

E-Commerce Myths and Reality

Yes, putting up a Web site is easy. And putting up a Web site to handle commerce transactions is pretty easy, too. But add words like effective, scalable, and successful, and it gets a lot harder. Setting up E-commerce is not easy or fast. Performance and scalability are the biggest issues. Even if a provider of E-commerce goods and services rigorously follows the key factors to devise an exemplary e-commerce strategy, problems can still arise.

Unfortunately, many e-traders assess the situation in the electronic market wrong from the very beginning. Therefore, they fail to understand customers, why they buy and how they buy. Even a product with a sound value proposition can fail if producers and retailers do not understand customer habits, expectations, and motivations. E-commerce could potentially mitigate this potential problem with proactive and focused marketing research, just as traditional retailers may do.

Failure to consider the competitive situation can lead to lamentable result too. One may have the will to construct a viable book e-tailing business model, but lack the capability to compete with Amazon.com. It is hard to predict the envir-onmental reaction to the emergence of the new business on the Net, but still it is worth trying. What will competitors do? Will they introduce competitive brands or competitive web sites? Will they supplement their service offerings? Will they try to sabotage a competitor's site? Will price wars break out? What will the government do? Research into competitors, industries and markets may mitigate some consequences here, just as in non-electronic commerce.

If existing reporting and control relationships do not suffice, one can move towards a flat, accountable, and flexible organizational structure, which may or may not aid coordination. Thus, failure to coordinate is another big problem.

Some of the Internet traders simply fail to obtain senior management commitment. This often results in a failure to gain sufficient corporate resources to accomplish a task. It may help to get top management involved right from the start. Lack of employee commitment is no good either. If planners do not explain their strategy well to employees, or fail to give employees the whole picture, then training and setting up incentives for workers to embrace the strategy may assist.

Setting up an e-commerce venture can take considerable time and money, and failure to understand the timing and sequencing of tasks can lead to significant cost overruns. Basic project planning, critical path, critical chain, or PERT analysis may mitigate under-estimation of time requirements failings. Profitability may have to wait for the achievement of market share.

Poor follow-through after the initial planning, and insufficient tracking of progress against a plan can result in problems. One may mitigate such problems with standard tools: benchmarking, milestones, variance tracking, and penalties and rewards for variances.

Becoming the victim of organized crime is easier today than it might seem. Many syndicates have caught on to the potential of the Internet as a new revenue stream.

In addition, today there have emerged several myths about online business. Here are the most widespread of them. Many people believe that E-commerce is cheap. Perhaps it is when compared with a full-blown enterprise resource planning implementation or the purchase of a mainframe. But for a number of reasons, a full-scale online commerce effort is never a low-cost proposition. Business-oriented commerce server software, such as Microsoft Site Server Commerce Edition, may start as low as $5,000, but that is just the first building block in a complex under-taking. Companies spend an average of $750,000 just for the baseline technology, according to a Gartner Group survey of 100 commerce sites. Then there are marketing costs and other non-IT infrastructure investments. Amazon.com, the paragon of E-commerce success, lost nearly $25 million on $153.7 million in revenue in the third quarter, and marketing costs were a big reason. Is Amazon gaining new customers from its marketing investments? Absolutely. Its revenue was up 337% from the year-ago period, and the company's stock price is up about 1,000% since its initial offering in May 1997. But the company is losing money – lots of it – proving the point that E-commerce is not cheap.

Another aspect of the level playing field myth is the assertion that the Internet gives small companies instant access to global markets. Access is one thing; leveraging it is quite another. Large physical-world companies have a huge advantage in overseas markets if they leverage their brands online, whether they are Boeing, Eastman Kodak, or Pepsi. There is a low barrier to doing E-commerce, but a very high barrier to becoming one of the leading choices.

And the most important thing. Doing business over the Internet the e-tailer must be ready for the unexpected all the time. Too often new businesses do not take into account the amount of time, money or resources needed to complete a project and often find themselves without the necessary components to become successful.

E-commerce is anything but a myth. It is a major trend that is reshaping businesses and the IT that runs them. But there's a common theme that runs through each of the myth dissections above: E-commerce, in almost all cases, doesn't change some fundamental rules of business. Doing business on the Web successfully takes capital, innovative leadership and execution, marketing shrewdness, perseverance, and the intelligent application of IT. As the Internet continues to speed the pace of change in the coming years, many aspects of business will be altered and transformed – but those guiding principles will always remain.

SYLLABUS FOR COMPUTER

(Theory 50 Marks)

1st Semester (3 Yrs)
LL.B. Courses

Unit 1: Computer and its Basics

- Block Diagram of Computer, Functions of Computer, Generations of Computer (1st to 5th Generation), Classifications of Computer, Characteristics, Advantages and Limitations of computer.
- Central Processing Unit (CPU): Computer Memory: Primary and Secondary, Type of memory, Storage devices: Floppy Disk, Hard Disk, Magnetic Tapes, Optical Disk, Pen Drive.
- Input Devices: Keyboard, Mouse, Scanner, Touch Screen, Bar Code Reader
- Output Devices: Monitor, Printers and its functions & its classifications
- Meaning of Hardware and Software (Application & System Software)
- Types of Languages: Machine, Assembly and High Level
- Meaning of Complier and Interpreter

Unit 2: Introduction to Windows Operation System

- Introduction, Benefits of operation system, Various applications of Windows Operation System, Graphical User Interface (GUI).
- Starting applications, creating shout cuts, Creating folders, Copying files and folders.
- Control Panel-Add hardware, add or remove program, date and time properties, mouse properties, sounds, system, User Accounts.
- Accessories-Notepad, Paintbrush, Calculator
- Recycle Bin
- My Documents
- My Computer
- Windows Explorer

- System Tool-Disk clean up, Disk defragmenter, Scandisk.

Unit 3: Networking and Internet

- Computer Network and its need: types of networks-LAN (Local Area Network), WAN (Wide Area Network), MAN (Metropolitan Area Network), VAN (Value Added Network)
- Concept of Network Topology, Types of Topologies (Ring, Bus, Star, Hybrid)
- Introduction of Internet, History of Internet, WWW (World Wide Web), Web Browsers (Internet Explorer, Mozila Firefox, Netscap Navigator, Macweb, Winweb, Google Chrome and Cello), Internet Servers and its types.
- URL, Internet Architecture, Cyber Space, TCP/IP Internet Service Provider, Domain names, Introduction of email, Communication using Email

Unit 4: E- Commerce

- Introduction, Scope, Definition, Traditional vs E-Commerce, Advantages and Disadvantages of E-Commerce.
- E-Commerce and the Trade cycle
- Functions of E-Commerce
- Types of E-Commerce-B2B (Business to Business), B2C (Business to Consumer), C2B (Consumer to Business), C2C (Consumer to Consumer).
- E-Commerce applications: Internet Payment System, Consumer Oriented E-Commerce, Business oriented E-Commerce.
- E-Services: E-Banking, E-Stock Trading, E-Investing, E-Auction, E-Employment, E-Governance and E-Jobs.

Books Recommended:

1. IT Today (Encyclopaedia)- *S. Jaiswal,* Galgotia Publications
2. Computer Fundamentals- *P.K. Sinha*, Priti Sinha, BPB Publications
3. E-Commerce- *CSV Murty,* Himalaya Publishing House
4. A First Course in Computer 2000- *Sanjay Saxena*

RTM NAGPUR UNIVERSITY
QUESTION PAPER FOR COMPUTER

First Semester LL. B. (Three Years)
Examination 2009 (New Course)

Paper-VII

COMPUTER

Time: Three Hours **Max. Marks: 50**

N.B. : (1) Attempt any Five question in all, including Question No. 1 which is compulsory.

(2) All question carry equal marks.

1. (a) What is computer Draw a well labelled block diagram of computer organisation.

   (b) Explain Primary and second Memory in details.

2. (a) Explain classification of printers. Discuss Laser Printer.

   (b) What do you means by scanner? Explain the types of scanner.

3. (a) Write a note on Windows Operating System. Discuss how GUI is used in it.

   (b) Write a note on :-

   (i) My Computer (ii) My Document

4. (a) Explain briefly the content of the Control Panel.

   (b) Discuss Internet Explorer in details.

5. (a) Describe the three most common network topologies.

   (b) What is networking? Explain the purpose of networking.

6. (a) Differentiate between LAN and MAN.

   (b) Define different types of Web browsers in details.

7. (a) Explain Electronic Commerce trade cycle with neat diagram

   (b) Explain benefits and drawbacks of Internet Payment System.

8. (a) What do you mean by E-commerce? Explain the scope of e-commerce.

   (b) Differentiate between traditional commerce and e- commerce.

Second Semester LL. B. (Three Years) Examination 2010 (New Course)

Paper-VII

COMPUTER

Time: Three Hours **Max. Marks: 50**

N. B. : (1) Attempt Question are compulsory.
(2) All question carry equal marks.

1. What is male merge? Explain in brief.

OR

Explain Bullets and Numbering option with all Tabs in details.

2. Describe formatting and conditional formatting with example

OR

What do you means by function? Explain different types of Statistical and Mathematical function of MS-Excel.

3. What do you mean by Master Slides? Explain all the features in details.

OR

Explain slide show menu in detail.

4. What is DBMS? Differentiate between DBMS and RDBMS

OR

Define Query. Explain different type of queries in detail.

5. Write the steps on creation of email-ID.

OR

What do you mean by uploading and downloading data?

[illegible] factors, [illegible] to [illegible] status quo in these areas.

[illegible] surveillance

[illegible] contact between government [illegible] citizens [illegible] government [illegible] to [illegible] [illegible] will be forced to interact [illegible] government on a larger scale. [illegible] private [illegible] their [illegible] [illegible] like system [illegible] develop. [illegible]

[illegible] surveillance [illegible]

[illegible] commerce has become a part of our everyday lives [illegible] [illegible] [illegible] are [illegible] [illegible]

[illegible]

[illegible] protect [illegible]

[illegible] the monitoring of internet chat rooms.

[illegible] devices [illegible] perform a digital wire tap [illegible] user's internet activity and [illegible] information specific to the [illegible]